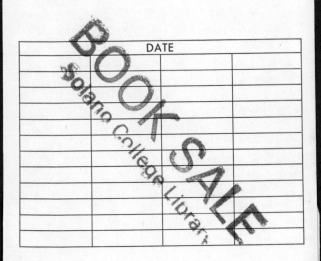

Paul Weiss
CINEMATICS

Southern Illinois University Press
Carbondale and Edwardsville
Feffer & Simons, Inc.
London and Amsterdam

Library of Congress Cataloging in Publication Data

Weiss, Paul, 1901–
　Cinematics.

　Bibliography:　　p.
　Includes index.
　1. Moving-pictures.　　I. Title.
PN1994.W394　　791.43　　74–20933
ISBN 0–8093–0671–9

Quotation reprinted with the permission of Farrar, Straus & Giroux, Inc.
from *Film: The Creative Process* by John Howard Lawson, copyright © 1964
by John Howard Lawson.

BOOKS BY PAUL WEISS

Beyond All Appearances (1974)
The God We Seek (1964)
History: Written and Lived (1962)
The Making of Men (1967)
Man's Freedom (1950)
Modes of Being (1958)
Nature and Man (1947)
Nine Basic Arts (1961)
Our Public Life (1959)
Philosophy in Process, Vol. 1: 1955–1960 (1966)
Philosophy in Process, Vol. 2: 1960–1964 (1966)
Philosophy in Process, Vol. 3: 1964 (1968)
Philosophy in Process, Vol. 4: 1964–1965 (1969)
Philosophy in Process, Vol. 5: 1965–1968 (1971)
Philosophy in Process, Vol. 6: 1968–1971 (1974)
Reality (1938)
Religion and Art (1963)
Right and Wrong: A Philosophical Dialogue Between Father and Son, with Jonathan
  Weiss *(1967)*
Sport: A Philosophic Inquiry (1969)
The World of Art (1961)

PRINCIPAL CONTRIBUTIONS BY PAUL WEISS

American Philosophers at Work, edited by Sidney Hook (1956)
*American Philosophy Today and Tomorrow, edited by H. M. Kallen and Sidney
  Hook (1935)*
The Concept of Order, edited by Paul Kuntz (1968)
Contemporary American Philosophy, edited by John E. Smith (1970)
*Design and Aesthetics of Wood, edited by Eric A. Anderson and George F. Earl
  (1972)*
Dimensions of Mind: A Symposium, edited by Sidney Hook (1960)
Evolution in Perspective, edited by G. Schuster and G. Thorson (1971)
The Future of Metaphysics, edited by Robert Wood (1970)
Human Values and Economic Policy: Proceedings, edited by Sidney Hook (1967)
Law and Philosophy, edited by Sidney Hook (1964)
Moments of Personal Discovery, edited by R. M. MacIver (1952)
Moral Principles in Action, edited by R. Anshen (1952)
Philosophical Interrogations, edited by S. and B. Rome (1964)
Philosophy and History, edited by Sidney Hook (1963)
Science, Philosophy, and Religion: Proceedings (1941–)

EDITED WORKS BY PAUL WEISS

Collected Papers of Charles Sanders Peirce (six volumes), editor, with Charles
  Hartshorne *(1931–35)*

FOR ERIC SHERMAN
Who inspired and enriched it

Contents

Preface

The literature on film is already quite large, and it seems to be increasing at an accelerated pace. One who, with me, has had no experience in film making, only a limited acquaintance with the literature, and just a normal exposure to film, will be inclined to use others as guides. He will surely have little temptation to add to the books already available. But I have been unable to find a work which not only treats film as an art, but examines its main contributors and constituents systematically, points up its similarities and differences from other arts, and tries to benefit from previous extended reflections on man and what else there is. This book is prompted by a desire to overcome these deficiencies.

Cinematics is an attempt at a beginning of a philosophically grounded examination of the film. In good part it is the outcome of thinking and reading begun over a decade ago, and of discussions with such knowledgeable students of the film as Eric Sherman, Arthur Knight, and Robert Thom. They have gone over the entire manuscript with great care. The work was also read by Richard Clifford, William Earle, David Slavitt, Jonathan Weiss, and Joseph Williman. I have done all I could to take account of the various criticisms, and have preserved many of them in the form of interjections. R. T. is Robert Thom, E. S. is Eric Sherman, J. W. is Joseph Williman, A. K. is Arthur Knight, and D. S. is David Slavitt. Their observations will provide the reader with a clearer understanding of the limitations of, and the alternatives to what is here advanced, and will surely yield insights into nuances that my inexperience led me to overlook.

I had originally planned to write the book together with Eric Sherman, but it soon became clear that we both had distinctive accounts of our own to present. How much of mine is dependent, positively and negatively, on what he has said and written, it is not possible for me to say. Nor is it clear just which ideas were primarily or initially his and which mine. He, and the others, in any case, have alerted me to central issues, raised important difficulties, and corrected serious errors. If the final result could win the approval of such men, I would be confident that I was on the right track.

Cinematics does not contain an extended examination of the nature of art.

This can be found in my *The World of Art*. The present work, and *Nine Basic Arts* — which treats of arts more widely practiced and longer established than film — can be viewed as coordinate sequels of the earlier book. But I have not presupposed an acquaintance with my other writings. Film is a unique enterprise and deserves an independent study. I have tried not to forget that fact. It has forced me to create some new terms to mark the differences between the agencies and objects of other enterprises and those that are peculiar to film. The whole, I think, will offer little help or knowledge to those who are experts in film making or film appreciation. It is my hope, though, that they and others will benefit from this attempt at a fresh and independent inquiry, grounded in philosophic reflections.
A grant from the National Endowment for the Humanities supported my research and enabled me to complete the book.

P. W.
Washington, D.C.
January 1974

The Art of Film

CHAPTER 1

Toward a Definition

From its beginnings until the present time, the appeal of film has been immediate and wide. Typically, it adds entertainment to drama, often splendidly. But it has not yet reached the heights attained by some novels or plays — or, for that matter, by some paintings, sculpture, architecture, poetry, music, or dance.* Vorkapich is right, I think, to remark that "there

---

* *Film is not an art and probably never will be. It may, however, be more important than art. It is history of unprecedented accuracy, and it makes history. It has revolutionized the world. It has changed the very character and function of politicians and statesmen — as well as wiping out one kind of universal naïveté forever, replacing it, perhaps with a more dangerous and volatile naïveté. This it has done everywhere, in all countries, under all forms of government. It is to be compared to the invention of the wheel and of the printing press. It may be the making or breaking of us — quite literally. Film will never be worthy of comparison with a Rembrandt. But it may make the adventures of Ghandi, Roosevelt, and Lenin seem trivial. Depression, flood, famine and fire, personal desires, ambitions, goals — all will be and have been shaped by it. No monk spends more time at his prayers or meditations than our children do before filmed television. Beware! Be joyous and be cautious. It's dynamite. The superlatives Hollywood press agents dreamt up in their prime may not have been exaggerations. Hitler, Stalin, and John Kennedy knew as much, and they were not particularly "brilliant" men. Film is Pandora's Box. When we enter the world of film, we are truly in the dark.* R. T.*

---

are extremely few motion pictures that may be cited as instances of creative use of the medium, and from these only fragments and short passages may be compared to the best achievements of other arts." [1] Those films in which new technological advances and skills were first exhibited are, to be sure, called classical, but the history of the film is of too short a duration to justify that designation. Also, classical works outlast their times, while so-called film classics are terribly dated. It is hard to adjust to their pace, to accept their turning points, to approve of their performances, or to follow their narrative lines appreciatively. The incidents, organization, and themes keep their import largely confined within the period in which they were made.* And, though great work in the

---

* No other enterprise can so quickly re-create time and place, be, in very fact, a time machine.   R. T.

---

film is still innovative, it has not yet achieved the status of great innovative art.

Some men are content only with what is dramatic; a few are content only with what is innovative. But entertainment speaks to all, the sophisticated and innocent, the old and the young. It also allows those who are appreciative of the dramatic and innovative to relax at moments with what requires comparatively less concentration and involvement. By and large, entertainment is the most persistent and dominant form that film assumes. It also makes it difficult to lose oneself in the art of film.

2

The modern film, whether popular, dramatic, or innovative, is both visual and audible. Visually it has at least three distinctive features.

1. It achieves a unity from within by a development over time. Yet with less and less frequency, but frequently enough, one hears it said that film consists of still pictures, which are united to constitute a shot. The shots are taken to express a single cinematic meaning, to be connected with others so as to constitute a scene. The scene, in turn, is treated as a unit to be added to other units so as to constitute a single sequence. Scripts are often written in consonance with this view, and the language and practice of film theorists is now so well stabilized around such conceptions that it seems foolish to question it. Yet it can not be allowed to stand, for it attends, not to a film but to a camera, and then to one that is not yet distinguished from a camera which takes photographs or stills, to be subsequently and externally combined. With equal warrant, one might suppose that a painting has distinct brush strokes as its units, to be externally combined in various ways so as to produce a larger whole. A painting is an organic work, whose units and relations are analytically obtained rather than presupposed. Though the brush strokes occur before the painting as a whole appears, the painting as a whole dictates what its proper parts are. Only

rarely are these brush strokes. And only rarely does a film have shots or scenes or sequences as its units.*

---

* I find myself constantly remembering or appreciating shots and
sequences far more than a film as a whole.   A. K.
And yet a film may be remembered, be significant, because of a particular scene or sequence. The stabbing in the shower in Psycho opened
up to modern consciousness, a violence which has since become street
knowledge, banal, frightening.   R. T.

---

2. The position taken by the film camera is approximately that from which an audience is to view the film. What a film records is there, like a monument or a document, for men to note, and which they are to try to live with by adopting something like the standpoint that the film camera once occupied. In the absence of viewers, the results are fixated. At some subsequent time, if viewers find it difficult to occupy the position of the camera, they will look at the film and not share in it, see it as that which had been viewed, and not view it themselves. This second characteristic is partly shared by photography. Photography, however, makes use of its camera as a surrogate for the photographer, and not for an audience.*

---

* This camera-provided position is often (perhaps even usually) one
which is normally unavailable or unreal to a viewer. E.g., in Birth of
a Nation (1915) the viewer travels with, ahead of, and facing a cavalry
defilade. It is almost never that film reflects an ordinary position of viewing
—the viewer is more normally an implicit interloper, voyeur, omniscience,
or spy.   J. W.

---

3. A film is completed by the viewers before it; they are transformed by the film into occupants of a world, part of which the film makes visible. Here, too, it is unlike a photograph. This is confined within the limits of a print, presenting a fragment of the world in which the audience is already a part, and therefore not to be transformed.
Bazin apparently believed that a film was photographic and, like other photographs, contrasted with a painting in showing a part of the very world occupied by the viewer. "The photograph as such and the object in itself share a common being, after the fashion of a fingerprint. Wherefore, photography actually contributes something to the order of natural creation, instead of providing a substitute for it." [2] It is not often that one finds Bazin off-guard, but here he evidently overlooked the difference between the two kinds of cameras employed, and the fact that photographs need

frames, whereas films do not. Indeed, he later perceptively remarks "the outer edges of the screen are not, as the technical jargon would seem to imply, the frame of the film image. They are the edges of a piece of masking that shows only a portion of reality. The picture frame polarizes space inwards. On the contrary, what the screen shows us seems to be part of something prolonged indefinitely into the universe. A frame is centripetal, the screen centrifugal.* Whence it follows that if we reverse the pictorial

---

* I like the formulation about picture frames as centripetal and movie screens as centrifugal, but you can make it more lively by alluding to the attempts, not entirely successful, to act on this truth. The change from the conventional screen to the wide-screen processes of Cinemascope, Panavision, Todd-AO, and Cinerama was an effort to enwrap the audience, to feed peripheral vision, to "prolong indefinitely into the universe." This tendency became silly with 3-D movies requiring special glasses so that tennis balls, breasts, or whatever could project out into the audience. The wide screen has taken over, but the special applications of Cinerama and 3-D have not succeeded. Mostly it was a matter of money, but there may have been philosophic reasons as well. D. S.

---

process and place the screen within the picture frame, that is, if we show a section of a painting on a screen, the space of the painting loses its orientation and its limits, and is presented to the imagination as without any boundaries." 3* A film thrusts itself beyond the limits of a screen.

---

* One should also note that a moving picture camera moves — in a way impossible for an eye, a microscope, or a telescope to duplicate. Seeing, in cinema, is not believing. All good cinema is irrational, unbelievable.

R. T.

Thus, the importance of the close-up is not what it includes, but what it excludes. A. K.

3

The introduction of a range of colors makes no difference in principle to what a film can present. Black, white, and gray are colors too; they do not differ in kind from red and green and blue.* These can in fact be so modu-

---

* It is a startling assertion that black-and-white film is not in principle different from color. One could claim that the distinction was that between

etching and painting. There are qualities in black and white, a sculptural and formal clarity, which seem diminished by color.   D. S.

---

lated that they pass into one another, and into black and white and gray, and conversely. But the introduction of sound has made a signal difference to the film. It has also given a new meaning to sound and thereby changed the import of film.*

---

* Of course, it should be remembered that silent film was infinitely noisy. Ninety-piece orchestras, gunfire, the toppling of towers of bricks (e.g., Intolerance) *were common and were expected at first-run theatres in the larger cities. Let us never forget that it was* The Birth of a Nation *(1915) which made Wagner a popular composer in the United States. Silents became silent only when mere actors began to talk.*   R. T.

Unlike the visible which the camera makes it possible to capture, sound awaits an audience before it can be itself fully. Every member of the audience occupies a center at which the sound arrives from different positions, at different paces, with different values. The audience, consequently, does not simply hear sound; it hears sound that comes to it.

A recording of sound by a faithful machine is not on a par with the product of a splendid camera, for the machine presents the sound from the position of its producers, and not from the position of an audience. If it tried to record what the sound was for an audience — perhaps by being placed where a listener normally is — it would subsequently be heard not by one who then adopted the placement, but by one who had a new place of his own. Sound arrives, but the seen is there to view.*

---

* But also from a particular angle. Why do children want to sit in the first row? What if one is forced to sit on the side of the theatre? The perspective, the absorption, in each instance, is radically different.   R. T.

Sounds are at once detachable, voluminous, insistent, directional, self-identical, interpenetrative, and interrelatable.[4] At its best sound exhausts an entire space, leaving no room for the addition of something to be seen. Music needs no visual aids. To be sure, the visible is also insistent on itself, but it allows room for the audible, providing that this is kept subordinate.

Montague, though, seems to hold that the visible is more determinate and articulated than sound: "in cinema, image *distracts* from sound, where sound is primary, and this because image is more explicit. For the same reason, sound adds to image. Being less explicit, it does not, except where it is most explicit, distract from the image." [5] But surely, sounds can be most explicit, while images may be blurred. And it is questionable whether sound is ever primary in film. At most it supplements.* When close-ups

---

* *Try watching a detective film like* Sleuth *without sound. Only a lip-reader could stay awake.* R. T.
Is this because sound seems *more physical than vision, and less intellectual (or shaped, formed)? Of course both are constituted by pulsations; but sound pertains more to body rhythms and pulses, whereas vision is associated with verbality, logic and reason.* J. W.

---

accompany dialogue, we often have sound both subordinate and supplementary.

Film dialogue, because it consists of sounds, is subordinated to what is seen; because it conveys a message, it also supplements it. Conflict is avoided by having the visible set the pace for the very dialogue that supplements it.* Part of the trouble with transferring classical plays to the

---

* *Not true. Frequently, film is cut to sound, even so-called silent film — i.e., the gathering of the Klansmen in* The Birth of a Nation *was cut to* Die Walküre. R. T.

---

screen lies in the understandable desire to have the visible paced by the excellent dialogue.

Sounds in a film are conditioned by what is visible. The visible dictates the pace, the turns, the beginning and the ending of the sounds, be they words, music, or neither. Because it is subordinate, however, sound in a film is unable to make the audience its center. Being bound to the visible, it can not reach to what is independent of the visible. Yet, seeking an audience, it can not be confined to the world fixated by the camera. Its achievement lies in between these two.*

---

* *Subjective sound requires a different analysis.* A. K.
This is confirmed by musical use of the sting — a submelodic tonal fragment which serves to intensify a visual given, especially in the absence of dialogue. J. W.

An audience is not only present at what is seen on a screen, but is also in the indefinitely extended region beyond the screen, into which the film intrudes. Consequently, what is on a screen is in effect only a focal point within a larger experienced world. Sound makes a radical difference to the situation. It places the entire cinematic event on a curve which continues to completeness in the form of a circle. The audience is also on that circle, exerting a counterthrust. The sound film and audience occupy the same world but with opposite emphases.*

Sound is one way of giving distance to a movie — with voice-over narrative. The close-up dialogue scene is not "subordinate and supplementary" but one of the interesting possibilities of film, immediate and direct. For one thing, the facial expressions of the performers work as in portraiture, with the audience unconsciously moving its facial muscles and participating in the mimesis. For another, the rhythm of cutting from speaker to reacting listener, and back to the reaction lies at the very heart of movie art. The usual sequence is an establishing shot showing where we are, a medium shot to focus attention, and then, at the emotional climax of a scene, this intimate close-up/dialogue exchange. There isn't any such thing as pure art, and certainly no pure movies.   D. S.

A film without sound is quite a different work in fact and for an audience than one which is made to be heard as well as seen. When a sound film is silenced the incidents are relocated. They are given new roles in relation to the environing space and in relation to the audience. The distinctions, punctuation, and pace which the sound made possible are no longer noted. The audience is compelled to occupy a new position, and must articulate the film afresh. The circle, where both audience and film are in counterbalance, vanishes, and film and audience become part of one place.

Emotional expressions normally continue to be manifest after the artistic occasion, which provoked those expressions, is no longer present.* The

---

This is terrific, but one wants more of it. Okay, emotional expressions continue to be manifest after the artistic occasion, but what expressions? What lasts? What made Bogart a great movie actor was a tonality (mostly through those close-ups), a map of experience in that lined face, a brave world-weariness that influenced a generation. Think of Cooper, or Ladd, or Marilyn Monroe. Her movies were not good, but the face, the innocence that survived all soiling — that lasted.   D. S.

---

manifestations are delayed in the case of film. One lives for a while in its world even when no longer attending to it. A longer time, apparently, is needed before one is able to become acquainted with what lies outside the world of film than is needed in order to become acquainted with what lies outside other arts.* Because film and audience are continuous, it is

* *Is the reverse not also true — that more experience of the outside world is required in order to judge films? Novels require more experience of the world than poems, and films require more experience than novels.*   D. S.

difficult for the audience to attend to something else, after the viewing. But, like every other art, a film leaves its audience emotionally prepared to face external realities in a way it had not before.

4

A film is an interconnected set of incidents, each with three sides. Spatially, an incident is a continuous, visible occupation of a region.* Tempo-

* *Although, it is well to remember that some of the most vivid and dramatic happenings in a film are never seen. A woman screams, is terrified. (vide Fay Wray in the shipboard sequence in* King Kong). *We do not see what she sees or imagines she sees; nevertheless our attention is riveted upon the unseeable. (Kong can never equal the limitless horror Fay Wray conjures up for us on deck. Film* does *enjoy some of the much neglected prerogatives of radio.)*   R. T.

rally, it has an indivisible rhythm, partly defined by sound, but primarily by what is seen.* Dynamically, it presents a single occurrence in which a

* *Of course, the visible plays, draws in, throws out its influence upon the invisible. Many films deliberately break the frame, the proscenium. Stanley Kubrick in* 2001, *for example, continually is plunging us by visible means into the nonvisible, the infinite. By this, one is not alluding to space in the science fiction sense, but into the continuation offscreen, that his images demand.*   R. T.

beginning is governed by and reflected in the ending, thereby making them relevant to one another. In dramatic works, the incident is equatable with the conventional, visible scene; in popular works it is often paced by an appealing musical score; in innovative works it usually involves some novel combination of sight and sound. In all, it is an extended, unified occurrence, requiring one or many setups, covering one or many scenes, and one or many sequences.

The three sides of an incident are independent of one another. It is possible for a single spatial region to be occupied for a number of moments and to be traversed by many occurrences. A number of places and occurrences can be encompassed in a single moment. A single occurrence may take many moments to unfold, and may occupy a number of different spatial regions. The sides can be brought into some accord by subordinating two of them to the third somewhat in the way in which actors supply voice and gesture for a required action. In dramatic film, the primary measure is the occurrence; in popular film, it is rhythm; in the innovative, both of these are subordinated to space. Film, at its artistic best, contains incidents in each of which regions, rhythms, and occurrences are organically united.

The incidents of a film are interconnected. Were a film made up merely of frames, shots, or scenes, it would be the product of an external relating of incidents, themselves the product of an external relating of static units. The film would be a mélange, an aggregate of single elements having nothing intrinsically to do with one another. In such a case, the rapid passage of the film before the eyes, the affinity of the characters, and the development of the plot would lead one to have an illusion of motion. * This, of course, is

---

* The idea of film as mélange is interesting, and you are right to point it out. The films of Stanley Brakhage do exactly this, and exemplify perfectly the idea of an illusory motion of unmoving objects.   D. S.

---

what many think does occur. It is a view entertained by those who say that nothing moves in a film; that it is nothing but a semblance; that whatever unity, meaning, artistic excellence we accredit to it is in fact nothing other than what we have read into it. But if we created a film by just looking at rapidly replaced still pictures and unit sounds, we must be doing something similar with every perception, every complexity, every work that we confront, experience, or live with. Such a contention ends with the paradox that even what we daily know, and where all evidence is to be found, is unreal. What we can not encounter and that for which we can have no evidence in experience alone would be. Art, history, common sense, law, engineering, politics would be occupied only with derivates, or with objects of our own construction out of elements no one of us had in fact encountered and, therefore, which no one of us could have used.

A halt, of course, could be called in the process of dissolution of what we confront. One might just insist that what is perceived, or used, or conventionally spoken of, is real, and that film and other arts give illusory imitations of these. Putting aside the fact that an art may turn away from daily life and its perceptions altogether, and that illusions are distortions of perceptions uncritically taken to be reliable, there is the fact that daily life and its perceptions blur, hide, and add practical import to what, from the perspective of art as well as of science, is purer, clearer, more intelligible, or self-sufficient.

It is always possible to adopt a position in terms of which what is confronted from other positions is simply dismissed as illusory, unreliable, unreal, and the like. But there would then be no resolution of the conflicting claims made on behalf of the different positions. A satisfactory decision requires one to attain an unassailable standpoint, in terms of which all others are properly viewed and graded. In the absence of this, we have to allow that different confrontations might yield equally reputable, irreducible data. If we are not able to occupy a final standpoint, we surely are not able to dismiss the distinctive claims of any discipline to put us in touch with what is real. That final standpoint, itself, might in fact justify the conclusion that a number of disciplines were equally basic and illuminating. Art, science, religion, and history could then be said to put us in touch with what is real, but from particular angles and under distinctive limitations. It would be a wise move to accept that conclusion and to proceed with resolute inquiry into the various dimensions of the world. A full-bodied philosophy will, of course, try to warrant the conclusion, but we need not here have to wait on it. As has already been suggested, and which will become more evident in the course of the present work (see, particularly, chapters 8 and 9), art elicits emotions which, to be fully satisfied, must terminate in ultimate realities. It therefore offers an emotional introduction to what philosophy, and particularly metaphysics, coldly affirms.[6]

5

The incidents in a film, like the actualities in the world, are connected by ultimate realities, whose presence and nature they reveal in the relations that the incidents have to one another. Five kinds of relations, and therefore of powers, are to be distinguished: (1) affiliations, (2) independence, (3) extensional connections, (4) structures, and (5) concurrent instantiations:

1. The actualities in this world have internalities more or less involved with one another. The other actualities with which one of them may be involved may be quite distant from it in space, time, or causality. It may have made no contact with them, and may have shared no content; yet it may resonate in consonance with them. The fact is conspicuous in human

life. We sympathize with and withdraw from men with whom we have had no previous contact. We blush, we fear, we rejoice, we affiliate and dis-affiliate independently of what we empirically have been or are. The incidents in a film are similarly related, but in an intensified form. The film's concern with what is seen and heard keeps it focused on incidents, but these are just distinguished parts of a more basic and more encompassing occurrence, expressed in the whole film. This, and the incidents, engage our emotions by addressing us on behalf of something deeper and more abiding than themselves, and therefore more appropriate to what we are, deep within ourselves.

2. Each incident is just as much an incident as any other. It may be more exciting; it may involve greater values; it may be more closely affiliated with certain ones and not with others. Nevertheless, it has its own integrity. That fact might be thought to support the supposition that the film is made up of distinct incidents. But the integrity of each, which places it on a foot-ing with the others, can not be known or made intelligible by dealing with the incidents in their severalty.* In their severalty, they are distinct, in-

---

* *The equality of incidents in their severalty is why any film looks good if one comes in in the middle. One sorts out who the characters are, what the situation is, what the structure is, and only then do most films fall apart and seem stupid. But the externality of film is absolutely seductive for a while. The contrast is with drama, which, according to Panofsky, has the reality flowing outward from character to spill out and enliven a palpable artificial set; in film, the reality flows inward from obviously true externals to the characters.*   *D. S.*

---

comparable; no one is equal to, or greater than, or less than the others. But the incidents of a film are all together in the film, each having signifi-cance in relation to others. To be sure, the development of a film will require that some be muted and others serve as means or carriers. But they will be so treated only because they have already been accepted as incidents together with the rest.

In a film, even the minimized and instrumental incidents are incidents equal in status with the others, though possessed of different values and carrying out different roles. The film gives them all the same status because it approaches them as equally worthy of a place within it. Each incident is completely present; nothing remains hidden; there is nothing promissory or latent.* A film, consequently, is one, not because

* I think latency is constantly more important (perhaps always more important in film) than what is seen.   R. T.

it is said to be so, but because it provides an occasion and base for independent incidents to be coordinated as equal, no matter what other purpose they may then be made to serve. The film is their common ground and condition.

3. Incidents are meanings in process. We classify, organize, and contrast them, without reflection, in terms of features which they share. We also move from one to another, logically, psychologically, and conventionally, by following routes reflecting the operative presence of rules governing those incidents. Together they are subject to a common structure. By taking account of them in this guise, the film as a whole can be planned, articulated, verbalized, summarized, and communicated.

4. Incidents are extended in space, in time, and dynamically. They are so many delimitations, bounded portions of these, intensified. Where one incident ends, another begins, without break. Were each just by itself it would be separated from the others by an indifferent emptiness, and would not, therefore, really be cut off at all. Each is selfbounded from all else, with an extendedness which is a limited portion of a larger extension. Films take account of this fact, demarcating distinct incidents within larger extensions.

Both incidents and films extend beyond the screen, but in different ways. Since a film encompasses many incidents, it spatially extends beyond the screen in a plurality of ways and for varying distances.*

* One of the astonishing phenomena is the way a good scene grows in your memory, although when you see the film again, you find it is really quite short.   A. K.

The audience, as a result, becomes involved in a complex spatial extension continuous with the extensions of the various incidents in the film.

A film also exists as a single present, contemporary with the present of its audience. The futures of the incidents and audience are gradually filled out by incidents in the course of the film, with the consequence that the film and the audience are made wholly present, framed by the beginning and ending of the film, inside an indefinitely larger time.

A film, because it encompasses many incidents, necessarily relates its audience's past, present, and future in complex ways.

Causally, an incident connects an audience to possible antecedent
conditions and to possible subsequent outcomes. By filling out the
positions of the antecedent and consequent with incidents, a film
exhibits the working of a single causal process. Because it lives through
the dynamic process which the film embodies, and which is punctuated
by the different incidents, the audience sees the film as a causal
whole.

The audience already has an awareness of a larger space of which
it is a part, a larger time in which it occupies an extended present,
and of a single necessitation which needs to be filled out with content.
And since, in its incidents and throughout, the film presents a part
of a larger space, time, and dynamics, its audience, by virtue of the
film, becomes part of their continuation into stretches that lie beyond
them.

5. Each incident is related to every other as an instance of a single unity,
characteristic of the film as a whole. Concretizations of the selfsame
unity, the incidents nevertheless differ from one another in range
and import. Some are subordinate to others, and some are interrelated
through a number of intermediaries. Together they give richess,
nuance, and development to the unitary whole.

Different films emphasize one or the other of the five types of relation
among incidents. Ideally, all the relations ought to play a role.
If this is done, the incidents will be interconnected in a fivefold way.
The purely spatial, temporal, and dynamic connections that are
obtrusive in a film are at best the surface of the extensions that in
fact connect incidents, and at worst hide the presence of the other
modes of connection operating outside the confines of space, time,
and causality.

6

A film is aesthetically excellent if it harmonizes radically diverse
sensuous contents, immediately experienced. Such excellence falls
short of what is attained in a work of art, with its luminous, grained
theme, its modulated, articulated, nuanced structure, its unitary meaning,
its self-sufficiency, and its ability to make one aware of the root threat
and promise that existence holds in store for man and what he prizes.
A purely aesthetic work which falls short of excellence presents one
with a disconnected set of immediately felt qualities. It arouses feelings,
but it does not, as an aesthetically excellent work does, sustain,

supplement, spell out, and control those feelings. It is two removes from a work of art, lacking not only beauty but also agreeableness. Too often, this is the only yield of experimental, avant-garde, improvisational films. They present sensuous contents, but without regard for the way in which these contrast and support one another. Film experimentalists too often produce what is not excellent, even sensuously. As a consequence, they challenge popular taste by confronting it with new and startling sensuous contents, but without satisfying the feelings that are invoked one after the other, or the attitudes which govern these. Nor do they appeal to emotions below the level of feelings.

The sensuously excellent is diversified and unified; it awakens diverse feelings and satisfies them to some degree. When it is an integral part of works of art, the appeal it makes to the feelings is continuous with appeals made to emotions below the level of feeling — emotions which no aesthetic content elicits and none could satisfy.*

---

* However! — to paraphrase: The divine discontent may be aroused by, may be the driving reason for film. Hence the star system — be it Bette Davis or Ingmar Bergman. ("Always leave them hungry" — or, let us say, film must make "hungry where most [she] satisfies.") R. T.

At its best, a film also has a dramatic form, alerting one to what can happen to cherished goods. Were it only dramatic, it would irritate while it disturbed. Were it just dramatic and popular, it would challenge and largely satisfy, but within the area of established ways and values. If it is to be a work of art, its dramatic aspect does not have to be singularly novel, but it must allow the film to affect more than a dramatically pertinent mood.

7

Unlike architecture, sculpture, painting, music, story, poetry, theatre, and dance, which differ so radically in different countries and in different cultures as to almost defy comprehension by one not long acclimatized to the values, practices, and mythologies dominant in a particular place at a particular time, film is truly international.* Men

---

* The internationality of film is partly illusory. The traditions in other arts go back over varying times and draw upon different systems of

belief and attitudes. All movies are contemporary; a twentieth-century Japanese has more in common with a twentieth-century Peruvian than he does with a sixteenth-century Japanese. Anyway, there are differences — Fellini is different from Satjajit Ray precisely because one is Italian and the other is Indian.   *D. S.*

---

with backgrounds, interests, educations, and religions, with arts and crafts hard for others to appreciate, readily respond in rather common ways to the same films. Not only films made in France and Russia, but those made in India, Peru, and Japan, have more in common apparently than anything else does, that is made in these different places. This does not mean that film need be superior or inferior to other arts, but only that it makes a quick appeal to most men. One might try to account for this fact by referring to the omnipresence of the camera and the use of technical devices by means of which the film is brought into being, since these allow for an escape from limited outlooks and interpretations, and overpersonalized outcomes. Or it might be said that the audiences in these different places are selected in roughly the same ways from men with some money and education. These contentions, though, do not cover the almost universal enjoyment of film on the part of the young, and by men uneducated and unsophisticated.

It could, though, be maintained with some justification that film does not have an absolutely universal appeal. If one were to go to primitive groups one would perhaps find that the films we enjoy are met by consternation, fear, and misunderstanding. Films, too, bear the imprint of outstanding film makers, and the film camera, like any other device, is used by men who inevitably intrude themselves. Still unexplained is how it is that the appeal of film is so broad, perhaps broader than that of any other art.

It is reasonable to assume that the grasp, acceptance, and enjoyment of the same films in many different areas which have distinctive mythologies, architectures, music, poetry, paintings, and dances is a function of the film's ready appeal to something at once deep and common to all men. It arouses strong emotions quickly. Is this not because it deals with crucial occurrences in the lives of all? Birth, youth, old age, sickness, death, love and hate, war and peace, victory and defeat, gain and loss of power mark sharp turns in the course of everyone's life. They involve basic values, and are of vital interest to all men. These the film brings to the fore, intensified, insistent, with a directness and vividness no other agency equals.

The film's unusually wide and deep appeal is not shared by the theatre. The effectiveness of the theatre is limited in good part by one's understanding of what is being said. This keeps its appeal confined to a comparatively small number. The theatre, too, is subject to many long-established conventions, making it difficult even to understand some of its pantomimes. A film, in contrast, not only need not be laced by dialogue in a particular language and subject to local conventions, as the theatre is, but it tries to focus on incidents, motions, and actions which all can grasp, no matter what their background. No other art has such a large, knowledgeable audience at ease with a plurality of works made at different places and times. Film viewers are citizens of a single world, aware of both the common and the individual, and of a vast unknown that lies just beyond what is well understood.

Though there are no films which deserve to be called classic in the sense in which the works of Homer, Aeschylus, Michaelangelo, Dante, Shakespeare, Bach, Rodin, Yeats, and Wright are classics, every film can be taken to be part of a single classic, to which it contributes a fragment, somewhat in the way generations of workers built the great cathedrals over the centuries. Film, as a single totality, has withstood seventy-five years of critical scrutiny * and, despite the supercilious attitudes of

---

What do you mean by suggesting that film has "withstood seventy-five years of critical scrutiny"? It has ignored seventy-five years of critical scrutiny.   *D. S.*

---

established art historians, philosophers, and critics, has won a clear place for itself as a promising art.* That it has as-yet no classics to its

---

* *No! No! No! More important than art, film is history "written in lightning," to quote Woodrow Wilson. Gone With The Wind tells us more about 1939 than about the Civil War, The Birth of a Nation more about 1915. Why was Vivien Leigh a nonvirgin a white man attempts to rape in GWTW, and Lillian Gish a virgin a nigger tries to rape in The Birth of a Nation?*   *R. T.*

---

credit is in part due to its comparative youth, in part to its difficulty, and in part to the fact that it is not sustained by a single well grounded traditional outlook shared by both producers and spectators. Film is helping create such a tradition. Not until this can be built on, and then as an independent reality with an overwhelming importance and power, will film be able to make great use of it. Only then will film achieve what is able to stand on a footing with the classical works of other arts. Only then will it, like them, have mountain peaks as landmarks. For the time being, its main hope lies with innovators, alert to the possibilities open to film. Innovators demand that one depart from established patterns and turn in a new direction where one can be solicited and controlled in ways that none can foresee. Their films can elicit the expression of guiding principles. They can also point up the inadequacy of such principles, thereby provoking the expression of emotions which prompt their correction, supplementation, and replacement. If what Jonas Mekas says about improvisations were true, it would hold even more surely of innovations — which are what improvisations become when they are successful: "improvisation is . . . the highest form of concentration, of awareness, of intuitive knowledge, when the imagination begins to dismiss the prearranged, the contrived mental structures, and goes directly to the depths of the matter."[7] I think he exaggerates, but improvisation and innovation do have important roles in the making of great film.

8

Great film is at once aesthetically satisfying, dramatically effective, and profoundly innovative. It makes an immediate appeal to the feelings at the same time that it arouses root attitudes of evaluation, and turns men in a new direction. The men then face realities, normally not discernible or surmised. Emotions, which the film elicited and which continued to be expressed after the viewing was over, are satisfied. Experience, learning, wonder, and inquiry are enriched and controlled. The experience is like that which the Taoist, the Yogi, and the mystic seek; the learning grips the sensitive young; the wonder is felt by those who are religiously inclined; the inquiry is the concern of speculative men. These explore in distinctive ways the realities whose presence is made most evident in works where innovations are integrated with popular and dramatic achievements.
A film satisfies the emotions it elicits, but not completely. The emotions continue to be expressed, even when an audience is no longer involved with the film. Those emotions are then in a less intensive insistent form and are directed at final realities — individual actualities and cosmic powers with which those actualities interplay. If these emotions are to be satisfied, it will be in that more diffuse form, after the film viewing is over.*

---

* *Or more direct. Hard-core pornography is not designed to drive the audience home in a detumescent state.*   *R. T.*

Film readies its audience to deal with realities outside it. If at once great and innovative, it leaves the audience face to face with what is irreducibly final. Once I distinguished just four such realities; [8] more recently [9] I found it necessary to distinguish no less than five, termed Substance, Being, Ideality, Existence, and God. These interplay with one another and with transient actualities. They ground the five types of relation discussed in section 5.

Initially, men encounter the modes of being inchoately together, not distinguished.[10] Special experiences and philosophic reflection enable them to focus primarily on some one of them. Film and the other arts provide occasions for them to attend primarily to Existence. The other arts, that are today recognized as basic, attend to some one dimension of Existence — space, time, or dynamics — and then as something which is primarily bounded, occupied, or exhausted.[11] Film, instead, tries to pay equal attention to all three dimensions. Its use of space tempts one to relate it to painting. It seems, too, to be somewhat like poetry, since it exhausts the time in which it is, though not without reverberations backwards and forwards. Dynamically, it seems to be like music, bounding off a causal region within which more limited specialized causal occurrences can take place. Confessedly, these comparisons are rather forced. The film is not like any of these, or any combination of them. It is a single, irreducible art, within which one can distinguish a kind of space, time, and dynamics, more analogous perhaps to painting, poetry, and music than they are to other arts.

Since this characterization runs counter to the strong tendency which many seem to have, to associate film more closely with story rather than with poetry, and with the theatre or dance rather than with musical performance, it is antecedently suspect. The film seems, like a story, to have a narrative line even when most episodic and fragmented, and not to have its own special intensity, language, and rules, as poetry does, needing considerable sophistication and experience to master. But this is to ignore the fact that films need no narrative, that poems may have a narrative form, and that some of the subtlest poetry — Homer, Dante, Yeats — also has had a wide appeal and can be understood and appreciated by men with little poetic experience. The film, too, seems, with the theatre and dance, to make use primarily of human performers and not to interlock a set of aesthetic elements. But this is so, I think, only for those who attend only to dramatic turns, and who ignore nonhuman performers and the way in which the incidents these sustain are united with one another.

Whether one chooses, in accordance with the common tendency, to think of film as more like story, theatre, and dance than, as I have suggested, like poetry and music, one can allow that film most likely is but one of many arts that try to give equal weight to space, time, and dynamics. The other arts have not yet been created. Just what they are like can not now be known, for to know what an art is and how it functions, one must attend to actual works. But it is possible to know in advance what conditions they must meet if they are to be great, and how they will have to operate on the audience if they are to be popular rather than innovative, classical rather than dramatic, or all of them together.

Like every other art, film makes us aware primarily of Existence, rather than of some other equally basic mode of being. If we are to be helped to attend to any of these other modes of being as effectively as the arts enable us to attend to Existence, use must be made of other than artistic ways of involving man's deepest emotions. It must be possible to arouse and control the same responses that art does, and to satisfy them for a time, but in such a way that they not only outlast the occasions which brought them forth, but are directed at modes of being other than Existence.

Film, and other arts, point us toward Existence rather than toward other finalities, because they present us with single extended wholes, in which terms are also relations, and relations are also terms. Such works are achieved by making use of the powers of Existence itself. The arts lead to Existence because they are produced through Existence's aid.

Existence, epitomized in a work of art, initially provokes expressions appropriate to the work and then sustains those expressions after one no longer participates in the work. But the more practical and limited interests of men soon come into prominence, and obscure the Existence to which the art had originally led. Existence, though, still continues to give faint indications of its presence, pressing in on the present from the past and future, locating one in relation to what is above and below, backward and forward, right and left, and placing one inside a larger causal process. But it does not become an object of attention except for those who continue to maintain that freedom from practical and limited concerns that had been exhibited in attending to the work of art. The help of Existence is needed if one is to arrive at Existence, but Existence provides that help only for those who have found a way of baring themselves to its presence — usually through the help of art, appreciated and lived through.

A work of art, because it has terms which are relations, and relations which are terms, is so far a simulacrum of Existence. But it is no mere semblance, imitation, or mirror. It vitalizes and sensuously intensifies extensions, reorders them, and charges them with novelties, to yield an organic whole that is to be lived with as irreducible and self-sufficient. By being made to terminate in the work, the emotions, which an art arouses, controls, and directs, are made into determinate vectors. On completion of the experience with the work, the emotions which were partly satisfied by that at which they vectorially terminate, continue to be expressed. By following their lead, one comes to attend to Existence, rather than to any of the other modes of being.

Film creates appearances revelatory of Existence, and incidentally throws light on the other finalities. When all the film makers are creative, independent, and cooperative, film has an ideal form. Specializations of this are achieved when one of the film makers assumes a dominant position, while continuing to be supported and supplemented by the others (chapter 7). The similarities and differences between the film, produced by coordinately cooperative men, and by men who work together but with one or the other in a dominant position, become most evident when the different film makers are dealt with in independence of one another (chapters 2–6).

At its best, a film is a work of art, at once complete and satisfying in itself, and revelatory of what is real in men and the Existence with which they are all involved. It is denied the opportunity to achieve this status when it is made in the interests of propaganda, education, disclosure, documentation, or escape (chapters 10–14).

We are now ready, I think, for a definition of the film, the import of which is to be clarified in what follows: *Film is a created (audio) visual ordered whole of recorded incidents,* providing one with a controlled emotional introduction, primarily to Existence, and secondarily to other finalities.

CHAPTER 2

The Script

A script for a film is a set of instructions indicating what is to be done if a film is to be made. This observation Coppola confirms, I think, when he says "A screenplay, of course, is not a finished piece of art; it's only the blueprint for a film. This becomes clear when you direct from a script you've also written." [1] It is also more than a set of instructions or a blueprint. The script presents a theme, a visualized idea. This, its plot, story, and dialogue, articulate in only some of the possible, justifiable ways.

A script may be changed in the course of its use without seriously affecting its idea and therefore its identity. Sensitive authors sometimes object to some of the alterations. They are right to do so if the changes mean that one then does injustice to or radically alters the meaning conveyed in the idea. They are right, too, to assume that their creation encompasses both idea and articulation. But it should also be admitted that an idea has a status of its own, even though it may not exist except when and as it is articulated. There is no *man* as such, but *man* has a distinctive nature which each individual embodies in a limited, specific guise. An idea is a unity for which articulations offer divisions and specifications, without necessarily compromising the integrity of the idea.

There have been films for which no scripts seem to have been provided. The camera was moved about at random; performers improvised or were caught off-guard; the only evident control was exercised by a director who had an unexpressed idea of what he would like to achieve, or by an editor who, in the cutting room, decided which sections of finished film were to be used, and how. But if there is no script, conceived if not written, followed even though not attended to, the film will lack an ingredient which is vital to it if it is to be a work of art. Were there no script, the film would be excessively immediate, sheer vision and sound, organized perhaps about some dramatic values, but without a controlling meaning or a verbalized structure.

The necessity that there be a script is one with the necessity that a film have a communicable form. The script commits one in advance somewhat as a promise, a nod or a raised hand in an auction, a declaration of love or war, or a chef's menu do. It points to limits or pivotal issues, and gives the whole a structure. We need it because creativity, if not externally guided, runs the risk of producing only an instance of willfulness. Without guiding control, the whole will most likely be overwhelmed by indecisiveness intersected by arbitrariness; it will be incoherent, confused, without development. These undesirable results could be minimized. Conceivably, they might be entirely avoided in some cases. But the longer and more complex the film, the more surely will the risks be great and hard to obviate.

A film must have some magnitude if it is to be a work of art. One can tautologically define that magnitude: It is greater than that which can be understood without a script, and shorter than that which goes beyond the point where the beginning and the unfolding determine and are determined by the ending. To have that magnitude, the film must exhibit an idea visually and audibly. The instructions that the script provide tell others how to make the idea cinematically evident. Conceivably those instructions could exist in the form of gestures, hesitations, withdrawals, and supplementary acts produced in the course of a filming. The film would still be one produced under the guidance of an articulated visualized idea.

A script need not tell a story; its development need not be in consonance with any dramatic rules. But it must express a meaning, and its development must unite beginning and end so as to constitute a single whole of contrasts and unions, tensions and resolutions. If that whole is to be given a cinematic expression, it is best first to visualize and verbalize it, so as to make the film not only something seen and heard, lived through and with, experienced, enjoyed, with a unity emotionally undergone, but intelligible, able to be thought about, summarized, and communicated.

Where does a film properly begin? Where does it properly end? The two questions are really inseparable, for the beginning defines what the end must be, and the end is what it is only because the film was begun at a certain place and progressed in a certain manner. The script stretches, in its own way, between those two points. The important thing is not that it begins in such and such a way at this place or that, but having begun in this way and in such a place, it proceeds cinematically to the relevant end.

We live both on the surface and in the depth of things. The surface
is the locus of contingencies; the depth is where necessity operates. A
good script makes room for both. It exhibits a necessary connection
between a beginning and end, but across a domain of contingency, where
the necessity is challenged again and again by the unexpected. What
happens, consequently, is seen to be both a result and a defiance of what
had gone before. The script allows one to see how the rational outcome is
achieved in the face of the unexpected, and how despite the necessity,
the contingencies support and oppose one another, and thereby determine
the meaning of the final whole.*

---

* *Scripts often function as you describe in theatrical movies.
Documentaries may be made without scripts, and often are. They are
assembled in cutting, and they do have a structure, a meaning to reflect
on. Documentaries are not what you were talking about, but they qualify
as films according to your definition in chapter 1, section 8 — as indeed
they should.* D. S.

It is good to be suspicious of words, with their conventional associations,
their unsuspected affiliations, their subtle commitments, and their
unavoidable ambiguities. Each art has its own kind of language, often
expressed in nonverbal forms. Even novels, poetry, and plays, which
make use of the established spoken and written languages, are forged
by constantly combating their routine use.
Film has its own distinctive language. Not only creators of film but all who
reflect on it need to learn how to speak it without accents derived from
other tongues. This is not yet enough to justify a decision to dispense with
anything resembling a script, and its use of ordinary language. The script,
though written in consonance with the requirements of verbal communication, can — and usually does — keep close to the rhythms and
requirements of film.
Not every filmed combination of images, of light and dark, of sound
and silence, deserves preservation. Creative work is too important and
difficult to allow it to proceed without the guidance and control that a
script provides. To dispense with a script is to dispense with what is
essential to the making of a great work of film art. Were a script written
for a sequence of filmed lights and darks, sound and silences,* it would

---

* *Scripts* are *written with lights, darknesses, sounds, and silences laid
out.* R. T.

---

not yet be like a musical score or a set of notations, for it would still benefit from, while not succumbing to, the conventional uses of words. Not offered as a novel or play is, as something to be enjoyed in the reading,* the script verbally expresses a visualized idea which is to be

---

* *No longer true. Many publishers do publish movie scenarios.*   *R. T.*

---

filmed as an interrelated set of incidents.

2

The unit for a film is the incident. This fact has been obscured by the technical limitations of the film. If one attends to the way in which a camera is used, one inevitably speaks of frames — what is captured in one exposure — and of shots — what is captured in a single use of the camera.*

---

* *Also of montages, double, triple, quadruple exposures, of dissolves and of wipes, of overcranking and undercranking, etc., etc.*   *R. T.*

Putting aside the fact that it is possible to make an exposure indefinitely long or short, frames and shots are not genuine subdivisions for a script, but for an animated work.[2]

An incident is a single event, an occurrence taking time to unfold. Usually it requires a number of shots. But a single shot can also embrace a number of incidents, particularly when there is a multiplicity of performers and short-spanned actions.

The metaphysics of the film, so far as this is expressed in a script, has been best stated — though without thought of the film — by Alfred North Whitehead. The irreducible basic unit, he holds, is an event whose being consists in the activity of uniting a possibility, grasped from a finite standpoint, with the entire past focused on from that standpoint. That single event, when it has come to be, passes away to become an indistinguishable component in the total inheritance of the next event. No event and no set of events, on that view, can act. An incident — which he calls a society — is a set of events. These events do nothing, their entire career is spent in coming to be. This is essentially what the script (but not the film) should convey — the coming-to-be of events.

A script presents a series of incidents linked together by an inheritance of a character. No one of its units operates on any of the others.* Still the

---

* *Split screens, dissolves, A/B/C/D dissolves seem to contradict this.*   *R. T.*

---

totality has a single persistent reality. The script presents that persistence. But unlike a Whiteheadean set of events, incidents have their own dynamic integrity, final and irreducible. Each, too, has tonalities and rhythms, ups and downs, quick movements and slow, produced and sustained by substantial individuals.

3

A script writer — or better, a scriptist — is sometimes compared with a story teller. His script, to be sure, can take off from some story, and it may take as its primary task the presentation of some tale or historic occurrence. If it does, it will break this up in accord with the necessities of a filming, and not in accord with the demands of a plot, a climax, or a story line.*

---

* *If the scriptist expects to make a living, he will, certainly, have in mind plot, climaxes, and story.* R. T.

Bluestone makes the point well: "when the filmist undertakes the adaptation of a novel, given the inevitable mutation, he does not convert the novel at all. What he adapts is a kind of paraphrase of the novel — the novel viewed as raw material. He looks not to the organic novel, whose language is inseparable from its theme, but to characters and incidents which have somehow detached themselves from language* and, like the

---

* *Language is, frequently, indivisible from character. W. C. Fields, playing Dickens's Micawber in David O. Selznick's* David Copperfield *was made to realize this.* R. T.

---

heroes of folk legends, have achieved a mythic life of their own. Because this is possible, we often find that the film adapter has not even read the book, that he has depended instead on a paraphrase by his secretary or his screen writer. That is why there is no necessary correspondence between the excellence of a novel and the quality of the film in which the novel is recorded."[3]

A script may do for a film something like what a written play does for one that is acted: indicate where crucial turns are to occur in speech, action, place, and attitude. Rarely,* though, does a scriptist have control over a

---

* *Not true. See Billy Wilder, Alfred Hitchcock, Stanley Kubrick and even, if you must, Robert Thom, who rewrote* Wild in the Streets *after*

filming had been completed. Would that the layman knew more about the
mysteries of editing, looping, and dubbing. R. T.

film. As a result, his work is used mainly as a tissue of indications of
what the others should do. Since he is then taken to be primarily concerned
with presenting instructions to the other film makers, he has no need to
embellish his material with novelistic language.*

* *Again not true—see Von Stroheim's extraordinarily novelistic version*
of The Merry Widow *(1924).* R. T.

Nichols sees the fact, but misses the reason because he thinks the film
must tell a story: "The most noticeable feature of a skillful screenplay is
its terseness and bareness. This is because the eye is not there, the eye
which fills and enriches. Nor does the screenwriter waste time with such
descriptive matter or detailing of photographic moods. These have all
been discussed at length with the director, art director, and others.*

* *In what studio? What film? What year? Circumstances vary*
enormously. Sometimes, the writer never meets the director, (the art
director!). Sometimes, the writer (as with Billy Wilder) is the
director. R. T.

It is the writer's job to invent a story in terms of cinema or to translate
an existing story into terms of cinema."[4] Margaret Kennedy also misses
the reason, but from another side: "A script is not meant to be read, as
novels, poems, and plays are read. It is no more a work of literature than
is the recipe for a pudding. So long as the meaning is grasped and the
recipe followed, it would serve its purpose if it were written in pigeon
English. The trouble is that the recipe is never followed. The orchestra
never plays the notes which the composer has set down." [5] But a script
need not be illiterate. And if it were, this need not preclude it from
excellently articulating an idea, and surely not from presenting the
governing meaning of a film, even one without a plot.
Scripts are to be read, but primarily to enable one to grasp an idea in
visual terms. They could be so made that they are worth reading as literature, but they must not be allowed to become so absorbing that they take
one away from the task of making a finished film. That other film makers
sometimes do not heed what the scriptist puts down is, unfortunately,
painfully true. "Most of the writers who share screen credits in Hollywood
have never worked together. One gets fired and the other gets hired to take

his place. . . . There is always something wrong with it because first drafts are not finished drafts . . . so he gets another writer who writes the second draft, only it is his first draft. Finally, after seven writers, the picture is shot with the seventh writer's first draft without ever having gotten to the second draft's stage." [6] But, despite Kennedy, "a writer can have a style which is unmistakeably his own, so that any one fairly knowledgeable in these matters doesn't have much difficulty in recognizing whose work it really is, regardless of non-writer claims to the contrary." [7]

It is possible to envisage a novelist who takes as his task the description of single shots from the position of a film camera, and the reporting of the appropriate sounds which supplement and enrich the seen occurrence. Dos Passos tried to do this. Had he succeeded he would have enabled the reader to imagine what occurs, and would then have completed his task. Were the entire product boldly transferred to a script, the writing presumably would have the same effect on the makers of a film that it has on the ordinary reader. A scriptist would, though, still have work to do. He would have to punctuate it according to the needs of film. If he does not provide instructions telling the camera where to point and how, or where incidents are to be begun, ended, and connected, he will nevertheless leave clear indications of what is to be done by the very way in which he conveys the meaning of the film.

The appeal to a reader of a novel is made through the help of a language detached from its practical uses. If that very same language is reproduced in a script, the readers of it will, to make a film, have to translate it into a language appropriate to the use of a film camera, and the practical need to make a unity out of its discrete items. "With the abandonment of language as its sole and primary element, the film necessarily leaves behind those characteristic contents of thought which only language can approximate: tropes, dreams, memories, conceptual consciousness. In their stead, the film supplies endless spatial variations, photographic images of physical reality, and the principles of montage and editing." [8] Film makers must implicitly, at least, interpose a script between a novel and a film, since a novel can at best only bring them to the position where they might imagine but not yet express what the outcome of the film is to be.

4

A script tells one how to mark out and reconstitute a region of ordinary space within which the film camera is to operate. The camera attends to a visual area in that region as having its own geometry, distances, contours, and fillings. By lights, walls, and other devices, it keeps the film in that area. The limits it sets are not the boundaries of cinematic space but of the incidents then filmed.

There is no time which is integral to a script. Though it may refer to a sequence of incidents and paces, and relate them, it does not in fact bring those incidents inside a distinctive time. It orders them in an abstract sequence, without requiring one to attend to them in that order. What it places in one order may be filmed in a second and, due to an editor, producer, censor, or director, may eventually be presented in another. More likely, the whole will then have a different rhythm from that which was originally offered in the script, and caught by the film camera.

The time of a novel is integral to it, constituted by the occurrences there. It has its own beginning and its own ending; throughout, the pace varies, partly because of the plot and partly because of the manner in which the story is told. Years can be skipped without disturbance; epochs can be displaced, shortened, and lengthened in accordance with the dictates of the events and the style. That time contrasts with the time of daily life; a story can cover aeons while the latter takes but a few moments. In order to tell the story of what happens in a minute, one may take up hours of ordinary time.

A script, like a story, is read in the psychological time of the reader. The reader of the story meshes his time with the time constituted by the story, to produce a new, distinctive time in which reader and story are synchronized. The difference between the way a novelist and a scriptist deal with the same incident is brought out vividly by Lawson, who confronts the beginning of Dickens's *Great Expectations* with the beginning of the script for it. It is good to have the two before us:

Ours was the marsh country, down by the river, with [*in*], *as the river wound, twenty miles of the sea. My first most vivid and broad impression of the identity of things, seems to me to have been gained on a memorable raw afternoon towards evening. At such a time, I found out for certain, that this bleak place overgrown with nettles was the churchyard; and that Philip Pirrip, late of this parish, and also Georgiana, wife of the above, were dead and buried; and that Alexander, Bartholomew, Abraham, Tobias and Roger, infant children of the aforesaid, were also dead and buried; and that the dark flat wilderness beyond the churchyard, intersected with dykes and mounds and gates, with scattered cattle feeding on it, was the* marshes; and that the low leaden line beyond was the river; and that the distant savage lair from which the wind was rushing, was the sea; and that the small bundle of shivers growing afraid of it all and beginning to cry was Pip.

"Hold your noise!" cried a terrible voice, as a man started up from among the graves at the side of the church porch. "Keep still, you little devil, or I'll cut your throat!"

A fearful man, all in coarse grey, with a great iron on his leg. A man with no hat, and with broken shoes, and with an old rag tied round his head. A man who had been soaked in water, and smothered in mud, and lamed by stones, and cut by flints and stung by nettles, and torn by briars; who limped and shivered, and glared, and growled and whose teeth chattered in his head as he seized me by the chin.

Here is the motion picture version:

---

1. *Exterior Thames Estuary. Sunset. The wind is making a high-pitched ghostly whistling noise.*
VERY LONG SHOT of a small boy, Pip running along the bank of the Estuary. Camera tracks and pans with Pip as he runs round a bend of the path and comes toward camera. A gibbet is built on the edge of the path, and Pip glances up at it as he passes.
DISSOLVE TO:
2. *Exterior Churchyard. MEDIUM SHOT Pip. He is carrying a bundle of holly. He climbs over a broken stone wall, and camera pans right with him as he walks past the tombstones and old graves. Camera continues panning as he makes his way toward one of the tombstones and kneels in front of it.*
3. *MEDIUM SHOT of Pip kneeling at the foot of the grave. Wind continues. Pip pulls up an old rose bush, which he throws aside, pats down the earth again and then places his bunch of holly at the head of the grave.*
4. *MEDIUM CLOSE SHOT. Pip kneeling near tombstone. Wind gets louder. Pip looks around nervously toward camera.*
5. *LONG SHOT from Pip's eyeline of the leafless branches of a tree, which look to Pip like bony hands clutching at him.*
6. *MEDIUM CLOSE SHOT Pip looks around as in 4.*
7. *MEDIUM SHOT of the trunk of an old tree from Pip's eyeline. . . . The tree looks sinister to Pip like a distorted human body.*
8. *MEDIUM SHOT Pip. He jumps up from the grave and runs away towards the stone wall. Camera pans with him, then becomes static as he runs into*

the arms of a large, dirty, uncouth and horrible-looking man. From his
clothes and shackles it is obvious that he is an escaped convict. Pip
screams loudly.
9. CLOSE SHOT. Pip. His mouth is open as he screams, but a large dirty
hand is clapped over it, silencing him.
10. CLOSE SHOT of Convict. His face is dirty and scowling, his hair is
closely cut. He leers down at Pip.
CONVICT: Keep still, you little devil, or I'll cut your throat! [9]

Lawson goes on to point up the distinctions between the two forms —
particularly the omission of the subjective experience in the script, its use
of conventional symbols, and its neglect of the psychological values
emphasized in the novel. The excellence of his account makes all the more
perplexing his failure to deal with the uses of time that also distinguish
story from script, and which ally it with film.

A script does not, as a novel does, have a time integral to it. It offers
nothing with which the reader's psychological time is to mesh. The film,
though, makes up for that deficiency. Like a novel, it presents a time which
has its own beginning, pacing, distances, and ending. Like it, the film
incorporates a time that is self-enclosed, wrenched away from daily time,
allowing one to live for a while in a new area. This new time is environed
by a larger time, which extends beyond it and into which the audience is
carried. That larger time is indefinite in extent and almost empty. The only
content that it has, the filmed incidents require one to place at times earlier
or later than those incidents.

The fact that the time of the film is newly created and, like the time of a
story, is cut off from daily time, stands in the way of the ordinary interpretation of film as inescapably realistic. That interpretation is based in good
part on the fact that the film camera must be aimed at a space which is
demarcated within a larger space. It forgets that the larger space is also
pulled away from a still larger, that it is given new structures and connections, and that it is then environed by another space which it in part
defines. More important, the interpretation overlooks the fact that, no matter
what may be the case with space, the time of a film is the time of the incidents in the film, and not the time it takes to see the film, or the daily time
in which filmed occurrences might conceivably occur.

The film camera and, therefore, the audience occupy a series of present
moments. These are not necessarily successive, and they may be remote
from the time when the film camera is used and from the present in which

the audience attends to the film. The audience is in the present, but sees only what is presented to it. And what is presented may be placed far away in space and given a very early or future date. Because it assumes the position that the film camera had occupied, the audience is able to be copresent with a multiplicity of incidents; because those incidents can be reordered and set at the most disparate dates and positions, the audience can be made present moment after moment at quite different, unrelated times and places.

The audience does not remain in the present of its attention; instead, it gives this up to be at the present of the film. The audience in 1973 attends to the film made in 1970 about incidents in 1900; to see the film, the audience, via the camera, is transported to 1900.* A similar transportation

---

* *And to 1970!*   R. T.

---

is achieved in the theatre and in fiction, but more directly though not as steadily, because not mediated by a mechanical agent, a projector. This allows the audience to take the position of the camera, not as something intruding from the outside, but as constituting a contemporary spatial limit of the actual incident that is being filmed.*

---

* *Not entirely true. Films have been made for 360 degree screens. We are about to enter the age of the holograph in which a filmed dancer may leap over the heads of the audience. Paul Newman may sit in the seat beside you. You may be able to walk around Jane Fonda.*   R. T.

An audience, in assuming the position of the camera, stands at camera distance from what is filmed.* The film, as stopped but not bounded by the

---

* *Not at all. It is at least a league* behind *the camera.*   R. T.

---

screen, brings the audience into a larger space and time than it itself presents. And, since the film as a whole is a single work, as a whole it constitutes a long, complex single here and now, within which there are distinguishable but not separate parts. The audience stands at the limit of the confronted space, contemporary with the entire presentation.

At one and the same time, an audience is at the different times and places occupied by the filmed incidents, at the single space and time of the film as a whole, and in the single space and time which extends beyond the confines of the film that appears on the screen. Yet it is often said that a camera records only what is here and now, and that the audience can do nothing more than persistently keep abreast of it. This is to forget that incidents are temporally and spatially interconnected in a cinematic space and time. Or it is to take the audience to be persistently freeing itself from its daily or psychological space and time only to fall back into it again, moment after moment. When an audience is watching a film it is, of course, occupying a position in daily and psychological time and space, but if it is absorbed in the film those positions are transcended to make it be at the incident, wherever this be in a cinematic time and space.

5

A story presents one with various transactions. Some of these demand that a particular outcome follow on some antecedent or, in some cases, that it be completely governed by an insistent prospect. Others allow greater room for some kind of freedom — spontaneities, luck, will, coincidence. Though both antecedent and consequent may be novel, the connection between them must match men's sense of what is reasonable and relevant, or be treated as absurd, foolish, dated.

A script makes provision for both necessities and for freedom. It need not, though, adhere as closely as the story does to what is reasonable or relevant.* Though readers of stories are presumably superior to the mass —

---

* Of course it must — although perhaps on a different level.   R. T.

---

because they know how to read and have the power to imagine what is reported — there is a greater willingness on the part of a film audience to accept implausibilities of connection. It allows itself to be oriented, paced, and guided by the filmed incidents.

A novel, at its best, gets readers to qualify their imaginations by invoked emotions. The story may then be projected on an imaginary space and time, and go through an imagined number of causal transactions. A script could have a similar effect on the film makers who read it. In both cases, the description of the way in which an incident progresses from antecedent cause to consequent effect could be identical. In both cases, the description could prompt an imagination of incidents. But for the readers of a story an incident contributes to the production of a climax. This does not occur for readers of the script, for in the script incident simply follows on incident. To unite cinematically the incidents that are described in a script, one must exercise a cinematic imagination; the story, in contrast, itself connects occurrences in a time that is ingredient in the story.*

** On scripts generally: you might consider that Hitchcock works from a
story board, a series of cartoons closer to Disney, really, than to anything
like writing. They are pictures which he gives the screenwriter, and the
writer's job is to connect up these frames. This makes some problem with
your notion of the frame as not basic. Hitchcock would probably disagree
with you. For him, even if not basic, frames are prior to everything else. He
also likes to work with hack writers who do what they are told. Why screen-
writing is hack work is obvious, but it is worth mentioning as part of your
argument about scripts, helping to put scripts into their proper perspective.*   *D. S.*

An awakening of the imagination of film makers by the descriptions of
incidents in a script is preliminary to the actual making of a film. As a
consequence, an audience on confronting the film is subject to conditions
which the reader of a story or of a script is not. "Of course I have read the
script before I go into the cutting room, but that's no substitute for seeing
the film itself. First of all, the script is usually a promise unfulfilled plus lots
of good intentions . . . many good scripts look ridiculous on paper." [10]
A film dictates the pace and direction of the emotions which it arouses.
To be sure, emotions are also aroused, paced, and directed by performances in the theatre, where the audience functions as a fourth wall.
They are also aroused, paced, and directed by the dance, for which the
audience provides limits and environment. In both these arts, audiences
help constitute performances, though usually not to a great degree. But
while film audiences do affect the nature and import of what they see and
hear, they can contribute nothing to an actual performance. A camera
stands in their way. Film audiences add interpretations and give new
meaning to what they confront; they are present at and help constitute the
performances that are caught in the film. But their interactions, unlike those
characteristic of audiences at plays and dances, are not with what is being
made but only what is shown after it has been made.
The spread of space, the passage of time, and particularly the dynamic
transition from cause to effect, present to the emotions, that the film elicits,
external insistencies through which one can faintly discern a single, final,
irreducible, powerful Existence. All arts arouse the emotions, and all lead
men to Existence, but none seems to take them so surely and directly to
it, an ultimate reality, at once spatial, temporal, and dynamic.
The imagination is awakened by the film, as it is by other arts. What is

then grasped is enriched and its emotional effectiveness increased. The emotions continue to be effective after the film is over. The imagination then need no longer be exercised for the emotions themselves suffice to bring one to Existence. A script also awakens the imagination, and may have some emotional effectiveness. But it does not enable one to be face to face with Existence. That is another reason why it should not be taken to be a work of art. At its best, it offers a way of imagining what Existence might be like, but that very imagining, by its vividness and particularity, keeps one from an immediate confrontation with what is dim but ultimate. Imagination must be left behind if one is to discern what is ultimately real. A story will do this. When the experience with it or any other art is over, we are left facing Existence, at once threatening and promising, ominous and benign.

A script is written for a film, and not for an audience, not even the audience of that film. Herman exaggerates when he concludes that "a screen play should never be written to be read" [11] because he supposes that a "screen writer creates only a set of directions for the director, the actors, the cameraman, and the vast horde of other craftsmen." [12] But the supposition does lead him to offer a good, quick way of evaluating a script: "The test of a screen play should be not how it reads, but rather how effective it is in describing scenes to be photographed, dialogue to be heard, and actions to be seen." [13] A script, though, need not stimulate film makers to imagine what the film might be or ought to be. It will be enough if it prompts them to make a film, even one quite unlike what the script led them to envisage.

A script is a single whole, though it allows its incidents to be detached from one another. One can note their beginnings and endings, and work inside these limits to modify their natures and development. Because they are so presented, it is possible for other film makers to connect those incidents in ways not specified by the script. The other film makers, though, do not simply set the incidents alongside one another. They, and particularly the editor and the director, set them within larger causal transactions, themselves set in a larger dynamic whole. That larger whole, which extends from the beginning to the end of the film, has the incidents as organically connected parts. By spreading beyond the limits of the screen, the organic larger whole also enables the audience to be embedded, with it, inside a still larger dynamism. The script says nothing of this dynamism,*

---

* Many scripts do—and could not be sold if they did not.   R. T.

---

and gives only faint hints of the organic nature of the actual film. A film is always more than a script made visible. The fact was remarked by Panofsky in 1934: "the invention of the sound track in 1928 has been unable to change the basic fact that a moving picture, even when it has learned to talk, remains a picture that moves and does not convert itself into a piece of writing that is enacted." *

Films learned to talk many times before 1927, but were rejected by the powers that be, including audiences. As Mary Pickford once pointed out: "It may be that the 'silent' film should have evolved from the 'talkie,' rather than the other way around."   R. T.

A script need provide only an articulate, paced, tensed, intelligible structure which enables others to make a fine film. It is not to be compared with the structuralizations employed in other arts. But if a comparison must be made, it should be with a musical composition rather than with a written play. Though a script uses language and communicates ideas, and though its intent is not to produce an aesthetic complex of sounds, it is pointed at the world of film making. Similarly, a musical composition is directed toward the music that is to be played. But, unlike a script, it usually also has an excellence of its own, allowing it to be dealt with as a work of art apart from the playing of it, at the same time that it gives primary place to sound.

A good scriptist has a good idea of the visual and aural impact of what he is outlining. It is not his function, though, to portray in advance what the performers will do,* what the camera will record, what the editor will con-

---

* Not true. He does not control it entirely, but when Burt Lancaster kisses Deborah Kerr as the surf batters them, you can bet it was in the script long before the actors were even damp — or cast for that matter. The screenwriter has a pretty good idea how a healthy male and female animal are going to act and react if their mutual desire is impervious to waves. Goosebumps can be foreseen.   R. T.

---

nect and preserve, or what the director will seek to express and exhibit. A Hamlet on the stage about to kill the king conveys his hesitation through his speech, and makes his acts conform to this. Were a film script to try to capture that situation, it would show a Hamlet hesitating because of something at once audible and visible which revealed what he had in mind about salvation, or fear, or hell, or retribution. Hamlet's hesitation would then be presented in the script as something which others are to translate and exhibit in a film.

Words denote in a play. In a script, they are more like the title of a painting or a sculpture than they are like parts of daily language or of the language of actors in a play. The words in a script mark out particular actions that are to govern the attitudes and gestures of the performers and the placing and use of the camera. They punctuate time, and thereby allow one to have an intimation of what time and, incidentally, the other dimensions of Existence really are.

If a play is used to make a film, it will have to be radically altered, not merely by translating the discourses into incidents which are their visual counterparts, but by shifting the focus to the visible, and making the speech incidental or supplementary.* It is, therefore, highly questionable

---

* *What about famous film solioquies — i.e., Charles Laughton's in the un-finished "I, Claudius"?* R. T.

---

whether a play of Shakespeare's could be put on film without being radi-cally altered.* Yet there is no reason why a play of his could not be made

---

* *It is just as difficult to recognize Shakespeare on the contemporary stage as it is in Roman Polanski's nude* Macbeth. R. T.

---

into a script and filmed — if one were willing to abandon or minimize many of the exciting speeches.* Factors which the playwright† did not mention,

---

* *Having brought up Shakespeare, you ought to say more about the vari-ous Olivier efforts, particularly* Henry V *and* Hamlet, *and some of the Orson Wells movies. Also, how about filmed plays — as with the Burton* Hamlet? *They aren't perfect, but they're better than your theories would allow.*

D. S.

† *As, perhaps, for instance in Orson Welles's* Othello. *But one hardly saw the Othello one has come to know and love in Orson's London stage pro-duction of that play.* R. T.

---

and which perhaps would be irrelevant to a staging, would have to be brought into sharp focus. Fine scripts are produced by men who are atten-tive, not to what the stage requires, but to the special needs of film. Some directors denigrate scripts. Some speak as if they never used one, or as if they took it to be unimportant. They are somewhat in the position of those conductors who minimize the value of a musical composition, and give themselves most of the credit for a musical performance. Both make the same error, the counterbalance of one made by those musicians who insist that they slavishly follow the score. Both film makers and musicians can faithfully follow a guide, but they still will do much the guide does not prescribe, invite, or even consider.

Scripts differ from scores in normally making use of language, and in allowing for distinctive visual developments. Both are guides to be vitalized by the creative work of those who utilize them. They are agencies for making something else possible; but this something else they do not usually control.

In a play, an actor confronts what makes a difference to him; the film shows the import of the confrontation for the performer. A written play reports *

---

* *Oedipus's bleeding and eyeless sockets, one would suggest, is a good deal more than mere reportage.*   *R. T.*

---

the effect a confrontation has on the actors; a script shows that it is an effect. The script sets the effect in the same world with the cause; the play first sees what the effect is on the actors before it allows us to see what there will be in the world in which the cause operated.

When an actor on the stage says hello to another, we await the reaction of that other, and then further discourse or other actions in response to that reaction.* In the film we can see what the greeting means to both;† its

---

* *No. No. Too simple. If the actor says hello, pulls a gun and shoots the other actor between the eyes, we will hardly be awaiting further discourse.*
                                                                                      R. T.
†*Not if the camera stays only on the speaker. We may be with Bernadette greeting the Virgin Mary.*   *R. T.*

---

intent can be conveyed even if there is concentration on the speaker. To achieve that effect on the stage, one would have to make use of asides or other devices which, for the moment, set the actor apart.

In a film, a concentration of one of the actors, through close-ups or portrayals of what he has in mind, is an integral part of his greeting the other. That fact will normally be conveyed in the script, though not necessarily by an explicit statement to that effect. The director and editor do not mechanically carry out what is there expressed; the script does not tell them what such carrying out demands.

Lindgren seems to deny this: "It is the script that guides both director and editor, and the pattern of cutting tempos that they produce in the finished film can only be one that already exists in more or less clearly defined outline in the narrative embodied in the script." [14] Were he right, directors and editors would be less creative and free than they in fact are.

A written play is so much a part of an acted play that changes in the one usually involve changes in the other, whereas considerable change can be made in a script without altering its thrust, value, or intent. This is due in part to the fact that changes in a written play are normally made preliminary to an acting, whereas the alterations made on what the script presents are usually produced in the course of the making of an actual film. It is as if one were to improvise on the opening night of a play, were it not that the changes made by other film makers are usually not unprepared improvisations but controlled, creative contributions to the making of a film. A script contributes significantly to any film that deserves to be termed a work of art. No such work is ever a purely spontaneous, random product; there is always an articulate idea guiding, controlling it. But the script is rarely dominant. When it functions as one among a set of independent contributions, it fails to exert the influence that the others do, mainly because it and its author exert little or no control over what is done to realize what it conveys. Yet it is important. Its idea and its spacings, pacings, suggestions, and distinctions, if they do not play some role in the making of every film, do play a not inconsiderable one in the making of a good film, even one which is exuberant, freshly made, with an emphasis on randomness, unpredictability, and the nonverbal.*

---

*I do not see that you have really told us the differences between play and script. A playwright rewrites his play during rehearsals, tryouts, previews — sometimes at the insistence of director, actor, or star. Playwrights have been known to be banned from the theatre in which their plays were being rehearsed. As for film, no one can tell you who did what in a film. It varies so enormously. The "auteur" — if there is any such animal outside Montmartre — may be the actor (Mary Pickford), the writer (Ayn Rand), the director (Hitchcock), the money man (James Aubrey), the editor or the producer (Selznick), the censor, the studio policy — whoever or whatever. You have to be there to know. Even that doesn't help most people: Lillian Ross is absurd on the subject of The Red Badge of Courage, as is Pauline Kael on Citizen Kane. Functions overlap. I have done makeup on my leading actors, written scenes in a cutting room, and have had dialogue that wasn't in the filmed version looped over a long shot. The actors hadn't been saying those words at all, but, at that distance, no one could tell what they had been saying. Filming had been over for months and the director long since dispensed with.   R. T.

CHAPTER 3

Performers

When enterprises reach maturity, appropriate concepts and words also begin to achieve a relative clarity and distinctness. It is conceivable that the enterprises exert an influence on the thought and language, though it seems just as reasonable to suppose that the influence operates in the opposite direction, or in both directions at once. More likely than not, the very same conditions which govern the development of an enterprise govern the formation and use of appropriate terms. In any case, film has now reached the point where it should be treated as a distinct art, demanding an independent analysis, and requiring one to forge ideas and to produce a vocabulary that are singularly pertinent to it.

Just as the first automobiles were conceptualized and spoken of as "horseless carriages," so some of the early films were conceptualized and spoken of as plays performed before cameras. We still speak of "film actors." Yet the problems, tasks, and often the abilities of those who are being filmed are too dissimilar from those characteristic of actors on the stage to make it worthwhile to deal with them in common ways. Grown men and children, humans and animals are so disparate in what they are, do, and achieve on the stage as to make one question the right to designate them all as "actors," while the performances of filmed adults, children, animals, inanimate objects, the skilled, and the unskilled are often so indistinguishable as to make desirable the use of a single term to refer to them all.

Only grown men deserve to be called "actors," for only they can act with some consciousness of what their parts mean in relation to others. A child can not know what it is to be a parent; it can not act the part of a child properly. Yet it makes more sense to speak of the child as an actor having some affiliation with what actors do on the stage, than it does to speak of the greatest of film stars as "actors," for it is one thing to carry out a role in a play in interaction with other roles and quite another to perform before a camera. To use "actor" to refer to both those who are filmed and those who assume roles on the stage is to mute radical differences. It will make for clarity if we hereafter speak of the one as "performers," and reserve "actors" to refer only to those who have roles in staged plays.

Performers need not take on any roles; they can be filmed as they go about their ordinary business; they may make up part of the background; they may, like props or stage settings, serve merely to allow some figure to stand out, or to be able to function. Strictly speaking, no one performer yields a filmed performance. A performance is an indivisible unity in which different performers are parts in somewhat the way that their gestures and clothes are parts of them, the main difference between the two consisting in the fact that performers have their distinctive, separate paces, whereas gestures and clothes normally do not, but are under the control of the performer.

Nevertheless, there are a number of striking similarities between performers and actors. Both engage in specified actions in limited contexts and for the limited time required by an incident; both submit to conditions required for viewing them; neither is able to control the work as a whole; both function under the guidance of a director.* There are also striking

---

*Charlie Chaplin, of course, was his own director. But Mary Pickford, Douglas Fairbanks, William S. Hart, Tom Mix, and many other stars used their directors as you or I would use a butler or a maitre d'. R. T.

---

dissimilarities between human and other performers. The maturity, sophistication, self-consciousness, and understanding which is possible to the one contrasts with the native innocence, lack of experience, limited intelligence, and insufficient self-discipline of the other. But the similarities between performer and actor can not hide their more striking dissimilarities, any more than the dissimilarities between humans and nonhumans can hide their similarities when they become performers. It is true, too, that an occasional actor, an Ethel Barrymore, an Olivier, a Brando may perform most successfully for a film. Olivier swings back and forth with considerable success from performing to acting, and Brando gave up a great career as an actor for that of a great performer. But instead of offering exceptions to the contention that performing and acting are quite distinct activities, such cases show that a few men are able to contribute significantly to more than one art.

Actors on a stage appear before an audience, and do so to develop a plot. Performers appear without an audience for short disconnected stretches. One can, with Nichols, take them to perform before a studio audience, but

then, with him, one will have to distinguish this from their true or "actual" audience: "On the stage of a film studio the actor still has an audience, though a small one; the half-hundred people who comprise 'the crew' — grips, juicers, cameramen, script girl, and all the familiar others. But if he acts in such a style as to affect the audience solely he is lost, for his audience is miles away and they will see him only through the uncaring single eye of the camera that looks on like a tripod man from Mars." [1]
An actor is governed by the play as a whole; a performer sustains a detached incident. A performer may be filmed in two incidents, one after the other, though the incidents may in fact belong to different parts of the film and have very little to do with one another. A performer might be filmed in a hotel room where the film is supposed to begin; if there is a return to the hotel room much later, with a number of new performers, as a consequence of an incident that was filmed at the seaside, the two hotel room incidents will nevertheless be shot one after the other. The performer in both cases is asked to function in a situation, to make an incident possible, and that is all. There may be nothing which he has to convey from within himself, but only something to exhibit for the film. He is audience-free and is caught up in incidents.
The living communication of actor with audience, and often of actor with actor, is denied the performer.* In compensation, the performer can be

---

One must not forget that the crew — and it is sometimes quite enormous — is a very professional audience and frequently reacts as such during filming. As Judy Garland said: There is a "large crowd of technicians behind a very candid camera . . . perhaps this professional 'audience' is a surer guide to achievement than any other. They are not there primarily to be entertained. So, when after I sang a song on the set [and] some of these veterans applauded, I knew that it was a spontaneous reaction and that I had made contact with their emotions."   R. T.

---

caught from many angles; he can be shown close up, in profile, from above or below. The film performer may speak, presumably to some one, and yet no one may be there. He need not have any experience, either on the stage or before a camera; his only function may be to typify a character, a way of moving, or a physiognomy. Some directors prefer performers who have had no training, and who yield completely to them. For Stroheim performers were "mere tools of his craft. They express *him* not themselves." [2]
A series of short performances can be pieced together by others to yield a single performance which never in fact had been carried out, and of

which the performer had no inkling. Griffith, remarks Dwight MacDonald, "used to keep his actors in ignorance about the plot in order to keep the control more completely in his own hands." [3]* But on the stage one wants

---

This was not always true of Griffith. Some directors demand weeks of rehearsals before they begin filming.   R. T.

---

professionals, who by training are able to give themselves to a particular part in interplay with others, so as to develop and carry out the plot in a single complex occurrence.

It is more than a pun to say that a performer knows nothing of the whole and therefore has no part in it.* Each incident is complete in itself; in each

---

Again, one would have to ask which performer. Some performers had and have complete control over every aspect of their productions — including the hiring and firing of directors. Among other examples: Mary Pickford, who imported Ernst Lubitsh to this country, also fired him from the picture she was directing him in. It is amusing to note that Mae Murray came back each night to reshoot her close-ups in The Merry Widow after Von Stroheim had left the set for the day. She made sure those close-ups got into the hands of Mayer, Thalberg, and Maggie Booth, and many of them are in the final film. She knew what she wanted and was a good deal more pleased with the final film than Von Stroheim was.   R. T.

---

he exhausts his status as a performer. As a rule, he does not rehearse. Nor does the performer learn a part which is to mesh with the parts provided by others. When called upon to repeat a bit of action again and again before the camera, he is not engaged in a rehearsal for some final, publicly viewed results, but is instead being asked to offer alternative renditions of what is wanted. Sometimes one hears of a film director who insists on "rehearsals," but these are usually dry runs of a final performance carried out away from the camera, presumably to cut down the expenses involved in making a number of alternatives. A rehearsal of an acted play is different from this. The actors are there helped, guided, interrelated as part of the process of making a theatrical work. A filmic dry run is the very performance that is to be given before the camera, checked on ahead of time; a rehearsal is a preliminary step in the course of getting a play staged. A performer, nevertheless, may rehearse before he presents himself for a filming. His rehearsal is not comparable to the rehearsal of an actor, but to an actor's solitary mastering of a role before he in fact comes to an actual rehearsal. Alternatively, if one takes what is finally filmed to be a performance, one can say that a performer does nothing but rehearse before a camera, again and again trying to present an incident. The performance that is chosen to be included in the final film need not be the last of his efforts, nor need it be the most successful. It is simply that which others take to be more suited to be together with what else is finally accepted for the film.* The performer here is taken to offer a number of ex-

---

* But, of course, this is true on the stage too. The director may choose in that instance too. And many a time one hears an actor complain: "But if I'd done it the way I wanted to. . . ." R. T.

---

hibits of a piece under the guidance of others; someone else decides which of these is to be a final performance because most in consonance with what is wanted in the work as a whole.

From this point of view, the performer does not even get to perform in the film; he is the source of new material which others will utilize. I agree with the tenor of Lindgren's remarks: "In a film that is not simply a cinematographic record of theatre acting the actor is not all-important; he is no more than one of the several technicians who combine their talents to produce a number of film shots, and it is those shots, not the actor's performance, that constitute the filmic medium. Not only does the film actor perform under the immediate guidance and control of the director, but the effect of his performance may be modified by his other collaborators, or by the way in which the separate fragments of his performance are cut and arranged by the editor.[4]

Jerry Lewis, himself neither a distinguished performer nor a distinguished director, nevertheless explicitly says what many directors fear to record: performers are irresponsible, without full awareness of what they are doing, they are to be indulged and humored. Such a view stands in shocking contrast with the attitude taken toward outstanding performers by the general public, the mass media, historians of the film, and critics. For most of them, the performer is a very important, perhaps the most important part of a film. He is a crucial factor, a focal point.

Both interpretations of the performer detach the performer from the film. To speak of a performer as irresponsible is to speak of him as though he had nothing to do but obey the director; to take him to be an exemplar of virility or pulchritude, virtue or villainy, charm or horror, or to be the one who gives the film its character or value is to speak of him as possessing or sustaining traits rather than as one who gives them a cinematic value.*

---

* And does not something similar apply to stage actors? R. T.

A related error is made by those who take film to be essentially a script

made visible and audible by a director, a camera, a cutting, and a splic-
ing. They forget that it is the final film which gives the performer his true
status; he is always more than one who appeared before a camera. In the
final film, he has supports, neighbors, and, most important, a significance
he could not obtain through his own efforts, or even with the help of other
performers.

A different but related mistake sinks the performance into the man, sometimes with a reverse twist, or into a performer, often idealized. Film maga-
zines and gossip columns are inclined to do the first; critics and students
of the film often do the second.

The first makes much of the fact that the screen villain is a good or bad
father to his children, that he does much for charity, or that he gambles. It
strains to find in a woman's four marriages some explanation of the way
she acts the part of an innocent, a tart, or a mother. Though everything a
man does, even when just performing, tells something about him, it might
be something quite minor, or highly general. It may merely show how
flexible or diligent he is, or how well he is able to sustain a sympathetic
imagination with appropriate bodily acts. The identification of man and his
performance is most common and least legitimate when the performance
is made to illustrate a certain type of man — usually one who incarnates just
one virtue or vice, such as courage or cowardice, honesty or unreliability.
That the identification is improper becomes glaringly evident when one attends to film farces and their performers — Keystone Cops, Chaplin, Laurel
and Hardy, Keaton, the Marx Brothers. The comic events and the characters that sustain them are accepted by everyone as being quite remote
from what the men are in fact. What is true of them is true of others who perform in films. Before a camera, men absent themselves to allow a performer
to be seen. Chaplin is no more a tramp than Laughton is a king or a glutton.
There is a tramp, having some resemblance to Chaplin, who eats the laces
of his shoes when hungry; there is a gluttonous king who looks like
Laughton. The one is as real as the Chaplin whose public remarks are
often petulant, and as real as the Laughton who was born and died. The
man of childish conceit and the tramp, the human Laughton and the gluttonous king are partial realities by means of which we can become aware
of something deeper, more abiding, and more fully real. There is some warrant, though, for identifying animals or things with their performances. It is
not absurd to say that they are what they do. But they, too, are realities
which the film — and perception, science, and common sense — exhibit
only in part.

It is at once true and false that a man is killed in a film. If it were not true, film would be just illusion, and only something like a biological death would be a reality. If it were not false, a murder would have been committed, and the police, we hope, would stop the film and take after the culprit. A death occurs in a film, but it is only a part of what really occurs. But, then, a biological death is also not the whole of what occurs, shorn as it is of the value which a death has for a family and in a film. The full reality of a death is not given by biology, film, or common sense; it is the terminus of the career of an actual man in an actual world, lying outside all specific approaches, but referred to and illuminated by them in different ways. Film tells us what is the case, via a distinct set of appearances related to the same reality to which other appearances, met with outside the film, also lead, along different paths and with different efficacies. A performance throws little light on what a man is and does when not being filmed. But it tells a good deal about him as a performer, i.e., one who carries out a role. Roles prescribe limited sets of acts to be performed in specific circumstances. Each by itself is general, indeterminate, achieving some specification through its interaction with other roles, while depending for its vitality, details, and full meaning on its embodiment in actual performances.

Personalizers overindividualize their roles; they crowd out all else by their personalities and idiosyncratic expressions. No matter what the role, it is they who are evident, not as individual men, to be sure, but as individual film performers. Arliss is a good example. *Types,* instead, carry out their roles in a series of distinct moves serving to illustrate specific traits or characters. These performers exemplify some virtue or vice; they are the character actors in grade B films, the performers in most westerns. *Carriers* go through the particular movements which a role requires, but instead of realizing the role, they dismember it, presenting required act after required act, without conveying a sense of the role. Inept performers belong here; so do personalizers and types when they are so badly cast that they can not express themselves or show what they can do. The best performers are *vivifiers*. When critics and students of the film speak of a "Bogie," a "Garbo," or a "Tracy" film, they normally refer to the fact that a role is being individualized without being overpersonalized. Vivifiers, however, usually have only a limited range; there are only certain roles that they are able to master. Given something else to do, they become just carriers.

These classes have no sharp boundaries. Performers who normally belong in one sometimes surprise themselves and us by their ability to perform well as members of another. An Olivier tends to overpersonalize, but in *Richard III* he shows himself to be a great vivifier. No complication of one class will take one into another. Guinness neither overpersonalizes nor vivifies. He is a character actor, but one who tries to exhibit many types of performance. These could never equal a single vivification of a role, for types always remain insufficiently individualized, severally and together. Each performer normally performs by himself. This is true even when he is struggling, responding, reacting. Nor can a role be displayed short of an entire work—something not usually permitted to a performer, though it is required of an actor. Actors, even when alone on the stage, act together with others, and as part of an entire play; performers, even when together with others, face the camera by themselves and then as engaged in only a limited set of acts. A performer is confined within the incidents that he produces; an actor is in the play. We have here one more reason why it is possible to use performers who have had no experience before the camera. They can be asked simply to make some incident take place. They may do this with some self-consciousness; they may lack the control and nuance characteristic of those who are well trained. But, by taking many different filmings from many different angles, through the use of dissolves, cuts, and splicings, it is possible to obtain a desired result.

A performer produces material to be used by other film makers, but an actor is constitutive of the play, helping make it be. An actor has to know what the play is about, what others are saying and what they mean, and what the proper response should be, but a performer need know only what he is to do in certain situations. He may have read the script, he may know what he is to do next, but not necessarily know how his performance fits in with what else is filmed.

An actor usually operates in a fixed area. He knows where he stands and how this functions in relation to other positions on the stage, to other individuals, and to the props. A performer, in contrast, does not know exactly where he stands. To be sure, he is placed here rather than there, but this placing here rather than there may be dislocated when it comes to relating this to what else is filmed. It is even dislocated in the very course of the filming itself, for as the camera moves close in, or moves away, or shifts from this angle to that, or as the lights change, the very position which had been occupied by the performer begins to change in meaning. An actor is located in relation to other actors and other things within a fixed and given and well-determined place; a performer, in effect, is given a definite place by others afterward.

An actor is presumed to know how to carry out his role. Asked to act as someone angered, he knows a number of fundamental things that he must exhibit for anger of such and such a nature in such and such a circumstance to be shown. Since a performer may be denied knowledge of the circumstance, and even against whom and for whom the anger is being utilized, one may be able to ask him only to enrich a particular momentary gesture rather than to illuminate a part. A director may tell him to move his hand here or there, to put his foot in this position or that, to look up at the wall or the ceiling, to close his eyes, to shift his posture — things that would not normally be said to an actor, except incidentally in the course of a rehearsal in order to subtilize a part which he already partly understood. The performer is here treated as though he were an amateur stage actor at his first rehearsal. Some performers, of course, are more talented than others, and some are remarkably incompetent, without a sense even of what a gesture involves. But both may perform equally well for a final film. On the stage, for the most part, we see the whole body of a man. On the screen we can sometimes see no more than his face, or just his eyes, his mouth, his hands, or his feet. These tell a great deal — and omit a great deal. They allow us to sharpen the perception of certain telltale gestures, and to exclude, for the time being, the contribution made by the entire body. Where the performance adds gesture to gesture, isolated movement to isolated movement, the actor carries out a role supported and specified by his gestures and movements.

A performance is something like a first night, arrived at without adequate preparation. Each is unique, and each is not altogether what it should be. More accurately, a performance is usually like one of a set of first nights, for it is one of a set of quite similar performances, not one of a series of performances, each benefiting from what had been done before. Though a mistake or misinterpretation can be remarked upon and corrected, the various performances are alternatives, not developments. Yet each is only a preliminary, since it is just material for what the performance will finally be in the film.

The fact that a performer is concerned with external behavior, with gestures and movements, within which perhaps some emotional content can be put by the skilled, makes it possible for there to be performers who are children, in a sense in which there can not be child actors. Child actors are props on the stage, but child performers are performers equal to any others; they, too, need do nothing more than fill out some particular kind of pattern, without necessarily knowing what it imports to others or what difference it makes to the entire situation.

It is possible, too, in a film, to have one individual substitute for another—in dangerous places, sometimes because an accident has occurred, or a performer is not available. This can not be done on the stage. It is conceivable, of course, that a new actor might replace one who had suddenly become ill, but there would then be a change in tone. In a film substitution, a good replacement is one that is not noticed. It is even possible to replace a great character actor or a great vivifier without affecting the tonality of the work, for the difference between the original and the replacement can be minimized beyond any preassigned degree by camera work and editing.

The restriction of a performance to detached incidents forces a performer to concentrate on a limited repertoire of movements and sounds. Since, as a rule, he does not know the import of the incidents he is helping constitute, he must so far be guided in quite elementary ways by the director. An experienced actor, in contrast, as he learns his part in solitude, has already told himself many of the things he is to do on the stage. He may be corrected and redirected, but these are all on the way to making his a polished piece of acting. A performer for a film, unless he is merely filling out the well-known lines of some established character—when his task is even further removed from genuine acting—has little to learn, but many instructions to follow. Some film directors prefer to use untrained men and women in their films, because what they want is not the assumption of a role but the exhibition of a particular movement, gesture, look, or appearance. Those directors then make up for the inadequacy in the performance by what they do with the results achieved—eliminating some, muting others, relating them in new ways.

A performer helps constitute an incident before a film camera, and for and before a film director. The camera, unlike the audience in a theatre or a dance, does not occupy a fixed position. It travels. It changes its place also through the use of different types of lens. Different techniques used in its manipulation allow it, while stationary, to film a performance as at a distance or as nearby, as clearly or dimly seen, as large or small, as envisageable from few or many perspectives. Because it is a machine, no one can perform for it. Since the performer has no audience, he must be content to perform not only before but for the director.

A director is not an audience; he does not help constitute a performance; he is not receptive, appreciative, allowing himself to be carried along by what he confronts. He is an instructor who helps a performer constitute incidents through which an audience is to live for a while. It is the director, not the performer, who is alert to what the audience will see and how it will presumably respond. The audience assumes the position of the camera because the director had taken this as the position from which the film is to be viewed. He sees the performance as a performance for an audience.*

---

* I think there is too much emphasis here on equating camera with audience. This seems to be a very popular approach in many books today, but I do think it is somewhat limited, and begins to set up a paradigm for the film-going experience which is not altogether true or consistent. Again, it is the film artist, I think, who establishes just what is to be the audience/camera's function and position with respect to one another. In one of Bazin's books, there is an excellent discussion of a film called Lady in the Lake, *which is shot entirely with a subjective camera. That is, from the point of view of one of the characters whom we never see. Bazin points out that instead of making the audience identify with that character (that is, because we see through his eyes, we should take on his role), the film has precisely the opposite effect. In other words, we feel most alienated from him because our view is so artificially constricted. In film, we identify with the character who is on camera. This is because of the mythic nature of film. We identify with the leading characters as we do in Aeschylus, etc.* E. S.*
There is, I think, no incompatibility between assuming the position of a camera and even of a performer before the camera, and identifying with the performer seen. In film, we normally identify with the performer seen, but from the position of the camera.* J. W.

2

Acting occurs in a theatrical space; a performance takes place on a set. Both differ considerably from ordinary space. Theatrical space is an enclosed region within which a play occurs; the space of a set is an enclosed region which is to be utilized by a performer. Ordinary space, in contrast with both, has a structure and an expanse independent of the objects which occupy it.
A theatrical space is integral to a play and is geometrized by it; it is divorced from ordinary space. To act in a play and to appreciate it one must leave ordinary space behind, and enter into a space having no reference to it. Ordinary space is a single homogeneous stretch of

minimum intensity, where each distinguishable position is a term and a relation; it is no container unaffected by the objects within it. There is not first a bare space and then occupants; there always is a multiplicity of distinctive, vitalized extensions interconnected by less intensive ones. The vitalized extensions are as integral to their objects as theatrical space is to an unfolding play. But the one is pluralized while the other is single.

The multiple objects in ordinary space charge the space with their attitudes, preparations, and activities, and thereby intensify it to some extent. In contrast, the spatiality of an actor is of little moment in the play; it has little intensity in comparison with the theatrical space. What the actors do in that space has repercussions on them, and this in turn has an effect on the space in which they interplay. There is, as a consequence, a constantly altering value both to the spaces of the actors and the space of the play.

The space of a film set differs from both the space of ordinary life and the space of a play. Like a theatrical space, a set is cut off from ordinary space, and has its own geometry, spacings, distances, and intensity. Like the actor, a performer is affected by the space in which he carries out his role, but unlike the actor, he is not coordinate with what else is there.*

I worry about your notion of space. The space of a set may or may not coincide with the space of a frame. The way in which a shot is framed by the cinematographer imposes the space, either on a set or on a location that may be natural and real. Space is less important, therefore, than composition, and a performer looms or dwindles not according to his space-relationship but according to the distance between his head and the lens. In any case, it is the director and cinematographer and not the camera that may be called the performer. To call the camera a performer or the audience is to indulge in animism.   D. S.

A performer may be filmed apart from any other and await the act of an editor to place him in relation to others who had also been filmed separately. The product will be a newly constructed, single, charged whole. This achievement exhibits in an obvious way what in fact happens during a performance. Each performer, even when in close proximity with others in a set is asymmetrically related to the others. There is no space which they share, but only a space that they diversely use, and vectors which they project, to be later manipulated by an editor.

Each incident has its own space. All other spaces are disconnected from it.

This has a corollary: any region of space, with its incident, can be connected with any other. The number of possible spatial wholes to be constructed out of filmed incidents is equal to the number of combinations one can make out of them. All combinations are possible — though not equally interesting or satisfying — because all spatial connections are adventitious. No thing is intrinsically remote or near something else. Though the particular juxtaposition actually confronted may shock the audience, and therefore arouse and frustrate or satisfy emotions not aroused, frustrated or satisfied by a different juxtaposition, the emotions can continue to be operative after the film is over, and lead one to know a space without locations, without a near or far, a here or there, an up or down.

3

Acting and performing also require different kinds of time. Their times contrast with the monotonous, homogeneous time acknowledged in physical science; with the experience-laden times of perception and commonsense; with historic time and its episodes of varying lengths pivoting about significant occurrences in the adventures of mankind; with a religious time which is under the control of eternity and is constrained, perhaps, by some final event; with the time of music with its distinctive rhythms, rests, and connections; with the time of a story, a dance; with psychological time — indeed, with any time other than that which is an inseparable part of the distinctive time of a play or of particular, detached, performed incidents.

The time which characterizes the scenes and events in a play slows down and quickens; it is interspersed with rests and transitions inseparable from the words, gestures, actions, and interplays of the actors. The very same play, which takes two hours to perform in ordinary daily time, can be incredibly long or short, depending on how it is acted. The length of the time is to be dismissed as "illusory" or "subjective," only if the ordinary time, or some other, is taken to be "real." * One will then make a

---

* True, and not true. There are deviations from real time in slow motion or fast motion, where the rate of film in the camera is deviated from normal. The psychological time of a blossom's opening is puzzling, but it can look quite balletic. A trick, of course, but art is a lot of tricks.　　D. S.

---

choice of some particular type of object or occurrence as alone truly real. In effect, one will have engaged in a "reductionism" or a denudation of the world, the one if the rejected times and objects are explained as being only complications or deviations from the accepted one, the other if they are just canceled out. But each reduction or cancellation not only accepts data to reduce or cancel, and therefore faces what it does not provide, but each can be countered by opposing reductions or cancellations. It is not too difficult to take the position of what was made to suffer the initial reduction or cancellation, and then go on and reduce or cancel what had reduced or canceled it.

An actor operates within the single indivisible present of a play. That present can be given dates at the beginning and ending which are very far apart, but this does not affect the fact that the play is a single whole occupying a single present moment. Within that present moment one can distinguish parts that are before and parts that are after; those parts can be presented in an order of earlier and later. Still, as parts of the play they occur within distinguished portions of an indivisible time. Those who would withdraw from this conclusion can not take recourse in the acceptance of some other present moment of time, without coming up against the very same problem of parts in an order of before and after, and which, as outside that present, may occur in a relation of earlier and later. Even if one were not to grant this point, and maintained, instead, that something less than the entire play was in the present, that something less would occur in an inseparable part of the time of the play.

A play is not a collection of scenes and acts; it is not constructed out of them. The play's the thing; all that one distinguishes within it is but a number of facets of it. In either case, if it be some bit of acting or the entire play which is taken to constitute the theatrical present, an actor helps create scenes which occupy only a limited portion of a single present. That present does not merely stretch beyond the acted scene; it intrudes on what is beyond it, and is intruded upon. What precedes the scene conditions it; the scene, in turn, gives it a new import. What follows the scene also conditions it, and the scene places limitations on the pace and length of what follows. An acted scene may even be conditioned by what has no place within the play, but which is presupposed or entailed by what does take place there, with the consequence that the time of that scene will have nuances which can not be accounted for in the play itself. Character casting, the nature of the role, references to past and future events all enrich the present acting moment by the nature of the time that is dramatically assumed to precede and succeed the events in the play. A performer contributes to the production of detached incidents with their distinct present times. He does not know where what he is helping constitute will appear in the film. Even more surely than the actor, he is affected by what does not occur in the scene, and may never have a place there, and which even affects the time that extends beyond the film itself. Conventions and tradition may carry the performer, and eventually the audience, far outside the confines of the film. But all the while the performance is confined within the incidents and their distinctive times. The pace and shape of those times is inseparable from what temporally occurs.

A film has a distinctive time within which the time of a performance is a subdivision, somewhat as the time of an acted scene is a subdivision of an acted play. There is no affecting of a performance and its time, by what goes on before or after, until the film is constructed. Until it is subject to the constructive art of making a film, the time of the performance is complete in itself. It is then like the time of an entire play, without a past or a future, except, in the sense just mentioned, where it presupposes and entails occurrences outside its confines. But unlike an entire play, whose occurrences are arranged in an order of before and after, and which does present scenes in an order of earlier and later, performances have no distinguishable components, and their times have no distinguishable parts. One can break up a performance, the incident it sustains, and the time ingredient in them, into smaller units, but these will not be subdivisions of it, any more than the movements of the blood, muscles, and tendons are subdivisions of the movement of an arm. The smaller units occur on a different level. They are supports, preconditions, not parts, not subdivisions, not delimitations.

An incident occurs as a single indivisible whole within which there is nothing comparable to a scene or act in a play. But the incident, scene, and act, and their times, are somewhat similar. Each is a complete unit allowing for no distinguishable components. The incident and its time, though, have boundaries that keep them apart from all else, whereas the scene and the act, and their times, are connected with others and are encompassed in the entire play and its time. There is a solidity, therefore, to the performed incident that is lacking to the acted scene. It makes sense to go over the performance again and again to perfect it. Repetition of this sort by an actor risks a disruption of the play. He may have to be coached to say his lines or to act at a particular juncture in a certain way, but this is preliminary to his acting of a scene that is to pass smoothly into another. Because an acted scene is but a delimited part of a whole, it is necessary to avoid treating it as a complete unit. Not all scenes, any more than all the roles, are to be given equal weight, but all incidents are to be performed as final and complete, their times closed off from all others, commonsensical or cinematic.

4

An actor and a performer are involved in distinct dynamic activities. The actor is part of a single whole into which everything else is pulled — the objects in the scene, his pauses and rests, his gestures, and those with whom he interplays — and the audience. The walls within which the scenes occur are, as mere barriers, outside the play, but the natures that they have are part of the play. The audience contributes its emotionality to what is occurring; the setting contributes nuances, agencies, and devices; the actors' pauses and rests determine the pace; each provides the other with material, occasions, limits, contrasts, and supports. Within the play as a whole, the particular situation which an actor then may bring about is caught up in a larger indivisible process with its characteristic beginning, development, climax, and ending, thrusting backward and forward into a larger environing causal whole.

The dynamism of a play does not depend on the players. There are in fact very few transactions that occur on a stage. Someone, to be sure, may be pushed, hit, shot, interrupted, surprised, helped; someone may read a letter, leave a house, enter a room. An envelope is torn open, a fire is raked, there is a sitting down and a standing up, movements back and forth, touchings, holdings. These can not be separated into illusory and real occurrences. All are significant in the play, and none of them produces in the play the very effects it produces outside. The actor does not look at the words of the letter he is reading; more likely, than not, there are no words there. But he does bend his knees and does sit down, leaning against the back of the chair. The letter reading may be followed by a cry of dismay; the sitting may be followed by a relaxation which cues someone else. Causality in a play is not linear but constitutive; it does not bring about subsequent effects but allows the play to unfold, somewhat in the way in which a people, through the agency of its daily activities, constitutes the daily history of a society.

There may be even less content to the activity displayed by a performer than by an actor, for the performer can have added to him, through cuts and splicings, any number of occurrences and effects with which he was never involved in the course of his performance. Also, less of the surrounding is brought into operation by a performer — and in a different way — than is utilized by an actor. Not only may a performance be cut off from antecedent and subsequent performances, while acting builds on and contributes to other acting in the play, not only may a performance eventually be joined together with what was performed at quite a different time and place, in contrast with the acting which belongs with acting before and after in that play, but a performer stands out against his set. A set for a performer is an environment, not a constituent of his causal activity. Where an actor is a focal point, pulling everything into his orbit, a performer is an occupant of a filmed area.

An actor includes within his dynamic activities whatever else there be, to enrich the meaning of what he is doing and conveying; a performer merely makes use of what he must in order to engage in a performance. The difference is like that between being at one's own home and being in a strange house. A man lives in his entire home no matter where he is in it, but he is never in more than a limited part of the home of another. An actor is at home in a play; a performer is a visitor to a set.

A performance can be accompanied by others. There can be accomplices, helpers, a costar, a supporting cast. But until the camera turns to them, and thereby defines them to be performers as well, they are just the limits within which a particular performance is confined. If the camera turns to the set, it treats this too as a performer, in which the original performer may be nothing more than a subordinate part. The camera will then do for the set what the actor does for the objects in a scene — makes it take on an active role within a dynamic occurrence. The camera does not add a set to someone's performance, but an actor can bring a scene into his acting.

5

A film is designed to exhibit the referents that a theatrical audience has to imagine. If the referents are not filmed, it is because one has engaged in a deliberate cinematographic act of exclusion. This affects what remains. To refer on the stage to what is absent is to make it present; to refuse to film what can be filmed is to absent what is cinematographically present. The meaning of an acted causal transaction is necessarily thinned out by being filmed. To recover what had been lost, the material used in acting must be reduced to a set, and that set must then be made into a performance. The performance of one who is filmed and the performance of the set to which the camera might then turn must subsequently be added together by the editor and director. The result will not be identical with the outcome of an assimilation of a scene by a stage actor. An actor subjugates a scene to his own dynamic course; an editor and director relate filmed set and performer, with the result that they produce a different dynamic whole from that which an actor produces by pulling within his orbit all that is around him.

Because the time, space, and dynamism are different in the two cases, it is not possible to transfer a play from stage to screen by filming it. Kept within the limits of the stage, the range of the camera would be unduly restricted. To get the same result in a film that is produced on a stage one might try first to film an actor who has caught up other actors within his activity, and then, from the position of the first, add films of those other actors to one another. An editor and director would, however, have to help make a film of that original actor's position, would have to add this externally to what they had filmed of the other performers, or would have to substitute for the performers an externally produced union of the action of others. The position from which other performers are brought into dynamic union would then be assumed by the camera and not seen, or that position would be seen but related externally to what else was filmed. Either way, one would fall short of a duplication of what had occurred on the stage. The converse, of course, is also true. It is not possible to duplicate on the stage what had been filmed, for actors are not able to repeat what performers do in a film. It is not lack of skill that stands in their way but a participation in a different art, having a time, space, and dynamics distinct from those which characterize a film.

CHAPTER 4

Cinemakers

Again and again in previous chapters reference was made to a "movie camera." It was also remarked that this had a distinctive function. Now is an appropriate time to see exactly what this is.

The determination of the contributions that a movie camera makes to a film as a work of art brings one almost immediately to the question of just how the problems and products of that camera compare with those which characterize a camera used in photography. To avoid allowing unexamined terms to make one unwittingly suppose that there are affiliations between items when in fact there are none, and at the same time to avoid multiplying terms unnecessarily, I will speak of the one as a "cinemaker," but continue to refer to the other as a "camera."

"Cinemaker" is a barbarism,[1] but like many another, rightly sacrifices elegance and legitimacy for a desirable accuracy and muscularity. It has two primary uses, a specific and a generic. Specifically, it refers to the instrument used in filming; generically, it refers indifferently to the instrument, the men who use it, or the product. When "cinemaker" is contrasted with "camera," one specific use of the term will evidently be stressed; contrasted with "photographer," another; contrasted with the photographer's final product, a third. But apart from all contrasts, "cinemaker" is generic. The context will have to tell us whether what is being referred to is an instrument, man, or product. But, in those cases where it is desirable to emphasize the man who uses the instrument, "cineman" will be used in place of "cinemaker."

There is much in common between cinemaker and camera, in use and in outcome. That is one reason why men have been so long content to use the same term to refer to the different instruments. A cinemaker and a camera both take account of contrasts of darkness and light, of different shapes, and of different positions. Both produce unitary objects having aesthetic values which are dependent on the ways in which elements are interrelated. Both isolate a portion of a larger space by the expedient of cutting off what is not wanted or can not be used. Both present the viewer with what is seen through a lens. And both make possible the production of works which are modifications of what the instruments originally provided.

A photographer, who is an artist,[2] is concerned with producing an excellent work. He does not begin by attending to what is aesthetically satisfying in daily life, but with what, from the position and through the operation of his camera, and through his creative work in a darkroom, will eventuate in an esthetically satisfying object. The final photograph may differ considerably from what was initially confronted and from what the camera recorded. The result can then be framed. If it is, what originally was an edge of the photograph becomes a bounding limit of it, helping to constitute and being constituted by the rest of the photograph. Both photographer and cinemaker can be said to make use of what can be obtained in a single click, but where the one uses this to make something that is to be framed, the other uses it as an integral part of a larger whole.*

*This argument about cameras and cinemakers is wrong, anyway. The single frame is not important, but the framed shot is important, and the extent that shot holds can be a way of punctuating the shot. The story board of Hitchcock is a clear example of how these still-shots are germinal and terminal. The backgrounds of people like Kubrick (a still photographer turned director) or Kurosawa (photographer or painter, I can't remember) suggest that you put too little importance on framing. The lighting of a Leon Shamroy or a James Wong Howe can be personal, distinctive, enhancing. The trouble is that the technical level of most films is so high, that we tend to take for granted the craftsmanship which is betrayed over and over again by writers, directors, producers, and, of course, audiences. How rare to see a badly photographed, badly lit, or badly printed and mixed movie! And how common to read badly written prose or verse, see badly performed dance, listen to incompetently played music!   D. S.

A photographer usually works creatively in his darkroom; similar work is normally left to machines and mechanical operators when we come to the film. A single photograph is what the one desires; its most creative aspects are introduced toward the end. But the end product of a cinemaker is not a single picture. Whatever creativity there is in a single frame comes in the shooting of it, and then only so far as this is a part of the shooting of an incident. A photographer, not a cinemaker, tries to turn the product of his instrument into something better, by working on it subsequently; a cinemaker, but not a photographer, tries to make something, not confined within a single frame, no matter how excellent this might be.

What a cinemaker produces is never final; it is to be used by other film makers as material for a film. His product stands to the film somewhat as a photograph stands to a gallery full of photographs, or to some artistic display of photographs — as having a place within a different art. But where a photograph is intended to be an excellent work in a setting, a single filmed frame is not. A cinemaker who concentrates on producing excellent single stills gives his pictures a disproportionate role, for they are intended in conception and place to be subordinate. Levinson, with some justice, takes the single frame to be an abstract unity, but the reason he gives, that it lasts for a part of a second, does not suffice to show this. "The isolated image normally occupying the screen for $1/16$ [$1/24$] second, is only an abstract unity." [3] But then he rightly goes on to remark that "it does not proceed as a whole, and does not function by itself. Like literature, the cinema is a living language not composed of isolated words drawn from the dictionary; it is their context, their fixed or free relation to other words which make them live." [4]

A cineman must avoid acting like a photographer who is willing to sacrifice something of his photograph in order to make it fit better with the other photographs that some gallery might display. Such a photographer is not an artist, but somebody helping make the gallery into a work of art by offering it material to be creatively used there. A cinemaker who is an artist attends to incidents stretching over time. He does not, like a photographer, concern himself with making single pictures and does not, therefore, have to ask himself what he must sacrifice in order to make them fit together. He is concerned with creating something else, from which single pictures can be removed. What he does will itself be reordered by others, but that is not his concern. If he filmed incidents splendidly, he has made his contribution to the art of film.

A cinemaker, we know, need not remain fixed when recording its unit incidents; it may move in and out, shift angles, approach from above, below, or the sides. And, of course, the lighting can be varied throughout. A cinemaker can reveal a rhythm no camera can, for this is forced to detach a location from the rest of space, a moment from the whole of time, and a fact from a dynamic process. The spatial region that a camera lets us see is a fixated abstraction, separated from the extended time and causation which in fact traverses it. A cinemaker, in contrast, is always concerned with a spatio-temporal dynamism. Even when it attends to what is at rest, it tells something of the causal and temporal antecedents and consequents; even when it attends to what takes only a moment, it exhibits a spatial setting and conveys some idea of the causality at work; even when it attends just to a cause or an effect, it shows them in a time passing over an extended space.

2

Both camera and cinemaker may be manipulated by men who have a good grasp of the aesthetic value of what is before them, and who can envisage the way in which it may interact with other aesthetic content. But this is not enough to enable them to produce a work of art. Works of art are worked over; they subject aesthetically satisfactory items to the conditions which govern the achievement of a self-sufficient unity. The aesthetically excellent pleases; an artistic work fulfills. The one is exhausted in being experienced, the other must be lived with and through, usually a number of times, and then reflected on. Its appeal is to emotions more deeply grounded than feelings, and more appropriate to what is ultimately real. When an experience with an aesthetic object is over, one is left in an easy calm; when an experience with a work of art is over, one faces realities which the work of art articulated in a limited, special, and revelatory manner. An aesthetic object is an appearance denied a practical bearing, and kept within a frame of our making; a work of art is an objective appearance made self-sufficient, but leading us to what is ultimately real. A camera may go beyond the point of presenting only the former, but it rarely if ever gets to the point of giving us the latter. For an object to have aesthetic value, it must be freed from its practical setting and grasped in its immediacy — sensuous, unrecognized, here and now. But a work of art stands apart from us; it is new and self-sufficient. Even a creative photographer can not, as a cineman can, forge such a self-sufficient work out of a plurality of independently considered factors, each allowed to mature over a period.*

---

* You don't mean (I hope) that a camera never gets to the point of giving us a work of art. You must mean a movie camera. That still cameras, or still photographers, can produce works of art is — or ought to be acknowledged. Photography is an art, isn't it? There are great photographs, great photographers. Cinematography, by itself, can not produce great art, or works of art.   D. S.

The cinemaker's units are incidents, with beginnings which control and are controlled by, determine and are determined by endings. A film has those incidents integrated in a whole; this has its own beginning and ending, its own tensions, its own problems and resolutions. As a rule, a cineman has no knowledge of what the final film will look like; he is rarely in a position where he can see the whole that is being produced from the incidents he has focused on. For the most part, he must be content to make each incident be cinematically excellent by working through it from different positions and in different ways for an extended period. And, to be at his best, he must have some grasp of the film's overall idea, of the way the film is developing, and of what the cinemaker is contributing. Incidents are filmed by cinemakers. Or, more precisely, by a cinemaker and cinemen. One of the cinemen, the "first," rarely manipulates a cinemaker. Rather like a chef, he sees to it that everything is properly prepared and carried out. The work of filming he leaves to his assistants, and concentrates instead on the supervision of the lengthy, difficult, and. important business of arranging the lighting.[5]

Again and again, distinguished cinemakers assure us that they know exactly what their instrument will do before it in fact does it. They tell us that they see "with their mind's eye," or that, having looked through a glass, they know exactly what will be accomplished. They have forgotten that there are countless incidental factors which make a difference to the whole, that there are fringes and details which they subsequently may have to cut away or be tempted to include, but which they did not anticipate. Every occurrence is subject to contingencies, unexpected turns, novelties; every created work takes account of their presence, eliminating some, compensating for others, and including what it can. The concrete outcome, whether it takes place in the world of daily life or in the world of art, has a texture, a depth, a multiplicity of unpredictable elements and developments which no one can know except through an encounter. To see with the "mind's eye" is not yet to see with the eye that a mind employs.

Musical composers, too, again and again contend that they hear all the different instruments with their different sounds even before the instruments are played. They can not, of course, *hear* those sounds. They may imagine the places the different sounds will have in relation to one another, but this is not yet to be aware of the sounds as they occur in fact. When music is played it has volume, luminosity, tension, drive, and forcefulness, and occupies the entire room. It then moves in, to, and through all the listeners. This it does not and can not do so long as it is merely imagined. For similar reasons, no one can really *know* what a cinemaker will actually produce before a cinemaker is in fact used. What is imagined lacks the concrete richness, the obstinacy and dynamism characteristic of what actually occurs. This is true, no matter what form of art we are engaged in, no matter how much in control we may be of our instruments, and how sure we are of the result before it in fact is produced. Texture, career, occupancy, the irrelevant, the accidental, and the intrusive all are part of the concrete occurrence, precluding this from being known before it in fact takes place. Some cinemen take advantage of just this fact, and even exaggerate its importance. They cherish the unpredictable; they like to have themselves caught off-guard. For them the enemy of art is the structured, the accepted, the law-abiding, the rational. Surprise and novelty are, for them, one with creativity and art. But no artist is ever completely surprised. Nor is anything completely free, completely unstructured, always original, nothing but new ground. All men are caught by the past, by their habits, by the medium in which they work, and by the state of the world. Whatever occurs, created or uncreated, is at once structured and unique, predictable and unexpected, anticipated and surprising, in varying proportions.

Some visible things are beyond the powers of a cinemaker — and of a camera — to deal with, except inadequately. They can not capture a dance, a theatrical performance, or a poetry-reading. The three-dimensionality of the dance, the accepted conventions of the theatre which piece out the meaning of what is said and pantomimed, and the pacings needed for a good reading must be transmuted if they are to have the same effect on the film that they have apart from it. If one tried to capture what is occurring in a dance, play, or reading by having a cinemaker function as though it were just a mechanical viewer, he would find that the cinemaker gave them a cinematographic setting, and that this altered the meaning they originally had. A sigh in a dance, play, and reading takes different guises, and requires different temporal stretches. To fit any one of the guises inside the others, or any of them inside a film, one would have to abandon their spatial, temporal, and dynamic stretches. Each art has its own requirements; what is done in one can be adequately expressed in another only by sacrificing something essential to one or the other.

This conclusion seems at first to be willfully paradoxical. A cinemaker is a surrogate for a spectator. Why then might it not take the position of a spectator at a dance or a play or a reading? A cinemaker acts with precision; it can zoom in and out and change its position and its lens.

Why should it not be able to get what a spectator does — and perhaps even better, precisely because it is technically excellent, without emotions or prejudices?

A cinemaker is a surrogate, not for a spectator at a dance or other art, but for a viewer of a finished film. It can not assume the position of a spectator at other arts, even when it is put at the position such a spectator might occupy, for it can not contribute what that spectator does and can. Spectators live with and through the dynamism of a dance, play, or reading. If a film is to catch a dance or a play or a reading as it actually occurs, it somehow has to include those spectators. But it will not show them making a difference to what they see, and therefore will not show them as living participants of the art which they are viewing.

A viewer of a film can not participate in what is filmed. A cinemaker will allow him to become acquainted with what was performed but will not allow him to contribute to it. The viewer adds something to what he sees; he alters its import, gives it values and meanings it did not have apart from him. If it be said that he helps constitute a film, it must be added that he constitutes what has already been filmed, and therefore contributes, not to the art of film, but to the art, if such there be, of seen-film,

Film, unlike a dance, play, or reading, is complete before it has spectators. In this respect, it is more like the spatial arts of architecture, sculpture, and painting, than like those that are primarily temporal or dynamic. Since a cinemaker adds to what it confronts it can not reproduce for us what a man directly confronts. And since what it adds is never exactly what a man adds to what he sees, a cinemaker can not even convey what art works are for living viewers. Works of art and experiences with art are given a new import when a cinemaker is brought to bear on them.

The Western theatre inherited from Aristotle the doctrine that all plays should have a unity of time, place, and action. The doctrine summarizes the practices that are pertinent to the simple dramatic presentations of the Greeks. But for later drama it has little value. Indeed, even in the Greek drama there were messengers who came in from other places and other times. To speak as though one then kept to a unity of place and time is to allow the single scene into which the messenger came to hide the fact that the message is oriented elsewhere. But the unit for a cinemaker is the incident performed. This adheres rather closely to the Aristotelian three unities. In fact, it gives one a good way to define an incident: a unity of time, place, and action.

A cinemaker sharply divides off what it focuses on from what it does not.

Men, in contrast, have peripheral vision. Even more important, eyes inevitably roam, allowing one to take in more than what is actually directly focused on. No matter what it is to which we attend, we attend to it in a larger environment. While we bound it through attention, we are aware that there is something outside the imposed boundaries. What is there may be glimpsed by the cineman, but only the extension it occupies has relevance to what is filmed. A film points beyond itself to the neighboring regions of space, time, and causality, with the consequence that what we see on film is located — not contained, as a painting or a photograph is — inside a boundary, actual or assumed.

The most honest and complete candid film has to cut out vagrant sights and sounds, the noise of the birds overhead, the light leaking through the door and window sills, the irrelevant horns of the cars at a distance, unwanted shadows and shadings, the peripheral presence and breathing of the stage hands — a thousand incidental things that actually do occur in the ordinary course of life and which, strictly speaking, are irrelevant to what one is trying to note. Cinemaking is artistic work, and artistic work eliminates what is irrevelant to a created excellence.

It is not even necessary for a cinemaker to be directed at anything. It is possible to work on the film itself, modifying it directly, in order to have new kinds of images to organize. It is also possible to film the monotonous and dreary, and any number of irrevelancies. But it is one thing to permit tedium and irrelevancies which one wanted to exclude, and another to bring them in so as to produce a desired result. When wanted and properly used, they remain unwanted by the focal figures while contributing essentially to a work of art.

A film audience is inclined to attend to the heroes, villains, and objects which are at the center of an incident, but a cinemaker must also attend to the empty spaces, to that which, for the ordinary man, is merely background. As in other arts, the empty has a place as surely as the full. For a cinemaker, the background is as positive as the foreground; indeed, nothing is merely negative for him, without cinematic value. The negative is that which paces and separates the rest. It can be barren or filled. Without it there can be nuances, but no distances or oppositions.

The cinemaker is a comparatively new instrument. We have not yet learned how to explore all its possibilities. Not only are new uses being discovered by experimenters, but no one yet knows all that film can encompass. Only recently have there been systematic attempts to explore the possibility of using multiple cinemakers at the same time, and in different ways, to film the same incidents, to be presented simultaneously perhaps, or in some other way. It would be interesting to see a film shot by two different cameramen each following out his own distinctive bent, and having these shown side by side — edited perhaps in the same way. It would be interesting, too, to see what results, different from those achieved in *Sisters,* e.g., can be obtained by cinemen following the same script. Other possible experiments come readily to mind. But just to mention them is not to advance the art of cinemaking; they have to be carried out, and then in the face of obdurate resistance, human, social, and physical. No one can anticipate the new uses to which the cinemaker will in fact be put, in part because new adventures build on the achievements of the past, and in part because what we conceive outlines but never can contain all that in fact occurs, nor actually overcome the obstacles that stand in the way of all practical efforts and artistic work.

3

Space, it has already been observed, is all that a photographer knows. A cineman also attends to what is spatial, but this is not alone of interest to him or to any other film maker. Film makers are time-conscious, incident-directed, at the same time that they are concerned with attending to what is spatially displayed.

It is sometimes said that the modern film was anticipated by or had its beginning in the use of machines to present a series of photographs of slightly different scenes, taken one after the other, and then flipped through quickly so as to give the illusion of the passing of a time. But the original photographs were photographs and nothing more. They offered spatial units which were then subjected to a temporal presentation. The result was an "animation," needing no performers but only items in frames. We come to film only when we begin with a genuine moving time, within which we can, if we wish, freeze moments and attend to purely spatial configurations. Time is essential to what a cinemaker records; that is why it is an integral part of a film.

4

Because the photograph is occupied with a space outside of time, it has no place for incidents, and knows nothing of causation. It produces its own excellent works, but these all have the fixity of paintings. They are not to be compared with paintings, to be sure, since they are produced in different ways, with different objectives, face different aesthetic problems; and yield different results. A painting, because built up part after part, is made more in a spirit that is cosonant with cinemaking than it is with photography. But it is also quite distinct from film because, like a photograph, it can not give much of a role to either time or causation.

In the Anglo-Saxon world it is a philosophic dogma that causality is not an object of perception but is, instead, nothing more than a restatement of a habit for associating items, or is a way of referring to the overwhelming presence of the past in what is now going on. The first of these alternative explanations stems from Hume; the other is presented by Whitehead. Both take their start with isolated sense data, i.e., qualities, and sometimes shapes and sizes: they see nothing in these which can tell us about what went before or what will come later, what is alongside or what is distant. Though the one is called "empirical," and the other a "process philosopher," neither in fact has a place for anything but fixities which, supposedly, we somehow are lulled into seeing follow continuously and causatively on one another. They offer excellent philosophic excuses for those who suppose that a film presents a visual panorama of surfaces following one on the other, and which an audience is somehow to interrelate and overlay with the supposition that something is moving and happening. But in fact these philosophies are not even appropriate to the film, not to speak of everyday empirical existence.

A causal situation can be analyzed in two ways. It can be broken down into stages, or into factors. To break it down into stages one distinguishes between an antecedent condition or "cause," a consequent outcome or "effect," and a transition from the one to the other, or "process of causation." Were causality just to consist of the antecedent condition and the subsequent outcome, there would be no temporal distance between them; effects would follow instantly and the whole of history would be collapsed into an unextended point. Were there only causation, without any distinct causes and effects, there would be only a single passage of energy, without anything being made to happen, and without any positions from which or to which the happening occurs. The Humean nevertheless accepts the first position, the Whiteheadian the other. They belong together.

The second mode of analysis distinguishes a formal from a sustaining factor, the former turning antecedent and consequent into mere terms in a formal whole, the latter sustaining that relational whole, but not without specifying and concretizing it. Were there just a formal relation between terms nothing would happen; were there just a reality in which the relation was ingredient, there would be no significant planning, controlling, or predicting. Spinoza attends only to the first, Hegel only to the second. But these two also belong together.

A formal relation connecting antecedent and consequent has them refer to one another. They are mutually relevant; each is and is to be known only as supplemented by the other. When that relation is sustained, the relation of relevance makes the antecedent be a beginning for a specified ending, and the ending an ending for that specific beginning. A relevant beginning never is and never is known until it has been departed from toward the specified ending; a relevant ending never is and never is known if it is sundered from a dependence on a specific beginning.

A formal relation defines antecedent condition and consequent effect as belonging together, apart from a process of causation. A sustaining of the relation is identifiable with a process of causation when this process is embedded in and dependent on some other, more basic reality. We know what is relevant when we know what an antecedent requires for its completion, and what the consequent requires if it is to be a completion. An account of causality in terms of factors rather than stages makes possible a distinguishing of different types of causation, in terms of the differences among their sustaining realities, or in terms of the manner in which the relation is sustained. There is a sustaining of limited activities by particular actualities, each adopting or producing an antecedent, and sustaining a relation to an outcome inside or outside itself. There is also a sustaining by perceptual objects which make otherwise indifferent appearances be relevant to one another as beginnings and endings of observable events. Still other kinds of causation occur in the theatre and the dance. These are just as objective and real as the other kinds, unless one unnecessarily restricts "causation" to cases where there is a compelling physical domination of one object by another. But in the other cases there is also a genuine passage from and relevance of beginning to ending, and therefore something more than a merely formal connection between antecedent and consequent. The causality in each case is inseparable from space and time.

There is more to causality than the exercise of brute force. Such force is in fact not observable, occurring as it does below the obtrusive phenomena. One who denied the reality of anything other than forceful causality would end by accepting as real exactly what no one can note. The most obvious cases of causality involve the presence of carriers of observable occurrences. Were a cinemaker to ignore these causal units, he would not only not see what makes outcomes relevant to beginnings but would separate off arbitrarily delimited portions of time in somewhat the way in which his lens and angles separate off arbitrarily delimited portions of space.

Both performers and actors sustain beginnings and endings of occurrences. These occurrences have no existence apart from them. The incidents and events are the substances in which the relations of relevance are embedded; in turn they are themselves sustained by living men or, in special cases, by animals or objects.

An actor reaches to the boundaries of a play; a performer is kept confined within the incidents of a film. An actor, too, must be a mature human being; a performer is whatever a cinemaker focuses on. A performance might be produced by operating on the film itself, or by attending, not to a man or even to a living being, but to things. I have already expressed doubt as to whether children can act, once acting be understood to involve not only the carrying out of a part, but the doing of this with a grasp of what the other parts are and how they bear on one another. But children can perform just as surely as anyone else, for they need to do nothing then but as they are told. They can even become great vivifiers—Patty Duke and Jackie Coogan—and, therefore be as good as any other film "star." What they can not do is sustain many types; it is doubtful whether they are even able to personalize a role. But because they can vivify a role, they can be compared with the best of adult performers.

Panofsky thinks that one of the important differences between film and play is that in the one the character is then and there constituted, and in the other it is merely exhibited for a time: "the screenplay, in contrast to the theatre play, *has no aesthetic existence independent of its performance, and its characters have no aesthetic existence outside the actors. . . .* Othello or Nora are definite, substantial figures . . . they most definitely exist, no matter who plays them or even whether they are played at all. The character in a film, however, lives and dies with the actor." [6] But the sense in which Othello or Nora live outside an acted play is the very sense in which Ben Hur or Dr. Caligari live outside the film. We can abstract a schema or outline from the script or written play, or from a performance on the screen or an acting on the stage. In both places, we can take certain lines or gestures to be essential to what we hold apart, and can therefore refer to any number of particular occasions as providing opportunities for exhibiting these.

A film audience, by accepting the position of a cinemaker, accepts the causality which is sustained by a role to which a living man has made an unspecified contribution. It can not, as an audience at a play can, attend to the role alone. To be sure, an audience at a play can not attend just to a naked role, but this is what it must try to do to appreciate what is happening there. But a film performance is what a cinemaker films, and from this no abstraction is to be made, even if it were possible. The causality that takes place on the stage is what is there sustained; what sustains the causality of a film is a performance in which a man has for the moment become a performer. The causality in the film has to do with the relevant beginning and ending, and not with him who specializes, qualifies, and sustains it.

Cinemaking is incident directed; the beginning and ending of its moments and the boundaries of its space are defined by the incidents it records. Since it is the film which makes the beginning and ending causally pertinent, it is the film that defines the incident. If its recording of the incident be called a "shot," a shot must be allowed to have any length. Warhol set a cinemaker in a fixed position with a fixed lens, and let the film run through it for hours. He filmed only one incident in a film in which a kiss was the only performer; in another film, he filmed another single incident where a building was the only performer.

Because a cineman sets the relevant limits of an incident, it is he who dictates what a filmed causality can do. Since he can start or stop at any time with any kind of content, he can create an indefinite number of causal situations, only a tiny fraction of which are to be found in daily experience. He is therefore able to reveal the unlimited capacity of causality to operate between any points, no matter what their nature or their distance in space and time from one another. That causality is only one dimension of existence; space and time are others. As a consequence, the cineman, though he himself attends only to particular incidents, is able to ready one to attend to existence as a fundamental reality having a power, reality, and nature not wholly exhibited on any finite occasion.

A concentration on distinct incidents precludes a grasp of what the incidents are together. This does not prevent a cineman from having a dominant or even an exclusive role in the making of a film. If he has, he will subject the different filmed incidents to the governance of the whole; muting some and emphasizing others, he will lengthen and shorten, add and eliminate in order to make the incidents filmed support one another. He might dispense with a script, turn objects and people into performers by the simple expedient of just focusing on them, and retain the order in which the incidents were filmed. But if he is the primary or only film maker, he will, more likely than not, produce a poor film. There is nothing in principle which requires that this occur. It is only that the other tasks demand so much experience and judgment, and consider so many problems which are not faced when one is filming incidents, that it is wise to give free rein to these others. It will indeed be necessary to do this, if what one seeks to make is a superb film, a work of art.

CHAPTER 5

Montagists

He who is now termed an "editor" of a film was, in England, once called a "producer." [1] Neither name is altogether appropriate. There are producers of films, but their task, like that of producers of books and plays, need not have anything to do with creating, but only with seeing that a work is made viable and available. Editors are employed by publishing houses and newspapers to give the work of others a better unity, form, and marketable guise. Theirs is incidental help, purgational, suggestive, coming after, or occasionally between the writers' bouts of creativity. "Editors" of films are today rarely also producers of films. They are creative men, making works of art out of filmed incidents, no one of which may have much value or significance. They leave it to producers to get funds and thereby make it possible to have a film begun, finished, and distributed. It is not their function to accept and polish, but to change rhythms, meanings, and values. They do not just suggest; they act.

A script offers directions; performers are confined to their performances; a cinemaker films incidents. None attends to the making of a single, unified film. That is normally the work either of a director or of an "editor." Both have a good idea of what the whole is to be and what in fact it has been made to be. Both gradually understand what the finished whole is like in the course of the forging of a single film out of a multiplicity of filmed incidents. Unlike a director, though, an "editor" has nothing to say about the script, and he does not control or guide performers. Usually he starts where a cinemaker leaves off, and, more often than not, is beholden to a director.

Since the creative work of an "editor" — montaging, the determination of what filmed incidents are to be related and how — is so unlike that of recognized producers or editors, it would be less misleading to speak of him as a "montagist." His is a task peculiar to the film, though it is not altogether unknown to arrangers, assemblers, advertisers, and novelists. "The development of film technique in fact has been primarily the development of

editing; it was a device virtually unknown to the earliest film makers." [2]
Kuleshov is said to have held "that the material in film work consists of
pieces of film, and the composition method of their joining together in a
particular creatively discovered order. He maintained that film art does not
begin when the artists act and the various scenes are shot—this is only
the preparation of the material. Film art begins from the moment the director [!] begins to combine and join the various pieces of film." [3]
The view has had its opponents, e.g., Spottiswoode thinks montaging is an
old psychological device: "the effect of any one shot differs sharply from
that of its precursor and successor, resulting in an impact of the sensations
and concepts derived from contiguous shots; and from this impact may
arise a third concept different from that of either of the components which
produced it. This we shall call montage. There is nothing radically new in
its nature." [4] Apparently, he thinks it characterizes, not the work of a film
maker, but of a viewer. "Montage, in various forms, permeates every stage
of the spectator's appreciation of the true film." [5] It is more correct to say,
I think, that it is a vital part of film making, and that its results can have
considerable effect on a viewer.
"Montage" literally refers to a mounting, an assembling, the producing of a
composite by combining elements through superimposition, overlapping,
and related devices. It is to be contrasted with "collage," the gluing or
pasting together of fragments, aspects of which produce some desired
overall effect. A poor montage is in effect a collage. The fact that something like montaging, in the form of cutting and synthesizing, occurs in
other domains, must not be allowed to stand in the way of the acknowledgment of film as requiring a distinctive type of montaging. The montaging
that is involved in film making is not duplicated elsewhere.
It could be maintained, with some degree of reasonableness, that a montagist does nothing more than select amongst various pieces of work in
order to see which of them will make for the best possible combinations.*

---

*You might admit to the cutter or montagist a little more importance, as
the directors and studios do when they wrangle about who gets final cut
on a film. The cutter has in his hands the rhythm and pulse of the whole
thing. Some directors, for this reason, do their own cutting. In any event, the
director directs the cutter—or should.   D. S.*

Like the owner of a gallery or a curator in a museum, and perhaps an
interior decorator, he could be said to just order or organize what others
had done. But this supposition overlooks the fact that montaging begins

with objects which do have an importance of their own, and that it makes something more out of them. A montagist might not select the most successfully performed or filmed incidents, but whatever he does select is an incident whose meaning and value, and not merely its aesthetic character, is to be creatively connected with those of other incidents, with the result that the values and meanings of all are transformed.

A montagist selects among many cinemade versions. He may eliminate what a director or a cinemaker or performers may consider to be important, to be works of art, or to be worth preserving for some other reason. More significantly, he juxtaposes what otherwise might have been made at considerable intervals, or what others think bear only remotely on one another. It is not as if there were a number of parallel works, a set of distinct films out of which he must select one; he himself must, out of a plurality of different incidents, select those which together are to constitute a single film. The emphasis here is on the making of an integrated totality, not on the selection, for the items that are selected are, for him, just so much material which he is to use creatively. It is his task to relate, in illuminating ways, portions of filmed space, time, or causality, and combinations of these, no matter how alien to one another the ordinary man takes them to be, and no matter how close or how far apart they are in nature, in a story, or in an actual film making. His treatment of sound accompaniments takes place among somewhat similar lines. It, too, is subject to a montaging. Without violating the conventional grammar of language or music, he produces new juxtapositions and tempos under the governance of what is seen. He may take either incidents or parts of incidents to be his units. In either case, he unites them not in terms of their proximity, aesthetic values, similarities, or differences, but according to the kind of contribution that they make to a final larger filmic meaning and value.

2

The conventional patterns which we live through every day are easy to utilize. But the more readily we utilize them, the less opportunity we give ourselves to look beneath and beyond them to what makes them possible, and what in the end is more real than they are. The radical use of portions spatial, temporal, and dynamic extensions by the montagist enables us to grasp the sequacity of these extensions. We gain a new insight into time when we see that a remote period can be brought into close juxtaposition to a present, without having to be intermediated by all the intervening times, as it does in the ordinary course of nature and daily life. The future can be made to work backward, and to be involved with the past, as surely as the past can be made to act on the future. Remote parts of space can be joined, and a geometry, not exemplified in the world or even pictured in any of the geometries that the mathematicians construct, thereby created — a geometry with hills and valleys, recesses and protuberances made then and there. The montagist's freedom from ordinary causal processes, similarly, allows him to make evident the relevance of anything whatsoever, thereby revealing their unlimited potentialities. When Warhol, in his early films, had his cinemaker run without supervision, he accepted the entire result without change. The outcomes were films, but not works of art. Indeed, they were films produced by negating one of art's essential conditions — the creating of a unity in which contrasting items intensify one another to yield a single whole, eliciting, contouring, and controlling man's deepest emotions.

Any condition essential to a work of art can obviously be deliberately defied. It is a great temptation for an artist to free himself from any condition which is set down as essential to art, for all conditions antecedently limit his freedom, and therefore his creativity. He should be allowed to follow his bent wherever it may lead, and no matter what the established routes are, for his fundamental task demands a defiance of all limitations. But this is quite a different thing from saying that he should refuse to accept this or that particular condition. This or that condition may have to be satisfied if a work of art of a certain kind is to be achieved. An artist ought to challenge every condition, at the same time that he conforms to whatever conditions should govern his working in that art. He must be like an airplane which works against but does not negate gravity, making use of the gravity in its own way and for its own purposes.

If one could show that works of art are the products of free, spontaneous movements, and that they demand an escape from all constraints and limits, it would be reasonable to maintain that one must try to negate all conditions. But there will always be conditions to meet, and there always have to be some constraints exercised and some limits respected. In the absence of all conditions nothing can be done, and a spirit of defiance at constraints and limits will promote the monotonous, the boring, the empty, the chaotic, or the ugly. Material has to be selected and discarded, worked over, improved upon, and purged, at the same time that its nature is respected. To heighten tensions, sharpen contrasts, take advantage of opportunities, and resolve discords and conflicts one must know what can and can not be done. A refusal to submit to any demand entrains a refusal to submit to the demands that excellence imposes. A beautiful work of art comes at the end of a mighty struggle in which self-expression may be a moment but can never be the motive.

There is warrant for a protest against the familiar. Sometimes traditions, habits, techniques hinder. When a work begins to lose its unity, when its opaque perfection begins to slip away, when its power to awaken an emotional grasp of what is real slackens, it is time to consider taking another tack.

An excellent work of art is beautiful.[6] But what it portrays does not mirror what is objectively real. Something ugly can be beautifully presented; a bore could be described in an interesting way; a poem on death might be a joy to read. And what is monotonous and trivial might be the topic of a film, which itself could be variegated and important. But then the film must be used just as creatively and interestingly as it is when the topic is exciting. To let a cinemaker run unsupervised before some tedious occurrence is not yet to make a great film. It is but to heighten the tedium by fitting it into another setting. Art neither tries to mirror nor to represent the very object it is trying to communicate; it creates an excellence which enables one to make a fresh and penetrative contact with what is real outside it.

The available mechanical agencies for bringing bits of film together are no more essential to the art of film making than typewriters are to the art of writing novels, for the important thing is to relate creatively one incident to another in such a way that the result is excellent. Machines can cut down time and sometimes imprecision, but the creative work is nonmechanical, and must be carried out by men.

It is good to try to get rid of all montaging, for the same reason that it is good to try to get rid of all scripts, all performing, all cinemaking, all directing. Each introduces restrictions worth rejecting. The success of the effort will, though, mean a failure to produce a work of art. The effort should be made, but it also should be brought to an end at the point where a vital creative dimension of the film is being lost. We will then become aware that something can be dispensed with, at the same time that we will see what is essential. A montagist may make the challenge to himself. After all, like everyone else, he is caught within patterns, rhythms, boundaries, and must, to work on a film, hold himself away from these, and see what in them is not necessary, what is only superficial, conventionalized, and even an obstacle to a fine creating.

A montagist is somewhat like a poet who plans to write a sonnet. He knows that he must keep within narrow confines, for these help define the kind of task he has set for himself. The conditions, instead of hobbling him, should sharpen the edge of his artistic perceptions. Given this and that material, the montagist is asked to exhibit his creativity somewhat as the poet is when held to fourteen lines. As a member of a film-making team, he should keep to the script, attend to performances, know what the cinemaker takes to be significant, and be aware of the overall unity which interests the director. But he should stop at none of these. They ought to be only pivotal points, guiding a creative use of what he is given.

It is rather easy to see how something can be added to something that had been filmed earlier. Accumulation, snowballing are familiar occurrences. It is difficult to see how what comes later can add to what had already happened. Still, we often embellish what we remember. It is the second World War which makes the earlier be the "first." In any case, the primary thrust in montaging is toward what comes later; this makes a difference to, while it is affected by what had gone before.

A montagist is primarily concerned not with incidents by themselves, with particular occurrences localized within limited areas, but with the difference the incidents make to one another and to the extensions encompassing them all. He knows no spatial, temporal, or causal affiliations or structures that might not be defied; every limit is to be passed beyond if it will make for a better film. The incidents that he finally selects are made into a new whole, his creation. The result makes possible a surer grasp of what space, time, and causality — and finally, existence itself, in which all three are one — really are. That this is the outcome which is best promoted by great film will, I think, become evident in the course of the discussion in part 2.

City planners and interior decorators aspire to be creative designers. The work of a montagist is analogous to theirs. All are engaged in relating a multiplicity of objects — even works of art — so as to produce a single work having its own structure, order, spacings, dimensions, and beauty. The best of designers, however, works within a given spatial region, whereas a montagist must produce his. By filling out the region creatively a designer gives it a distinctive geometry and content. A montagist not only does this; he creates a new space.

A montagist begins by accepting all filmed spaces as on a par. No one of these is more real for him than any other; the relations they may have to one another in the film give them diverse weights and roles, but this does not affect their status as equally legitimate subdivisions of a single, larger space. Some of the filmed spaces will be used to constitute the outermost boundaries of the entire space; the others will be placed within those limits. The way in which he spatially connects spatialized incidents by means of spatialized incidents provides the entire space of the film with a distinctive structure. The resultant total filmed space has distinct areas, planes, volumes, sinuosities, angles, protuberances, and declivities, back grounds and foregrounds, each a delimited part of it.

Only a fraction of all that is filmed, as a rule, is selected by the montagist, and this is altered in rhythm and intensity by the way it is creatively interrelated by him. The choice of the spaces he will interrelate, the determination of those which are to be at the limits and those which are to be within these, and the decisions regarding the devices that are to be used and how, in order to produce the desired result, are up to him. Cuts, fade-ins and -outs, dissolves, wipes, and related agencies enable him to pass from one spatial region to another in the course of an effort to produce a single, new space. No one gives so much weight, as the montagist does, to the well-known fact that the import of an occurrence is affected by its neighbors. He has an opportunity, denied to others, of relating in any one of an indefinite number of ways a whole range of filmed extensions, and thereby making evident that they are independent, with distinctive configurations and capacities to be related.

Sometimes it is said that what is shown on the screen is two-dimensional, and that we read a third dimension into what we note there. Similar claims have been made for paintings. But in both cases one then confuses the carriers of created works with the works themselves. A painting and a film are placed on the surface of canvas and screen, but they themselves have their own distinctive spaces. If one were to deny that those spaces were three-dimensional — or, more accurately, n-dimensional, where "dimension" refers to a distinct direction — one should for the same reason deny that it has two, since the dimensions that are exhibited by a painting and a film are distinct from the dimensions of a canvas and a screen. To be sure, one does not confront the created dimensions except within the boundaries of a canvas or a screen. But just as a painting is bounded away from the world in which a canvas is a part, so a film extends beyond a screen, but not into a space in which the screen, as a physical entity, is located. The space in which a film is and into which it continues is not the space where its screen can be found.

Is there no relation between filmed, perceptual, painterly, and scientifically known space? If not, we seem to be confronted with a multiplicity of spaces which can not be brought into connection with one another, despite the fact that a space seems to be precisely that which is spatially related to other spaces, no matter what their contents. But if they are all located within a single common space, painting and the film would apparently be where their canvas and screen are, with the consequence that in each case there would be distinct spaces competing for the same position.

Neither painting nor film can be located in the space of physical objects. Other spaces and items are already there. Instead, we must say that both they and physical space subject a more fundamental, real space to special conditions, but that, unlike physical space, they are not occupied by solid, gravity-governed objects. In compensation, they epitomize real space and not merely, as physical space does, specialize it. That is why the emotions, that painting and film evoke, can effectively lead one to confront space, as it is by itself, after an experience with the works is over.

However, the space of a painting, though an epitomization of the same real space that a film epitomizes, is not identifiable with the space of a film. Distinct paintings have distinct spaces; distinct films have distinct spaces, too. But if this is so, do we not have a plurality of distinct epitomized spaces?

Because different portrayed spaces elicit the same type of emotion, we know that they epitomize the same space. But because the actual emotions are played out in different cases, we know that the portrayed spaces are nevertheless different in nature. To confront them, we must look toward the canvas or screen to face, not the space of the canvas or screen, but a more fundamental space in a new form.

Real space is at least as malleable as the range of experiencing reveals it to be; it has the fixity of being and structure that thought discovers. The space dealt with in film re-presents it, reconstitutes it, and intensifies it, to give it revelatory guise, thereby providing an effective beginning for an acquaintance with that space. The spaces of filmed incidents have less than maximum intensity, and control an emotion less than is possible. A poor film will reduce the intensity and control even further. A film, that is a work of art, instead emphasizes the harmonies between the spaces of different incidents so as to produce a single epitomized space of maximum intensity, in full control of the expression of the emotion that it elicits.

3

A montagist is concerned with time as well as space. The time of each incident is in the present; there it has a distinctive span. But it is sometimes said that there are no extended presents. How then account for the fact that there seem to be such presents? To explain this "seeming" one must somehow occupy an extended present, for that is where one ties together the different units—all presumably not in time or in the past and therefore never identified or encountered.

The different presents of different incidents have different lengths. Some are crowded with subordinate occurrences, each lived through and with; others are quite empty. Some take a considerable amount of ordinary time in order to be seen; others are over in a fraction of this. The different presents of the different incidents are brought together by the montagist to constitute a single time. His work may take days and even months to complete; what he produces may take hours to unfold before an audience. Yet he can work only in his present; the film can take place only in its present; and the audience can view it only in its present.

We work, we see, whatever occurs must take place in a present moment, for what is past is gone, inert, inaccessible, excluded by what is now the case, and what is future is not yet, a mere possibility which action is to make present. All that can be seen and all seeing, all that can be heard and all hearing, all that can be experienced and shared in is in the present. But now we are faced with difficulties which also haunt the theatre, symphony, dance, and poetry, as well as history and daily life. All face us with what must pass away before something else can be. If all are in the present, how is it possible to have causes and antecedents, and tell about what happened in the past?

Any sentence that we might construct or utter, any thought, any act in which we might engage, has distinguishable parts *before* and *after* one another. Yet the sentence, thought, and act are themselves undivided present units. Their parts are not *earlier* and *later.* And what is true of a sentence is true of a paragraph; what is true of a thought is true of an argument or series of thoughts; what is true of an act is true of an entire career; and what is true of these is true of history, dance, poetry and, surely, film.

Can there be presents of different lengths? Can different presents be ordered serially without being set earlier and later than one another? Can we be required to pass through one present in order to be in another present, without thereby making the previous present be past, and therefore no longer an integral part of a single present? Other related questions are particularly pertinent to the film: How are the presents of the incidents and the present of the film related to one another? How are they both related to the present of the time when they were filmed? How are they related to the present of the audience to which, and to the place where, the film is shown? What is the relation of the present of a film to the present of a viewing of it? How is the film's present related to the present of real, objective time?* How is the film's present related to the whole of time? How can a

---

* A film made about a particular time, subject, story, or person will tell us at least as much about the time when the film was made as about the time depicted. When The Birth of a Nation was made, the attempted rape of Lillian Gish was made by a power-hungry "nigger." When Gone With the Wind was made, although Vivien Leigh, too, stirs up the Ku Klux Klan, the Klan is never mentioned by name, and the attacker upon the "woman of virtue," although he lives amongst blacks in what is euphemistically called "shanty town," is strangely enough white. On the screen today, our white heroine of the Civil War would, doubtless, be seducing the black superstud. He would be bestowing his favors if he chose to descend to her.

R. T.

---

montagist take a series of incidents and make them be together in a single present time which he just created, and which, therefore, no one had ever lived in? It would take a treatise to do justice to all of these. But the previous discussion of the relation of the spaces of filmed incidents to the space of the film, and of the relation of the space of the film to space as a whole, opens up ways of seeing what the upshot of such a lengthy discussion will be.

When experienced moments are distinguished as being earlier and later — and not merely as being before and after one another, the way numbers are — they are abstractions. The experienced time of a filmed incident and the time of a film are as real as any other experienceable time, but they also epitomize the whole of time. Each filmed incident epitomizes the whole of time, but with less intensity and control than is possible to an entire film. Montaging interrelates the present times of different incidents to make them subordinate, nonisolable parts of the film's single, indivisible, more intensive and controlling present. There, the incidents occur before and after, not earlier and later than one another. Held apart from the film, they are earlier and later filmed incidents for a montaging, while still in an order of before and after in the single present enterprise of cinemaking.

A montagist cuts into the single time of cinemaking to isolate distinct incidents with their distinct times. He thereby inevitably takes each one to stand for the whole. This is preliminary to his bringing those incidents within the present time of a film. Before he arrives at that point, however, he inevitably makes the incidents, that he isolated, into parts of the single enterprise of montaging. It is the purpose of that enterprise to allow the incidents to be integral parts of a film. But this is only to say that montaging is a creative activity which ends by placing the material with which it works into a new unity, where it has a new import. The daily time when the incident was filmed, the time it purports to exhibit, the time of the cinemaking, the time when someone might fasten on it, are all replaced by the time of the film, where the incident is caught up within a new present.

The space of an incident is encompassed within larger spaces where the cinemaking and the montaging occur. The larger spaces enable the incident to be located in the world of film making, and then made an integral part of a film. The limited present time span of an incident is part of the present time of some enterprise, such as cinemaking or montaging, and of the present time of a film. In the time and space of cinemaking and montaging, the times but not the spaces of incidents are denied boundaries; in the film, both the times and spaces of incidents lose theirs.

4

In ordinary life, an incident has causal as well as temporal and spatial boundaries. The causality of an incident is like that of its space and time in being locatable inside a world which is not part of a film, but is unlike them in the film, because the boundaries of the causality, and not the boundaries of the space and time there, remain unaffected by what is outside the limits of the various incidents filmed. Causality, in and outside a film, occurs within the borders of an incident, but neither the time nor the space of that incident is bounded from the whole of the film's time and space. In a film, consequently, the incident loses its spatial and temporal but not its causal boundaries. Incidents, causally remote or quite irrelevant to one another, can be brought quite close in the course of a successful effort at producing a single filmic causal whole. In every incident, and throughout the whole, the montagist thereby makes evident how particulate, how diversified, how omnipresent causality is. Causally viewed, the entire film compresses a final universal dynamism. Within it are smaller causal occurrences, all occurring within a single filmic present and a single filmic space. The montagist is forced to respect the causality of incidents more than he must respect their times or spaces. This fact prevents him from ever making a film in which all trace of the elements out of which it was constructed has been removed. But this does not prevent him from producing a single causal whole by relating causal situations in any one of an indefinite number of ways.

5

A writer of science fiction attempts something like what a montagist does. But the writer is more deliberately confined. He views space and time in somewhat the ways in which they are viewed in ordinary life, and tries to adhere quite closely to acknowledged causal patterns. There is no rejection of the ostensible course of the world. The monsters that he conceives and the careers of those on his distant and imaginary planets are subject to established laws. These limitations are ignored by the montagist, even when he is concerned with a film devoted to the telling of an ordinary, routine story. Instead of trying to envisage law-abiding, though baffling and outrageous occurrences, he moves freely over all space, time, and causality. Items quite remote in position or in bearing are brought close together; others which occur close together are set far apart. What he does must be in accord, not with the demands of science, but with those of drama, feeling, and reflective understanding. His juxtapositions are not intended to report what is supposed to be the case, but to illuminate what space and time and causality really are. The challenges that he invokes by his manipulation of incidents are for the purpose of bringing us back to reality, not to make us question common suppositions or daily routines. Science fiction offers an escape from the accepted; montaging provides agencies for getting to a reality beyond anything encountered.
In making a science fiction film, montaging, of course, is employed. Without destroying the story line, or the overall space, time, and causality which is to characterize the whole, incidents are then given new neighbors and thereby new roles and meanings. The montagist acts here as he does with any other film. The oddities of the science film are not due to him, but to the script, the performers, the cinemaker, or the director; his task is to convey the import of the whole by his creative relating of the filmed incidents to one another. In helping us to escape into an odd world, he at the same time allows us to become aware of the reality that underlies this as well as any other particular set of occurrences.

6

When, as is the normal case today, the montagist works in close harmony with the director, and sometimes with the cineman, he occasionally watches the film being shot and usually looks at the rushes.* He wants to

---

* *The collaborative harmony you talk about is largely idealistic and unreal. There is almost always one man in charge. It may be the producer. In some cases, as with Fellini or Bergman, it will be the director. Committees do not make art, but men do. One man, usually. Innovative film making requires an absolute identity of intention and sensibility on the part of cutter and director. This makes the cutter both more and less important than he seems in your description, if I read your description correctly.*

D. S.

---

decide, in harmony with them, just what should be retained and what should not, since he is trying to make a film which is the outcome, not of his activity alone, but of a team of cooperative men.

It would be interesting to have the same material presented to a number of montagists at the same time. It would be helpful to make the experiment of having one or two incidents given to a number of montagists to see just how they would bring these together, and what selections they would make out of the number of alternative versions that were possible.* Their different

---

* *ACE (American Cinema Editors, the film editors' guild) did this a few years ago, and it bears out your theory.* *A. K.*

---

products would tell us something about their different creative styles. Or a montagist might be urged to make two or three different films, utilizing the same basic raw material but selecting according to different principles and rearranging them according to different devices. One might experiment in letting some know and others not know the script or a director's intent. Some montagists we might deliberately mislead; others might be made aware of the theories that are now coming more and more into philosophic and literary attention about different types of time. Will the different outcomes give us new insights into the world? Will they all have the same revelatory power? We can not know, until the experiments are tried. But a shrewd guess can now be made. Reality is so rich that an endless number of approaches can be taken to it. They will tell us the selfsame thing, but in distinguishable ways. Different films, though taking us to the same reality, do so with different degrees of effectiveness, and from distinctive angles. A different sequence or utilization of the very same filmed incidents will provide a new opening into the same endlessly rich, never wholly fathomable reality which we already dimly glimpse, and to which every art inevitably takes us.*

Philosophically, the cutter selects from raw film as the intelligence selects from the raw data of existence to construct patterns, to interpret or impose relationships, to inform and give structure.   D. S.

A montagist is no more and no less essential to the making of a great film than is any other film maker. He may, though, assume a dominant role in the making of a film, and still be able to make it great. That film will be different in kind from that which is the outcome of his working coordinately with the others since it will not allow the contributions of the others to be placed on a level with his. It is even possible to produce a great film, with him in a subordinate position, provided that he continues to be a creative contributor to it. Only when the montagist or one of these others becomes the only film maker, with the rest having nothing but supportive roles, does it become impossible to make a great film, since it will then be denied the essential contributions which the other film makers provide. Montaging can not, therefore, be identified with film making. Nevertheless, it can be taken to distinguish the film from other activities which also depend upon a number of distinct contributions made by men working cooperatively but still independently, and which provoke and control expressions of man's fundamental emotions.

A montagist's mastery of space, time, and causation point men toward existence, only one of the modes of being. The contributions of other film makers, even when they are coordinated with montaging in the making of a film, direct one to other beings, via the existence that montaging directly focuses on. It is possible to go just as directly to these other beings, but this will require one to engage in something other than art. One will then do something analogous to what is done by scriptists, performers, cinemen, or directors. Thus, a religious man, in his efforts to make better contact with a final unity, is focused on the very reality that governs a director. This, the director can grasp only through the mediation of existence. Unity interests him but for the sake of making a film; a religious man is interested in it in order to make a life. A director misses what the religious man obtains, but in compensation, he strives to, and may, create a work of art.

CHAPTER 6

Directors

For many, a director is the most important creator, and perhaps even the only creator of a film. Some suppose that he alone is an artist and all others — scriptists, performers, cinemen, and montagists — are just craftsmen, standing to him somewhat the way in which builders stand to architects, stage designers to plays, assistants to master painters, or horses to jockeys. He alone, they think, is the "author," leaving an unmistakable signature on every work in which he is involved. The position exaggerates what was initially intended by one of its earliest and most effective exponents; "I first employed the term 'auteur theory' in an article entitled 'Notes on the Auteur Theory in 1962' (*Film Culture*, No. 27, Winter 1962–63). The article was written in what I thought was a modest, tentative, experimental manner. It certainly was not intended as the last word on the subject. Indeed, it invited debate of pooled scholarship." [1]

"Ultimately, the auteur theory is not so much a theory as an attitude, a table of values that converts film history into directorial autobiography. The auteur critic is obsessed with the wholeness of art and the artist. He looks at a film as a whole, a director as a whole. The parts, however entertaining individually, must cohere meaningfully. This meaningful coherence is more likely when the director dominates the proceedings with skill and purpose." [2]

"Not all directors are auteurs. . . . Nor are all auteurs necessarily directors. . . . Players, particularly comic players, are their own auteurs to varying degrees. . . . The director is both the least necessary and most important component of film-making. He is the most modern and most decadent of all artists in his relative passivity toward everything that passes before him." [3]

Sarris and other defenders of the auteur view hold — correctly, I think — that without the director the film would be a mélange, a sheer aggregate of pieces, not a single film at all. Just as an excellent orchestra, containing none but skilled musicians, will inevitably break up into a multiplicity of players not altogether in harmony, were they not all under the control of a conductor, so will excellent film makers break up into a multiplicity of discordant workers in the absence of a dominating director. But this is far from making the director *the* film maker. Wollen has underscored that fact. He remarks that the director is only one among a number of film makers, and that the auteur theory, despite what Sarris intended, is now the view that the director's style is to be uncovered in a film, and everything else dismissed or minimized:

Of course, the director does not have full control over his work; this explains why the auteur theory involves a kind of decipherment, decryptment. A great many features of films analyzed have to be dismissed as indecipherable because of "noise" from the producer, the cameraman or even the actors. This concept of "noise" needs further elaboration. It is often said that a film is the result of a multiplicity of factors, the sum total of a number of different contributions. The contribution of the director — the "directial factor," as it were — is only one of these, though perhaps the one which carries the most weight. I do not need to emphasize that this view is quite the contrary of the auteur *theory and has nothing in common with it at all. What the* auteur *theory does is to take a group of films — the work of one director — and analyze their structure. Everything irrelevant to this, everything nonpertinent, is considered logically secondary, contingent, to be discarded.*[4]

It has even been argued that directing is not a matter of great difficulty. "As a matter of fact, it's a very simple thing. Of course, directing an extraordinary film is a little more difficult . . . any intelligent person who wanted to could direct a film. . . . They're made at home all the time . . . by college students, high school students, even illiterates. Directing films is nothing mysterious." [5] Putting aside the fact that good and great directing should be distinguished from the efforts of amateurs, it is to be added that the degree of difficulty of a task provides no measure of its importance, or of the contribution it makes to an art.

A director is needed. But even this has been denied. "With the exception of *Strangelove*, of the films I've worked on there isn't one which would not have been infinitely improved by the absence of the director. . . . In his present mode the director is wholly superfluous, an interfering parasite. His proper function — that is to say, a knowledge of lighting techniques and the use of lenses — has been taken over entirely by the Director of Photography. A good script, of course, does not leave room for interference — at least, not *legitimate* interference — it covers every move and every contingency, even anticipates those little areas where you know the director will go for overstatement." [6] And, again, "Directors with an exceptionally strong visual sense may be useful in improving the moves and actions of a scene — but never in improving dialogue." [7]

Southern here speaks on behalf of the scriptist as others do on behalf of the director, or some other film maker. He overstates a case which would have been improved by qualifications and subtilization. He is like those who speak as though performers were the essential or the only significant factors marking off one film from another, like Pudovkin and fellow Russians who focus on montaging, and like those historians who hold that the entire creative work of filming was already fully marked out by Mèliés, Lumière, Porter, and others who first made films that were more than photographs quickly flicked before the eye. In each case a truth is dislocated and turned into an error.

A director usually makes use of a script; he controls performers; he gives orders to a cinemaker; and he passes judgment on the work of a montagist. No one else normally has his authority; no one else has as his task the critical examination and control of the work of others; no one else has as firm an idea of the film as a whole.* But like a conductor, who is nothing

---

What director? When? Why is it that through at least two decades one could distinguish a Warner Brothers movie from an M.G.M. movie — even if the director or the players were the same? One must deal with the artistic impact of an impresario. One can no more understand The Good Earth *without reference to Thalberg than the Russian ballet without reference to Diaghilev.* R. T.

---

without an orchestra, he is nothing without those others.* Something simi-

---

* *The producer David O. Selznick referred to himself as the conductor, the director as his first violinist — and on most Selznick productions, this, indeed, was the case.* R. T.

---

lar, of course, can be said about a horse and its jockey. Still, like a conductor, who neither makes music nor provides a score, a director neither films nor provides a script, while a jockey makes the running a race, and dictates the pace. Without a rider there is no contest, but without a director a film can be made.

Without a director, one can write a script, indeed the very script that is to be used. Without a director, one can perform, sometimes better than the director insists upon. Without a director, cinemaking is possible, particularly by one who has read the script. Without a director, montaging does take place, and may be more successful the less the director interferes. But, also, without the director, there will not be a deliberately made, unitary film in which every incident offers an instance of the very meaning that characterizes the whole.

2

The first task of a director is to translate a script into visual and auditory cinematic terms. Unlike a composer who marks off the parts of a score that are to be played by different members of an orchestra, a director does not concern himself primarily with writing instructions which others are to follow in his absence. Once again his work is more like a conductor's, guiding those who are present.

An actual playing, it has already been remarked, does not simply duplicate what is imagined, making it available to a multitude. A conductor (or a composer) does not actually hear the music while he is reading (or writing) the score. He remembers the different timbres, colors, and weights of different sounds, and he can imagine what he has not heard. But his imagination does not yield sounds any more than his memory does. He can imaginatively distinguish a wide range of sounds and imaginatively interrelate them; he can anticipate the way they will contrast, conflict, mute, supplement, or enhance one another when they are in fact heard, but he can not hear them, no matter how hard he tries. The playing of music gives the music volume and power, allowing it to move toward the listener from above, below, sideways, front, and rear. What one then hears has a texture, an insistence, and a rootage not available to what is imagined. The one is confronted, the other projected. They differ to the same degree that a verified occurrence differs from a prediction. Envisaged and performed incidents also differ in these ways; so do an anticipated and a completed film. The incidents and film that are to be produced are only possible, no matter how vividly they be conceived and projected; the incidents that are performed and the film that is made are actual, no matter how poor they be.

A director projects the incidents and film to be; he confronts the incidents that are being filmed; he works on incidents already filmed. When he projects the incidents and film he is at the beginning of acts of creation; when he confronts the incidents that are being filmed he attends to the raw

material for a film creation; when he works on filmed incidents, he creatively uses filmed material. When he imagines what the whole film will be
like, he is at the beginning of his creative work as a director; when he sees
the completed film he attends to what has already been created. As a
projector of incidents and film he is about to engage in a film making; in
the course of a process of creation, he confronts performed incidents; but
when he views the completed film he functions as a critical member of an
audience.

Like a composer and a conductor, a good director pays scrupulous attention to details. Each incident is treated as a unit to be set alongside others
in such a way as to maximize the excellence of the final whole. No one of
these units, even when held apart, is independent of the others; each
makes a difference to what the others are and mean. They not only belong
together within a single envisaged whole but are subordinate to the final
film. A completed film has incident passing into incident without break:
it does not allow for the isolation of any one except at the price of distortion
and misconception. The director sees each incident, as no one else does,
within an imagined final whole; he works with the others to make all the
incidents be integrated within an actual final unity. The author of the envisaged film which conditions the making of incidents, he is still only a co-
author of the actual film produced through a creative union of those incidents.

A conductor of an orchestra is essential to its production, but does not
really make a contribution to the music heard. He stands away from it,
directing those who play. A director of a film is in a different position. If
he were like a conductor, he would coordinate the various performers and
perhaps tell the cineman and the montagist just what they should do. He
would keep them working together, each concerned with a different task.
There are directors who take this to be their function, but the director,
properly speaking, is a man who represents not the unity of the different
makers but the unity of a film.

A primary unity is one which takes whatever is distinct from itself to instantiate it. Consequently, it faces nothing other than a plurality of fragments of itself. A director expresses such a unity, and wants the other
film makers to see that it is realized in the film. Each is to exhibit, in his
own distinctive, limited way, the unity that the director has in mind. In one
sense beforehand, and in another sense in the course of making the film,
he entertains the whole as that which is to be vivified and presented
through the help of them all. Because of his capacity to deal with them as

producers of instantiations of the single unity that he represents, and because he often has the entire film within his control and has an awareness of what the filmed beginning, middle, and end are, will, and should be, one readily looks to him as the source of a single consistent style manifested in all the dimensions of the film.

A director of a film shares with a director of a play and a conductor of an orchestra the obligation to provide an interpretation. But it is not his task to try merely to provide a visual interpretation of what is offered in a script. Instead, he has just as much an obligation to interpret what is to be done with a cinemaker and through montaging. The interpretation that he gives to the script is just the beginning of a more complete and radical interpretation, since it embraces the work of the other film makers as well. Performance, cinemaker, and montagist all offer the director intensifications of and additions to what the script envisaged. Let there be a script which calls for a quiet street scene in which nothing is happening. The director might imagine it running downhill, with narrow pavements, coming to an end at a factory. In place of human performers he might imagine different objects placed in various positions. But he can not stop there. He* will have to decide whether the street is to be

---

* or, more likely, the scriptist.   R. T.

---

seen in daytime or nighttime, and he will have to decide from what angle it is to be approached.* Keeping just to this particular scene, he may have

---

* or the scriptist, producer, budget, cinemaker, or chance. As for chance, one must be cognizant of the fact that the sun does set and the entire production may have to move to another location the following day. On the other hand, night shooting may be more expensive than day shooting and, therefore, be impermissible — i.e., budget, contracts, when a particular performer is due to leave the company because of prior commitments, etc., etc. How one wishes there would be a chapter in a book on cinema about and entitled simply "Money."   R. T.

---

to think of various ways in which it could be filmed, one of which is to be selected because it brings out best how various incidents fit together on that street. He might imagine juxtaposing one end of the street to the other; he could have the same part of the street shot from many angles and distances.

Some professional critics seem to be interested in the director primarily for evidences of innovative techniques which show how one is to be able to produce various effects otherwise not achievable. Griffith and Welles are for them the major figures in the history of modern film. This is understandable. In all enterprises, the men who are often most honored by professionals are those who produce new devices, who show how to meet old challenges in new ways, or who create new problems and solve them with novelties. They point the rest to the next level of attainment. But some of the greatest writers, painters, sculptors, playwrights, and poets are not innovators. Though great innovators begin periods, great artists often close them. The emphasis on innovative directors' works by close students of the film today is an indication of the youth of film, not of its maturity.

A director gives the unity of a film a role at the beginning, throughout, and at the end. In addition, it is his task to attend to the role each of the others has by himself and in relation to the rest. He has much to learn from them even when he is in full charge of what is done. Were he to do nothing but direct others in the making of a film, he would do less even than an architect, who sees to it that his projected building becomes a reality in a particular environment. One who was just a guide in charge of creative men at one and the same time would deny full functioning to others and yet allow them to function independently of him. A director contributes because he imposes the idea of the unity of a film on every aspect of it. He sees to it that others vitalize the single unity he has in mind. Since they together bring about a film he never envisaged in its full concreteness, to have an idea adequate to what in fact is produced he must allow the actual film to change his mind.*

---

*Your discussion of directors is good, but incomplete. I think it should be balanced by a discussion of the producer's role. And that brings me back to the camera and your curious idea that the camera is the audience. Really, the director is the audience, making the performers go through a take over and over again until he is pleased, selecting the cut he likes, accepting or rejecting the designs of set decorators, costume designers, etc., etc. But the producer, the man who puts together the deal, is the movie-maker. Too little money, and the film is doomed. Too much, and it must appeal to too wide (and therefore too stupid) an audience, which means it is doomed. The wrong actors, the wrong budget, the wrong director, the wrong scriptwriter, and the whole thing is a mess. In no other art form does ethics play so great a part, nor is there anywhere so poignant an overlap between ethics and aesthetics. And there seem to be very few rules. *A man like Howard Hawks thrived at the old Warner Brothers studio, working on low budgets. A man like Buñuel did some of his very best work on a shoestring, working against the limitations imposed on him. Others, like Bergman, thrive on independence and autocracy. But it is a matter of general agreement, I think, that the producer's role is the central one, and that he is the enabler or disabler of everything that happens. This is all very messy, I know, but it is the nature of film making, and you ought to deal with it.*   *D. S.*

3

A performance takes place *for* a director and *before* a director. As the first it is the making of an incident in an imagined whole, of which the performer knows little or nothing. As the second, it is the making of an incident for one who is assuming the position of a cinemaker and therefore of an audience, a critic, and a coach. A performance for a director, when most successful, is a single occurrence to be placed alongside others; a performance before a director, when most successful, produces what will be a part of a final film. To perform just for a director is to perform within a presupposed but unknown whole; to perform solely before a director is to accept the position of a cinemaker, i.e., from where the viewers will see what is filmed.*

---

* *This is dangerous stuff, reasonable but probably wrong. It is not necessary to tell the performers anything at all. They perform for a director—as Lassie does, or Flipper, or Jennifer Jones—who, by the way, did one of her best films in* Beat the Devil *without having been told that it was a comedy. She is not very bright and never suspected. And she was rather annoyed when she saw the movie and found out.*   *D. S.*

A good performance takes place in a film that was envisaged by the director.* Though that performance will lose its spatial and temporal

---

* *Yes, that's true about Welles, but then how many movies can Welles make, getting on as he does—badly—with the money people and the producers? The interdependence of all these people is fascinating, and you don't get enough of the richness and the agony of it. This is what you would like to be true, and what may be sometimes true, but not always, and it's too pat. In the old studio days, there was a Fox look, and an M.G.M. look, and any director working for one of those studios would get a picture*

that looked like any other picture coming out of the same studio. Today, with independents working in impromptu ways, one picks a cinematographer for the look of his work, and that selection of personnel is an aesthetic action! You hire James Wong Howe and you'll get a lot of back-lighting. You hire Boris Kaufman and you'll get a clean, hard-edged look to everything. Leon Shamroy is fantastic with color and spectacle.   *D. S.*

---

boundaries in the film, it will continue to retain its causal limits and its position in relation to the cinemaker — considerations which the director has to keep in mind.

Because a performance does not have an audience, it necessarily has a different spatial, temporal, and dynamic character from that which an actor provides. Its limits are those of an incident whose beginning and end are determined by a cinemaker. By being given a place by a director within an envisaged whole, and eventually a place within a film through the cooperative work of a director and other film makers, a performance is made part of a single unitary work, comprising many interlocked incidents. Professional film making also requires expert cinemen. The work is so complex and difficult that it is usually divided among a number of highly trained competent technicians. They can not be interfered with without loss of excellence. Nevertheless, they, too, are subject to the director, for they also, like a performer, have not usually mastered the entire script, and do not know how particular incidents are to be placed in the projected or final film. At the same time, it is the director who must attend to what it is that cinemakers can do. To prevent his own anticipation of incidents and film from outstripping its capacities, he must act somewhat as a trainer of a dog does: watch where the dog goes, and then tell it to go there. The "somewhat" in the comparison is well-advised. A director may decide on the light, the angles, the lens, and the duration of a cinemaking; he has to attend to the way in which the others work together. He is a one for their many, with them and yet over against them, the condition which enables them to function and interplay maximally. Without a director, there might be fine performances which are not recorded; without him, there might be excellent cinemaking of performers having only a peripheral position in the film. It is the director who relates performer and cineman in terms of what he sees is now required by his idea of the film, and how these men ought to conspire in order to make the film that ought to be. It is he, therefore, who makes cinemaking the cinemaking of a performance, and performance the performance for a unitary film. But the director must also work for and with a montagist. He, too, is a professional. A director might have a good idea of the way in which incidents are to be altered and interrelated in order to be together in a splendid, unified film, but it is the montagist who must produce that unity. Avakian speaks for the montagist: "Any director in his right mind will leave his editor alone until the first cut is finished. The notion that the director works continuously with the editor in cutting the film is a myth. It only happens that way when the director is also the cutter. . . . there are whole large portions of a film where a director will just say, 'Go.' " [8] There is no formula which a director can follow; he can not decide in advance what is to be discarded, what is to be retained, what is to be put here and what is to be put there. No one can make these decisions without assuming the montagist's role. What the montagist produces must be used by the director as a control over what else is to be filmed, and how. A director works to bring about a unitary film; though this requires him to envisage the whole in advance of its achievement, he works inductively, changing his idea in the light of what he has been given and how this has been utilized.

A director is not oblivious of the alteration a film undergoes in the course of a film making. But he determines and controls the changes even while he yields to them. His idea of the whole is restraining and insistent; a montagist's idea is conditioned by what is available, and is subject to what a director has in mind.

A director interprets the script, coaches the performers, suggests to the cineman, works together with the montagist, and interrelates them all, incident after incident, thereby articulating what was initially considered. He begins with a vague idea of the entire film and uses this to help him determine what is to be done. Usually he expresses that idea in the form of a narrative line; marks a beginning, ending, and vital turning points; imagines an aesthetic whole with its major contrasts; and makes use of a space, time, and dynamism which encompass and are embodied in all the incidents. These factors are distinguished in being specialized; and they are specialized in the course of a film making.

The film that a director initially envisages plays only a slight role to begin with. Attention is focused on the incidents, with the idea of the film serving both as a possible area in which the incidents are to be placed, and as an agency for making connection with other incidents to be subsequently produced. During the course of a production, a director comes to a point where the initial envisaged film no longer functions solely as a possible area and connection, but becomes more and more the actual place where incidents are located. The incidents then fill out the film, and the film encloses the incidents. As the production progresses, the director comes to still another point where the initial envisaged film is replaced by the actual film so far produced. As a consequence, the unity of the final film turns out to be both a function and a determinant of its parts.

Were there no envisaged film, there would be no purpose, no direction, no directing. The result would be discontinuous improvisations, chaos, or just material for someone else to work over. If a projected film did not become a possible area to be filled out by incidents, it would be just a goal to be striven for, but never realized. If the filled-out area were not eventually replaced by a film that was a function and a determinant of its parts, the parts would not belong together and there would be nothing in them which could acquaint one with the nature of the whole.

What is not a work of art can arouse the emotions; what is not a work of art can control the emotions; what is not a work of art can satisfy the emotions. But it is only a work of art which controls and at least partly satisfies the emotions that it arouses. By attending to the emotions, a director can partly check his judgment that he has produced a work of art. The aroused emotions are spelled out and directed by such a work, and therefore are neither as crude, nor as violent, nor as debilitating as those brought out into the open by other means. When a screening is over, the emotions are not yet entirely quieted, and of course, are no longer controlled by the film. Drained though they are of most of their energy, they still can take one toward realities rarely discerned in daily life. If a film is truly innovative, the residual emotions place one in a position to inquire about, as well as to have some experience of, the endless malleability of space, time, and causality. A director, because he stands away from the film making in order to understand and produce a single unified film, is in a position to know this. But, because he can see that what is known through film can be known in other ways as well, he is at times tempted to be "philosophical," a "thinker."

The deepest probing film is innovative. This does not mean that it is experimental. An experimental film maker asks himself what the established constraints and conditions are to which film has been subject, and then sets about to defy them. He might refuse to use a script, or he might use one that is not designed for a film. He might not use any performers, and content himself with marking up his negatives. He might refuse to coach, or he might have his performers do what is alien to their natures, habits, experience, and interests. Poor light and mutilated film might be preferred to good. Incidents might be disjoined, conjoined, and interwoven in new ways. These technical novelties do not necessarily bring him closer to the making of a work of art than he had been before. But they do have shock value, and they could make possible a better work of art on the part of a director. For that double reason experimental film should interest him, as it interested Kubrick, particularly toward the end of his *2001*. A director's usual concern with the film as a whole, as a possible area, and as integrated with its parts, tends to make him take too many established procedures for granted. Experimental film is the enemy of the clichés of habit; that is reason enough to make an alert director want to attend to it.

It is possible to insist on innovation regardless of popular or dramatic demands. The result can be an effective, disturbing work, which irritates and confuses, not by what it portrays but by its incidental occlusion or defiance of normal feelings and established attitudes. Such an innovative film, with the experimental, breaks away from familiar forms. Unlike the experimental film, an innovative, though, can be popular and dramatic as well.

A director's perspective is only one of many. Still, it is all-encompassing. But just as a philosophical position, no matter how comprehensive and thorough, is no substitute for the world, so the totality that a director conceives is no substitute for the concrete occurrence that is produced. The fact is even more obvious when other film makers are also at work, even though they are under his direction, and create within the encompassment of the idea that he has before him, and in terms of which he directs their functioning.

4

A good director knows what the desired end is, and how to make it control all that goes on. That end, of course, is not the terminus of a film or the last incident. It is a meaning pertinent to every part. A one to be made immanent in a many, it is to be carried out in all the ramifications of the film. When the film is completed, it should be possible to find the end to be at once realized throughout and to have been enriched by every incident. A director learns from the film that is being made what his unity visually means, for it is initially only schematic, general; it is made determinate through the actual creation of the film.

Performers make what a director can only suggest or demand. He does not direct them as a painter might direct his apprentices, or as an architect might direct contractors and workmen, for he requires them to help create a film with him. Even in the extreme case where a director has to tell them how to lift their hands, what kind of gestures to make, whether or how to frown, where to look toward, even where he makes them present an incident over and over again until they show exactly the right expression, the performers help make the film. They are always contributors, never mere props.

An Orson Welles keeps his cineman under fairly tight control, telling him what angle to shoot from, what lights to use, how slowly or rapidly he is to move. Welles is confident that he knows better than anyone else what is to be filmed. As a result, his cineman is reduced to the status of a craftsman. But even under such restrictive conditions, it is conceivable that his cineman could contribute to the making of a work of art by the way in which he interpreted the instructions Welles gave him. If too autocratic, of course, a director will not allow his cineman much rein; as a consequence, the film will not be enriched by the contributions that a creative cineman could provide.*

---

* In Hud, *Ritt made many good cinematic points by leaving James Wong Howe in almost total control of the visual texture.* J. W.

It is possible for a director to be in control, and still allow for other men to make contributions to a film. It is conceivable that some director may himself be a cineman, a performer, and a scriptist, as well as a montagist, all in one. Such a man would have to carry out the different roles at least as well as those others can. It would be strange, though, if there were no cineman who was as gifted in his own area as a director is in his. It would be very strange if there were some director who was so extraordinarily gifted that he was superior to any cineman whatsoever.*

---

* Yet this certainly was true of Von Sternberg, very probably of Von Stroheim, and perhaps even of Hitchcock and Chaplin. R. T.

There need be no destruction of the unity of a film when others are allowed to add their own creative elements to the creative work of a director. Unity is not necessarily lost by giving some freedom to others. Full control need not be exercised in the beginning, nor even throughout. It is sufficient that the director take hold and see that what would otherwise appear to be discrepant, or what does not help produce maximum excellence, be altered. If a director insists on having a point of view in advance, which he keeps to regardless of the contributions that others are making, he will end with something which bears the unmistakable mark of his peculiar kind of ability, but it will be less of a work than could have been made. He gains most when others are given their freedom to show what they know.

Good directors in the theatre bring out the potentialities of an actor, precisely by not insisting on their interpretations of his every move. They do not want to deny to the actor an opportunity to contribute maximally to the total result. It is odd that what is so well known in the theatre is not so well known in the studio. The reason, perhaps, is that in recent years a number of distinguished directors have been able to bring the film to levels which it had not previously attained; we owe so much to their achievements that we tend to overlook the achievements of the other makers. It also offers another indication that film is still a young art.

A great film conceivably shows a director's impress more than it shows that of any other, but ideally others make their distinctive styles also evident, while instancing what the director has in mind. Film that is dominated by a director is only one possible form of film. But film without any director, or film which shows no influence of a director, is film which is less than it ought to be. A good director makes sure that all the parts are creatively produced and brought together in a single totality. That totality should reflect his fundamental idea. Together with the others he should provide determinate, limited, vivified versions of what initially is quite general. This the scriptist articulates, and the director envisages — both before anything is in fact filmed.

There are directors who do not begin with an overall idea, but instead constantly improvise. The early films were made in something like this spirit, particularly the comedies. In these, incidents frequently provided occasions for determining what next was to be done. The opposite extreme is entertained by those directors who claim that they have the entire film, from beginning to end, already in mind. If they really saw the entire film before it was made, they would see much less than the film might be. The fact that they might then see far more than others does not in any way affect the point that the films could have been greater than what they actually produce, great though those films might be in comparison with what others do or could have done. A tyrannical film director stands in his own light just so far as he prevents others from being as free as he himself would like to be. What he has in mind is always general, transcending script or plot, or any other articulation. It is to be conveyed in cinematic terms, and therefore by making an actual film. This might exhibit the very idea originally entertained by the director, but it could well exhibit an idea which had been much later discerned, and actually realized by the other film makers.

The account that has here been given of the film deals with it as a work of art to which different men, together with a director, contribute essential components. Each one of these can make a film in which he has a primary role and the others only secondary ones. But in the ideally perfect film each makes an equally indispensable, valuable contribution. Any one of them, though, could be given a primary role, without precluding the production of an excellent film. If this is so, there will be at least six different types of film, each a possible work of art on a level with the others. In addition to films where the different contributors are equally important, there will be others where the scriptist plays a dominant role; others where the performer is outstanding; others where cinemaking becomes the principal factor; still others where montaging is to the fore; and others where the director is the main "author." An examination of these variants exposes both the strengths and the weaknesses of the different contributors to good film.

CHAPTER 7

Five Varieties of Art Film

The filming of great plays, such as Sophocles' and Molière's, has been only moderately successful, in good part because there was an understandable, but too great a desire to keep to the traditional treatment of the plays, characters, and roles, and in good part because almost everyone is so intimidated by greatness that it is hard to be maximally creative with long-established, outstanding works. And then there is the unavoidable task of preserving well-known lines and scenes, despite the fact that they do not have the rhythms, the lengths, or the relationship to the rest that film demands. But there surely will come a time when the texts of great classical plays will not only be used as material for a shooting script, but will be produced on film in all their greatness. Undoubtedly sequences will be altered, emphases shifted, and the language modified so as to retain in the new medium the distinctive import of what was originally written. Today, stage directors shorten and omit scenes of classical plays; new interpretations are read into familiar characters, turns, and speeches—some of them in response to the need to present the plays in a modern theatre before an audience not altogether familiar with the language or the customs of the time when the plays were originally given. Film will require still further changes, if it is to do as much justice to the plays as modern play directors do to them. The dialogue and narrative line will have to be more or less preserved by the films, however, or the films will fail to be films of classical plays.

If one can justly alter the dialogue or the narrative of a great play for the sake of making a great film, there is nothing in principle in the way of also making great changes in it, or of introducing into it narratives newly made, or even dialogues of no great import. One will then sacrifice good writing for the sake of retaining or improving cinematic insights into the nature of man and the world. It is possible then to go on and emphasize to a degree, that the texts do not, minor dramatic turns, characters, causes and effects, and interconnections. Zeffirelli's *Romeo and Juliet* is an example. The result is quite different from the play originally presented in manuscript or on the stage, but surely has as much emotional impact, is as interesting, and reveals as much.

Though written in language, a narrative need not be primarily at the service of speech. It may be descriptive, having to do with the course of the world in relation to man, where the world may be the primary factor, overwhelming in its relentless movement, unrelieved by sound. The narrative time will then mark the world's rhythms and direction, point up its crucial turns, and thereby give it a meaning from beginning to end. But if there is an overemphasis on the narrative, one will turn the film into a vehicle for a message, make it didactic, or keep it confined to the merely dramatic.

Language should enrich what is seen; what is seen will gain meaning if it is paced by what is said. The silent film made much of posture, grimace, gesture, and movement, but even it pieced these out with language in some form, in order to point up a place and meaning in a world where men spoke together. The scenes were often filmed with sound accompaniments and, when shown, were often supported by spoken dialogue or music. It is a mistake, therefore, to take silent and sound films to be polar opposites. They are on a continuum. The one can have long stretches of silence, the other can have sound added when filmed or viewed. In both, the visual is of primary concern. But modern film, because made with deliberate attention to the need to have a place for sound, has to have a distinctive pace and a development.

A film can tell a story and still be a film, even a great film. This, of course, is known to all film makers. Theorists, urging the primacy of some other contributor, or anxious to justify experiments, have vainly tried to undercut that fact. An acknowledgment of the rights of a dominant narrative need not stand in the way of the dominance of other contributors in other types of film. But when a script, instead of having a coordinate or outstanding role, supported by the others, is alone made essential, with performance, cinemaking, montaging, and directing forced into incidental positions, the narrative it contains will be given a false prominence.

A script's demands may not be heeded by a performer. Some performers in fact are inanimate, and when human they may not have seen or understood the script, or may be forced to follow the suggestions of a director. But if a performer is dictated to, he will tend to act woodenly, mechanically, doing what he is told, somewhat in the way in which he might try to make love by following the rules laid down in a sex manual.

An actor, since he knows the narrative, and the place that his part has in it, would seem to be more subject to this risk than a performer. On the other hand, a performer, because he produces isolated incidents, might be thought to escape the constraints of a script, since this is precisely where incidents are kept in relation to one another. This is not the case. An actor who has mastered his part makes it subject to the way it is to mesh with those of others. A performer runs the risk of becoming subject to a script, directly or indirectly, because he can so readily offer an isolated visual reformulation of what is set down in words.

A cinemaker, too, may be comparatively unaffected by a script. He may not even have seen it — this is more likely — and may simply follow the recommendations of a director. But if he does know the script, or follows it as mediated by the director, in such a way that it dominates him, he will tend to begin and end, to pace, angle, and emphasize in accordance with something said, and not in accordance with what is seen. What he confronts has rights of its own which it is his task to respect. To allow himself to be subject to the script is to make himself tend to minimize these rights, to do less than justice to contours, rhythms, and forces, to gradations of light, and to the ways in which different incidents can enhance one another.

Though a photographer also pays attention to the aesthetic value of the different parts of the scene before him, and the ways in which they might be made to enhance one another, he is both more and less likely to be subject to verbal controls than a cinemaker is — more likely because he attends to only one moment at a time and therefore is more in accord with words, and less likely because he does not need the extended verbal guidance that keeps a cineman abreast of a course of development. A photographer who allows words to dominate him will be insufficiently attentive to the different demands made by sight and language, while a cineman who allows a script to dominate him will be insufficiently attentive to the demands that movement makes on vision.

Montaging begins after a script has been used. As a rule, the montagist has read it, often is present at the day's shooting, and understands the director's interpretation of what has been and is yet to be filmed. Like other film makers, he can allow a script to have a predominant role; his comprehension of what is written will then excessively govern his determination of what is to be seen. He will adhere to the sequence the script presents and will take its emphases and pace to dictate what he is to do.

Decorators and landscapists are more likely to be subject to what is projected than a montagist is, since these men are usually employed by architects, developers, and others who have some particular work they want enhanced but not significantly altered. The enhancement, though, is their own work, outside the scope of what architects and developers are able to do or properly control. A montagist, who is subservient to a script, does not have that much freedom. He pieces incidents together, but primarily to allow what a script presents to be cinematically visible. It is as if a landscapist used trees solely in order to make a building be more or less conspicuous.

A montagist is tempted to give most consideration to a clearly stated, persuasive, attractive script which promises him great scope for his activities. A director would be even more tempted. A script structures, outlines, and pivots the idea of the film as a whole; it can easily pass from being suggestive and directional to becoming an unswerving condition, and even a measure of success. But if a director allows a script to have a predominant role, he will be inclined to substitute coaching for directing; translation into visual terms for the creation of a film; a possible unitary nature, not integrated with what is filmed, for a unity developed in the course of a film making.

A director of a play is more inclined than a film director is to follow what is verbally laid down. But a director of a play has no need to start with a vague idea of what is to be, and gradually enrich and concretize this; the play is the idea to be maintained throughout.* Though it will be somewhat

---

* And yet Tennessee Williams found it necessary to publish two third acts of Cat on a Hot Tin Roof. His own, which ended in utter despair, and Elia Kazan's which left you with that damnable hope for the future, that pox which inflicts movie and play producers alike.   R. T.

---

altered in being vitalized in the acting, a play has a definiteness and an articulation that a film director's initial idea does not have. A director may nevertheless be tempted to allow a script to dictate to him, as no play director allows a play, for a shooting script spells out directing details. It may explicitly state where performers are to be, their distances from one another and the cinemaker, and how incidents are to be begun and ended. A director, subservient to a script, will do less than justice to the idea which a script expresses. The script may subdivide the idea but can not visually express it. The visual expression is for film makers to provide; a script should be their guide, not their master.

2

Audience, mass media, and performers differ from scriptists, cinemakers, montagists, and directors most sharply in their estimates of the importance of a performer. They think that, at his best, he deserves to be given, and surely is to be acknowledged to have primary status in a film. They speak of him as a "star," who gives a film its characteristic tone, value, and interest.

Most performers can not act.* Their performances are often controlled by a

---

* Not absolutely untrue, but, surely an injustice. Here, I will mention only John Barrymore — the early Barrymore, who had quite a comfortable reputation both before the footlights and the cameras.   *R. T.*

---

director, and are highlighted and in part constituted by cinemaker and montagist. The narrative gives them the meaning they are trying to portray and convey. Often they merely fill out roles, repeated in film after film. Some had never appeared before a cinemaker; others are little more than focal points. Primary emphasis on a performer usually falsifies what is in fact the case, and where justified, spoils the film. Still, some performers can outperform others; the task set to them by a film is carried out superbly. A great performer could exhibit the meaning of a whole film at the same time that he gave various incidents their full value. He could be the main contributor to a film. He would not then have to be present throughout, any more than a general or a hero has to be everywhere in a battle or a war. But this is not yet to say that a performer should be a "star." A star not only obscures the work of other film makers, but denies them their place as genuine contributors in the making of a film;* they are placed at his

---

* There are instances in which this is not true. One thinks of Marlene Dietrich in The Blue Angel, *the nominal star of which was Emil Jannings. The director, Von Sternberg, has always been remembered for this movie — and even Jannings I'm afraid. But Dietrich and* The Blue Angel *constitute one of those great artistic accidents in which film and newly created star fused with all of the other elements of the production, and a great star film was the result.*   *R. T.*

---

service, allowing him to stand out, no matter what this does to the film.*

---

* If a film is essentially a star-vehicle, like Camille, *this can only help.*   *A. K.*

There are crucial and great performers. These have a primary position in the making of a film. But they are not the stars of which the public speaks; they become stars when the other film makers are neglected or treated as just occasions or supports. Stars stand to outstanding performers somewhat as codes stand to narratives. The one needs translation, the other enriches and completes. The line between a star and a great performer differs from that which separates message and script. A script turns one toward a film, a message away from it, but both stars and great performers keep one focused on the film. A star is a pivotal figure, whose absence spells slack, tedium, emptiness; a great performer is a vitalizer of incidents whose achievements illuminate what occurs apart from him. A great performer is present where he is absent, making a difference to what there occurs; a star is missing where he is not present, someone who is wanted there.

It is possible to fill out the places, where a star is not seen, by making use of other stars. One will then produce a plurality of foci, a series of pieces, but no single film. Great performers intermesh, enrich one another, not because they make contact, but because what they do casts a light over what else occurs. But stars just replace one another. The result is a series of nouns, atoms, not a single integrated whole.* The dark places where a

---

* *Forgetting* The Blue Angel, *one must remember the relationship between movies, stage, circuses, and carnivals. Movies to be art must, also, in a special sense be fun. Stars* are *fun. They walk the high wire, they do triple somersaults from trapeze to trapeze. Those who do not appreciate the absurd merits of* Grand Hotel *(Garbo, both Barrymores, Crawford, Wallace Beery, etc.) or of* Dinner at Eight *(Harlow, Beery, again both Barrymores, Billie Burke, etc.) should perhaps not be allowed to be ringmasters; perhaps they can* only *be critics or philosophers.* R. T.

---

star is not could be filled by arresting incidents, or even by incidents which provide a needed continuity. These would then provide connective tissue, verbs, transitions. But every incident should be a verb as well as a noun, a connection as well as a term, a resting place as well as a transition, a substance as well as a process.

A role is not to be simply carried out, but vitalized and individualized. A star both fails to turn it into a fine performance and overpersonalizes it, even when he does nothing more than take up the same role in film after film. He may repeat the same mannerisms and intonations, wear the same kind of clothes; he may even be encouraged to emphasize these in order to make him readily noticeable. Even then he will overpersonalize, and not yet produce a great performance. His individual self will, of course, not come into play, being well hidden behind the established role and its requirements, but the role will still have been overwhelmed by him. A fine performer, in contrast, sustains an incident to make it and his performance find a significant place in the film; he takes a role to be an outline to vivify in such a way as to make the result an essential part of a work of art.

When performers are given dominant positions, with the other film makers also contributing to the making of a film, a distinct type of film is produced. Incidents are then no longer just units; they are dynamic thrusts, epitomizing the entire film. When a star usurps the place of a performer, the incidents lose much of their status to become just occasions making possible the exhibition of a distinctive mode of personalizing, while still leaving the role insufficiently concretized. When a star becomes the story, there is no story to be starred; nothing is evident but the appearance of the star. The film is his vehicle, but he takes it nowhere.

A truly great performer vitalizes a role. He does not intrude his person into it; he does not call attention to himself as a performer. Instead, he exhibits a character, and quickens the role in the course of making incidents be. The result is self-contained incidents, nuanced, aesthetically unified, in which a character in a role, a performer exhibiting that character, and a man assuming the task of performer are presented together. The man is in the incident in a restricted form. As an actual living man he has psychological, social, as well as biological and other histories; he is also substantial, self-centered, and has an unreachable privacy. Via the incidents in the film, he has a limited number of relations to a limited number of other performers in the same or other incidents. The incident is an appearance in a limited context, differing from what is daily encountered, from what science might know, or from what happens in society because of the way it is related to the other incidents.

To hold that a nonperforming, actual man was being seen on the film puts an opposite stress on the error which holds that an incident or a performance is an illusion.* Neither position takes film seriously; both

---

*For Cleopatra Fox ordered fake horses from some Italian workshops, which made them, and killed horses for hides to put on the fake-dead horses. Were these dead horses performing? Were the fakes real?   D. S.

tacitly suppose that what is real is only what men daily encounter. Were they right, there would be no need for science or philosophy — or what these reported would be unrealities. And there would be only illusions to be found in history, society, as well as in the various arts. Incidents, and the performers that make them possible, are affiliated in distinctive ways in film; the fact that they are inseparable from substantial beings which also exist outside film is a fact about their grounding, their presuppositions, not a fact about them. Brando is a "Godfather" who dies a death which has distinctive relations to other filmed incidents. That death is inseparable from Brando. But the man, Brando, does not simply die the death of a Godfather any more than he will ever simply die biologically. With his biological death Brando will be unable to engage in a multiplicity of activities he had been able to carry out, one of which was dying the death of a Godfather in a film. But, conversely, the death of a "Godfather" is forever affiliated with other incidents in the film and will not be affected by Brando's death apart from the film. In film, the incident's the thing, and catches up men within itself. But film is not all there is, and what it exhibits are only fragments of what is ultimately real. That ultimate reality is not an actual man. A film tells us about a more ultimate reality; this is more persistent and encompassing than any man could be, but is conveyed in film only in the form of limited occurrences.*

---

* Once more, one would like to relate The Godfather *to the problem of the star. There are, as I once pointed out* (Esquire, *March 1967*) *certain performers the public wants to have die or be beaten. Garbo was one of these. Montgomery Clift was another. Think how many times we've seen Brando, for example, die* — The Nightcomers, The Young Lions, Mutiny on the Bounty *(in the same story, Gable didn't). If he doesn't die, he is hideously beaten* — One Eyed Jacks, On the Waterfront, The Wild One, *etc., in both categories. It is not right to ignore the "fate" certain performers have either wished on themselves or are steered into. Art is art* — *perhaps. But we do not expect Monet to paint a crucifixion.* R. T.

An incident in a film is related to other incidents there in two ways. It has its meaning added to at the same time that it adds meaning to other incidents. A death is related to a funeral, the taking over by a successor, and the like. The other incidents in the film serve as background, pacings, obstacles, which prevent the first type of relation from being a merely formal structure. When a death in one film is related to a death in another, the deaths will either be taken as inseparable parts of the films, or will be abstracted from these. If confined to their films, what is outside the films will function as background, pacings, and obstacles for relations of comparison. If the deaths are abstracted from the films, the other incidents in the films acquire new roles.

When a man dies a biological death, a cluster of other activities also cease. But they do not all end at the same time; the economic status may have stopped earlier or may continue for a while after the death; so may familial, social, and other careers. But all of them, rather directly, are to be referred back to one individual who ceases to be a single organic being, with the consequence that he ceases to be a ground for them — and for the making of a film. A death in a film is a death we can view again and again, and is therefore quite removed from the individual in whom different activities have their common origin. In compensation, a death in a film refers us to any and every death occurring outside the film, on the way to referring us to insistent, ultimate realities.*

---

* Death is an interesting subject, one I hadn't ever considered in film terms before. I wonder if you aren't being too reasonable and too pure. There is a special frisson, reflected in box office receipts, at seeing the film of a recently dead actor. Bruce Lee, the dead actor, has helped the new Kung Fu film by having died. It helps The Carpetbaggers *to know that this was Alan Ladd's last part, and that his puzzled and hurt delivery of his last line in movies is in this, "I haven't the vaguest idea," he says, and disappears, forever and for real.*   D. S.

A cinemaker may be given a subordinate though essential role in a film which pivots about a great performer. The task of the cinemaker will then be that of recognizing the performer's central position in various incidents. Though the incidents will still have outstanding importance for the cinemaker, they will depend upon the performer for focus. A star, instead, denies to the cinemaker any other function but that of attending to the star's distinctive features and activities, even though such concentration diminishes the cinematic value of the incident, the work of the rest of the cast, or the nature and meaning of the film as a whole. The star might move but the film will not; he might say something but still nothing will be said. There will no longer be an immanent controlling force giving meaning and direction to a plurality of otherwise indifferent and unimportant occurrences; everything but the star will be in shadow. Stars shine too brightly to allow for the contrasts which incidents and film require.*

---

* *A star is simply a performer with a box office appeal to an audience.*
This is neither good nor bad, but another contingency with which the film
maker can work, more or less creatively, more or less successfully. It is a
more neutral thing than you make out, this stardom.   *D. S.*

A film, governed by a great performer, offers a special challenge to a
montagist. Without curtailing the performer's creativity, a montagist has
to cut, splice, merge, divide, and unite a multiplicity of incidents, but
in such a way as to maximize their values. He may eventually be forced to
break into them, to cut them down, to make the performance less than it
originally was on film, but these will be outcomes reluctantly arrived at.
When a performer is a dominant, but still only one of a number of
contributors to a film, he compels a montagist to see how the others can
support or supplement the performance. But if a montagist has the task of
making a film centered about a star, he is forced to highlight him, no matter
what this does to the film. To be sure, conscientious about his obligation to
produce the best possible film, he will try to give value to those other
incidents — but only so far as that will enhance the presence of the star.
It is not enough if he sees to it that nothing grays the star's presence;
everything must add to it. This may require great ingenuity, even great
creative powers; a montagist may then be needed even more desperately
than he would were there only minor performers. But the ingenuity and
creativity will still not be at the service of the film, but of the star.
A star can not be a star in a film, but only in parts of it. This is true even if
he is present in every part, for there would still be nothing which made the
parts into a whole. Though the presence of a star throughout a film
provides a thread of identity maintained from beginning to end, this is
not yet a unity in which script, cinemaking, montaging, and directing also
make equal or subordinate though essential contributions.
A great director may elicit great performances. Those performances
could be governed by the director's initial idea of the film as a whole. This
is what happens when he has a coordinate or a dominant role in the
making of a film. But a star too often dictates to a director. The initial idea
that the director has is then destroyed to leave an idea primarily defined
by the star. Instead of helping transform the idea that the director initially
had, another is set in its place. The star's performance is designed to
realize that idea; it is not intended to supplement the contributions
made by others.
When it is a star rather than a true performer with whom a director has to

work, his primary task is to see, not that an excellent film is made, but that a star is presented excellently.* Of course, the director would like to have

---

Are you saying that there has never been a great film that had a star in it? A dangerous doctrine, indeed! Chaplin? Keaton? Even John Wayne? Fernandel? Jacques Tati? Ingrid Bergman? Peter Lorre? None of these ever appeared in a great film? If this is what you are saying, then your category is empty, which is possible, but your observations are mostly irrelevant because the judgments you make about how films ought to work is without basis in history as well as in economics and ethics.   D. S.

---

a star presented excellently in an excellent film, but this is not possible if he is subject to the condition that he do nothing that reduces the magnitude of the star. The star shines alone, in a setting provided by the others; they must be blacked out if the star is to be seen.*

It is not unthinkable that a star might germinate a great film. One must consider the great comedians: Chaplin, Pickford, Keaton, and (although he is not frequently considered a master of comedy) Fairbanks. The star has, frequently, not been an employee (in any sense), but the maker of the film.   R. T.

Today it is common to take great performers to be stars, but not as common to take stars to be great performers. The two should be distinguished more radically, for it is desirable to separate sharply films in which all film makers have a significant role to play or where performers are dominant, from those where only stars are to be counted. To make and maintain the distinction should not be difficult. One need only to determine whether an entire film or only a succession of parts is able to be presented. Since a man may be a star in one film where he overwhelms all the others involved, and in another film may show himself to be a great performer who works together with others coordinately, or with others assuming essential but subordinate positions, no one, though, should be classified as a star or a true performer apart from a reference to particular films. Fragmented films provide no adequate place for great performers; unified films have none for stars. A great performance may, of course, occur in sections of a film; but though it is always confined within incidents, through the work of the montagist and others it will be possible to integrate it with the rest of the film.*

For you, star is a pejorative word, and it ought not be. It necessarily implies imbalance and economic domination. But if you admit this

---

economic domination, you should admit all of them. The distinction is worth making, perhaps, between great performances and star performances, even in these peculiar and cumbersome terms. But truthfully, admitting that from a great performance there arises, almost inevitably, the temptation to star performances. Lorre in M was great, and in one of those American International horror flicks a star.   *D. S.*

3

A cinemaker's task is to bring out the full value of each incident — aesthetic, dramatic, supportive, supplementary, and intelligible. When, instead of working coordinately with others, he becomes the dominant figure — as seems often to be the case with Japanese cinemakers — there is an overemphasis on visual effects, with a correlative diminution of the contributions of script, performances, montaging and directing.* Incidents

---

* *If the Japanese are different give them credit for both their peculiarities, for they are painterly and also extremely bloody — as our own Westerns have become. The fun of a Japanese film is in the tension between this punctilious picturesqueness and the messy violence.*   *D. S.*

---

are then no longer the primary object or product of cinemaking; that position is assumed by the scene, where the incidents are given their aesthetic due, but only as together with other aesthetic elements, and with a comparative neglect of the incidents' other dimensions. Narrative line, performance, relation to what else is to be filmed, and relevance to the idea of the film as a whole will be forced into the background, still essential but of less importance than the purely aesthetic character of the detached scene.

When a cinemaker becomes *the* maker of a film, denying any role to the others but that of occasions, supports, instruments, or aids, he turns himself into a movie photographer, one who produces scenes one after the other, without regard for any other need or objective. In effect, he makes a series of stills. Motions and changes, of course, will continue to be filmed, but the entire film itself will be one extended fixity, somewhat like a Japanese screen, where a number of separate events are portrayed, to be looked at sequentially.

There can be films which owe their greatness to a cinemaker. These have a progression that is not identifiable with any expressed in a script. A cineman speaks there in a distinctive language whose words are splendid aesthetic units in splendid aesthetic sentences. He does not offer a new creative interpretation of the script in the way a classical pianist does for a score, but functions more like an innovative musician, taking off from the script for the sake of attaining his own goals. The result may well be better than anything which the script itself promised. But this will rarely occur, if he does not allow the script to contribute to the nature of the final result. A great film has a progression, its "narrative line." This need not involve the telling of a story, realism, a concern for plot, development of character, or a well-defined beginning, middle, and end. A narrative line may concern the way in which images are to succeed one another; it may give great weight to aesthetic values; and it may ignore meanings and familiar references; but it is always verbally expressible as well as cinematically experienceable. Without it the nature and course of a film could not be communicated except by being seen. A cineman who is interested in nothing but aesthetic experience, the sensuous living through of something encountered, grants a performance only as much play as it needs in order for the experience to be enhanced. He neglects both aesthetic and art objects, the one having the status of something held apart from all else, and to be appreciated for what it is, the other having an excellence which is the outcome of a creative making. Confronted with a performance, no matter how great, he attends mainly to its lights and shadows, its contrasts and complements, the way it fits in with the entire setting. What is said he values for its sound, not for what it says. It would be just as satisfactory to him if he were to attend to an audible display of colored shapes one after the other.

One of the paradoxes of experimental film making is that, in the attempt to avoid the telling of tales, in the effort to see what can be done by treating film in new ways, and in the recognition of the incompatibility between the role of star and the demands of the art of film, performances are used mainly as occasions for the production of aesthetic experiences or aesthetic objects. To be sure, ordinary sensitivities are challenged and defied, but this is only to say that the result is often not aesthetically satisfying. Experimental achievements could, though, be used in a great film to enrich and be enriched by the work of the various film makers. If a cineman, alert to the achievements of experimental film, were to work with others, what before was aesthetically unsatisfactory would not be taken by itself, but would be interlocked with other contributions.

Given a dominant role in an hierarchy of film makers, a cineman is able to make a great film. That film could be an art object. It would be different though, from those made by other dominant film makers, or by all of them working together, more or less on a common footing. A work of art is a sensuous excellence, self-contained, appealing to man's basic tone; it is beautiful, not merely pleasing; it has a place for climaxes as well as for contrasts; it introduces us to a world beyond itself; and instead of giving us something to be merely lived in, it gives us something to live with. A film work of art is an achievement which requires one to attend to incidents as well as to qualities, to performances as well as to differences in light, shape, and movement.

It is difficult for a cineman to assume a position of dominance over a montagist: a montagist works on the results provided by a cineman. But it is possible for a montagist to put himself in a subordinate position or to so shrink himself that he does nothing but patch together what a cinemaker presents to him. If he does this, he will deny to himself a creative role in the making of a film. A cinemaker, dominant or not, needs a montagist to make a unity out of what was produced at many different times, under many different circumstances, and perhaps without any understanding of how the disparate items were all intended to fit inside a single final whole. If a montagist does not make a contribution to the creation of a film, but works solely to make whatever unity he can out of a cinemaker's products, the outcome, more likely than not, will be just an assemblage of parts.

A montagist who is an assistant to a cinemaker puts together as well as he can what is not even material for a single film, since it is nothing more than a set of occasions for aesthetic experiences, or — where a cinemaker has been joined by everyone but a montagist in the creative making of a film — nothing more than detached aesthetic objects which the montagist may bring together, but is given no opportunity to unify. A cinemaker, if he is to make a great film has to make room for the creative work of the other film makers as well; a montagist will start with what the cinemaker was then able to produce. Were there no contributions made by others, the material presented by the cinemaker would not be rich enough to make possible a great film.* Only if a montagist is alert to those other contribu-

---

* And yet most (although certainly not all) powerful directors — or at one time producers, at another time stars — control the final cut, are over the shoulder of the montagist every moment, giving direct orders as to the precise frame at which a cut, a dissolve should be. One may say the film is lacking, but one would have to omit from one's list of great films all of

Chaplin from The Gold Rush *on, most of Hitchcock since at least* Rebecca, *almost all of D. W. Griffith's films, the Pickford-Fairbanks films, Eisenstein's films, etc., etc. The montagist is supervised by one or many hands — in all countries of the world. Frequently, he has a brilliant idea and it is used.*

R. T.

tions will he be able to help make a film which is more than a felt whole. Consequently, he must try to preserve the values of the different parts, as he goes about his task of trying to make a unity out of them. Though he will not allow those values to take precedence always, he will favor them, do what he can to maximize them.

The work of a cinemaker is highly specialized. The best results are achieved by a film crew which backs creative insight and sensitivity with technical proficiency. Some directors, it has already been noted, are so knowledgeable, perceptive, and controlling, however, that they are able to impose tight conditions on the work of cinemakers, and yet bring about splendid cinemaking, sometimes beyond the imagination of distinguished cinemakers. Such cases are rare, but they suffice to show that it is possible for a cinemaker to play only an incidental role in a film dominated by a director. The discussion of this situation does not belong here, since it has to do with the kind of film that results when a director takes on a dominant or an exclusive role — and will be deferred. What is now relevant is a different situation, where a cineman is the dominant or the only film maker, with the director having just a subordinate or incidental function.

A dominant cinemaker, who would produce a great film, needs the help of a creative director. That director will start with the idea of the film that is to be made, and end with the idea of the film that is made. But the film will be one in which aesthetic values override all others. The director, consequently, will be required to provide a restrictive interpretation of the script. He will also have to mute performances so that they serve primarily to give body to what is to be seen and heard. With the help of the montagist he will produce a unified film which is to be felt or appreciated more than it is to be understood. Alert to the contributions of others, he will nevertheless see to it that they remain confined within the limits that fine cinemaking requires.

When a cinemaker takes the position of an exclusive creative film maker,*

---

* *This is a situation, which, to the best of my knowledge, is purely hypothetical, except when a cameraman graduates and becomes director.*

R. T.

---

a director can have only the minor task of a supervisor who sees to it that the others work in harmony with one another to provide a needed support for the cinemaking. Neither he nor the others will contribute to the making of a film, but only to making it possible. At times, the director may be compelled to restrain the others and to encourage the cinemaker, but his work will still be incidental, not essential. The result will be a film in which the parts will be greater than the whole. Movements and rests, postures and shapes, sights and sounds will have replaced human performers, and montaging will be reduced to the provision of nuances and contrasts within a single, satisfying, aesthetic unity. Were the director denied even this minor task, the film would be just an aggregate of images and sounds, a sequence of units which remain distinct no matter how closely they are pressed together.

4

Russian film makers have for a long time insisted on montaging as the most distinctive, the most basic, the most genuinely creative part of film making. Montaging, they have made clear, has a crucial role to play in great film making. Everything else, some of them go on to say, can have only a comparatively minor part. Sometimes they even speak as though everyone other than a montagist had merely a supportive role, providing only occasions, material, or opportunities for him. That they have produced distinguished films goes without question. That they have produced them only by montaging is less evident. They have, to be sure, minimized the role of performers, and do not seem to have been overly concerned with the subtleties of cinemaking.* But they do seem to have strong narra-

---

* *Evidence does not bear this out. Witness the recent Russian production of* War and Peace, *in which the actor who played Pierre also directed the film. He certainly was not unconcerned with minimizing performances.*

R. T.

---

tive lines, and their different directors do produce distinctively different films. A case, therefore, can be made, at least for those who, in contrast with the Russian theorists of the film, insist also on the role of a scriptist or of a director. But to this one might reply, on behalf of the Russian theorists, that these alternatives merely point up a failure to achieve what a film should achieve. It is surely possible to conceive of a fine film made by a montagist, with all the others in secondary positions.

When a montagist is dominant over a scriptist, the film can have a structure, a direction, perhaps even a story to tell, but this is made subject to the demands of the art of montaging. The montagist will not ignore the performances, the cinematic aesthetic effects, the unifying idea, any more than he will ignore the script, but all of them will be given a place only so far as they are consistent with his creative union of the parts of the film with one another.

Were a montagist to become the exclusive film maker, he would break through these restrictions. The resulting film would then offer an exhibition of the ways one can assemble and disperse, superimpose, dissolve, cut, and cross out. It would be a unity of compressions, affiliations, and transitions, rather than of a story, of what was performed, of what was seen or heard, or of an idea. He would see the script as marking out the units which he was to separate and connect, and would ignore what it might indicate as to just what order should be followed.

A montagist who paid attention to the narrative line of a script would, by that very act, reveal that he was not taking himself to be the only maker of a film. Without foregoing his dominant position, and therefore the exhibition of a mastery of space, time, and causation, he would be in a position to make a great film, the whole as well as the parts of which were expressed in the script. He could depart from the script again and again, but if he is to make a great film, there will still have to be a structure which owes its presence to what the script originally expressed. If he departs sufficiently often and sufficiently widely, that structure with its articulations might be hard to relate to what was originally in the script, but it will nevertheless be a translation of it, under conditions required for good montage.

A montagist might make a great film by attending to nothing but performances. These, without reducing his creative activity, may tell him what he is to organize, interrelate, distinguish, unite, and thereby enhance. He would not have to sacrifice every other value for the sake of the performance—that would be to treat the performer as though he were a star. But, by montage he would star the performance, make it the outstanding fact in the film. Different parts of an action, different actions, different performers would be brought together in such a way as to complement one another and thereby yield a filmed performance which in fact never had been performed before a cinemaker. When this remarkable fact is kept in focus, one is almost ready to agree with those who take montage to be that enterprise which marks film off from all others.

A montagist who took only himself to be a film maker would see performances as opportunities for the exhibition of montaging techniques and skills. Incidents would be separated and juxtaposed, broken into and connected in order to produce a film whose only unity was the method that was being employed to make a single work out of a multiplicity of parts. Since there would be nothing in it which was being consistently preserved or which had been insistently imposed, it would not have a true unity; there would be just fragments that had been attached to one another in a sequence. It could not be a great film.

A montagist works with the material that a cinemaker provides.* It is

---

There may be a question of sequence — does the work of the cinemaker precede or follow that of the montagist in a given film? For Eisenstein, Hitchcock, Bertolucci it would follow; for Godard, Anderson, Fellini it would precede.   J. W.

---

tempting, therefore, to suppose that he or the cineman might assume a relatively subordinate position, or even perhaps that one of them will have no significant role to play in film making. As we have already seen, they can work coordinately. But a montagist can be comparatively dominant in relation to a cineman, and still make a great film — so long as he is appreciative of the contribution that the cineman makes. If he is, he will restrain tendencies to exhibit his ability to break up and unite incidents, so far as this would result in the loss of the cinematic values of what was filmed.

Much that a cinemaker provides must be discarded, not necessarily because it is defective, but because he films the same incidents again and again, because some of the filmed incidents are not sufficiently different or sufficiently relevant to what has already been accepted or to the idea that has begun to emerge, or because of limitations in the time allotted for showing the film. Ratios in commercial studios today run to about one foot of film retained to nine rejected. Ideally all ten are excellent products of the cinemaker's art. Presumably any number of splendid aesthetic objects could be made out of the discards. The discarding must, therefore, be governed by other than aesthetic considerations.

A montagist's choice among incidents to be retained should take account not only of filmed aesthetic values, by themselves and in relation to one another, but also of the contributions made by other film makers. He is to attend not merely to the aesthetic values of the parts and the kind of aesthetic whole they can be made to yield, but to the narrative line, the nature of performances, and the idea that the director intends to have exhibited.

These must not, of course, be allowed to block out the contribution of the cinemaker, even when he has been given only a subordinate role. There could well be filmed incidents that were not as satisfactory aesthetically as others, which the montagist may have to choose for the sake of doing justice to the intentions and achievements of the other film makers. But the choice must not be made in disregard of all good cinemaking. A great film is a film one can enjoy seeing.

Where a montagist is the only film maker, the same outcome is to be expected that is found when some other film maker denies creative roles to the rest—no single fine film is made. When he operates in abstraction from the results of cinemaking and what might be done to preserve and enhance them, he will, more likely than not, end by spoiling what should have enriched, dulling what should have been brightened, contraposing what should have been contrasted. The result will lack aesthetic excellence and can not, therefore, be an excellent film. If the other film makers be ignored as well, the result will, of course, show still other defects.

A director could have only a subordinate role in relation to a montagist. When this occurs, there is no initial idea to control the course of film making until the film as a whole takes shape. There will be such an initial idea and it might be well expressed. The montagist might even have knowledge of it. But it will not be allowed to dictate just what he is to select and what he is to discard. The idea could control the interpretation of the script, the nature of the performances, and the use of the cinemaker, but if the director is subordinate to the montagist, the idea will be replaced, sooner than it need be, by the idea of the actual film that is being produced by the montagist.

A director must eventually give up his initial idea for one which answers to what is in fact embodied in the finished film. The replacement occurs before the film is completed. But when a montagist is in charge, the replacement is preceded by the idea that the montagist is seeking to express, and leads to the production of a film more alien to what the director intended than it otherwise would be. The film might nevertheless be great. Great film making does not require that a director be dominant over all or throughout. He could conceivably dominate over or be coordinate with the scriptist, performer, and cineman, and still have only a subordinate position in relation to the montagist. He will then guide the film making until the montagist takes over with an idea that takes account of the director's. Avakian observes that "There are basically two ways an editor can work with a director, and these aren't dissimilar to an actor's way with the director. (1) The editor can read the script, look at the dailies, and then question the director as to specific intentions of narrative, dialogue, character, actor, or camera, within a given scene or section of the film, then try to execute as close as he can to specific direction, or (2) The editor can ask for maximum exposure to the material and people involved making the film, and ask that he be allowed to find for himself the director's intention, within the many takes of the scenes, narrative, the actors and camera imagery playing within it all. The second is the way which allows for the creation of a great film. Usually the director is there to screen the material after it has been cut in some form and when he's needed, that is, when something isn't going right." [1]

Were a montagist to ignore the director altogether, the film on which he works would be just raw material to be organized solely in accordance with his own ideas. No unity would be discerned in it, and he would see himself to be the source of the only unity it can have. But a film is not merely put together out of miscellaneous parts; it is developed through the articulation and finally the overcoming of an idea initially had. The overcoming does not involve the substitution of one idea by another altogether different; an initial, vaguely grasped, hardly articulated idea is gradually and then suddenly replaced by one which is embodied in the very product that the initial idea made possible. Otherwise, the resultant film would have at least two quite disparate parts, one of which reflected the use of the initial idea, and the other of which had to do with what was in fact produced. Two half films would in effect be made, one of which had no place for a montagist and the other of which had none for a director. Each half would be defective, the one because it failed to use the parts of a cinemaking to produce a single, unified film, the other because it failed to follow a coherent line of development from beginning to end.

Montage enables film to stand over against the outcomes of other arts and other enterprises.* Other arts and enterprises, like film, evoke and control

---

* This excludes a film like Hitchcock's Rope which contains no traditional montaging.   E. S.

---

the expressions of man's emotions, but the other arts do not enable one to confront existence in all its dimensions at once, while other enterprises, though they may enable us to confront a final reality, do not get us to existence. Montage emphasizes the fact that film is concerned at once with the spatial, temporal, and dynamic,* and that it can place any objects in them

---

* *It seems to me that all arts are montages. You move around a statue. Your eye travels over and into a painting, through glazes and glazes. One arrives at the Umbrian sky (to steal a bit from Berenson), moves forward toward the figures in the painting, through a clear, exhilirating atmosphere. Time is involved. There is no such thing as seeing a painting or a statue at once! Or even comprehending it at one moment in time. Good luck to the mystics and the epilectics, but I do not believe any art does not involve you with the "spatial, temporal and dynamic." Nothing exists now only. Perhaps our difference is semantic, but I don't believe it.* R. T.

---

in any order. It is sensitive to the nature of existence, in which time, space, and causality are one, apart from all occupants, where part merges into part, where part relates part to part, and where every occupant is necessarily extended. It does not, to be sure, portray existence, but what it does portray enables us, after the film is over, to face existence emotionally with a directness we could not otherwise achieve.

Russian theorists of the film are more in the right than their opponents. They know that montage is essential to and can make a great contribution to great film. But an implicit materialism leads them to minimize the roles played by other film makers. Though these others do not contribute as much to make one sensitively aware of existence while viewing a film, they do enrich the awareness that montage provides, and do allow one, after the film is over, to discern, behind the veil of existence, the presence of other ultimate realities. Those realities are directly confronted through the help of other enterprises somewhat in the way in which film helps one to confront existence. This fact will become evident when we turn to the distinctive nature of the propagandistic, educational, disclosive, documentary, and escapist film (chapters 10–12). But first it is necessary to see what happens when a director, rather than any of the other film makers, assumes a dominant or an exclusive role. Again, but now full face, we stand before the theory that it is only a director who can be the true maker of a film.

5

The claim that a director is the "author" of a film may take one of three forms: (a) He may be taken to be the only begetter of the film. The others will then have to be said to be engaged in just incidental tasks, supportive, helpful, but not essential, not creative, not contributive to the making of a film. (b) A director may be taken to be the principal creator of the film. All the others will then have essential, creative contributions to make, enriching rather than supplementing his. (c) Or he may be taken to be but one of a number of cooperative creators, everyone of whom is essential to the making of any, or any great film. He could then be said to be the "author," because it is he who makes a film be an art, in contradistinction from all other arts or other products; because he alone makes it possible for the film to be great; or because his signature, his style, his intent is the most conspicuous in any, or any great film.

a. Were a director the only maker of the film, other men would still have to be employed. At the very least, there would have to be a cineman. But he and the other workers could be used just to provide occasions for the director to exhibit his creative powers. The others would be puppets at worst and technicians at best, means to be used, making no contributions of their own. It would be the director alone who determined how the script was to be interpreted; it would be he who dictated all the moves of the performers, allowing them no decisions, no improvisations, no interpretations; it would be he who determined the angles, the lens, the lights, the distances, the shots, and the span of each use of the cinemaker; he would be the true montagist, using some assistant to carry out his instructions as to where and how to cut and unify.

The director would here have a role apparently analogous to that of an architect who normally goes no further than to provide blueprints, mockups, and the supervision of the contractor and the builders as they proceed to carry out his demands. The analogy holds only to a point. It breaks down because a filming, but not necessarily a building, forces a change in the kind of idea that is embodied in the final work. A building often is already in outline in the blueprints. Changes are introduced and the original idea inevitably altered in the course of the building, because of discoveries made about light and shadow, materials, neighbors, and the like. But the changes are mainly changes inside the original idea, and do not compel its abandonment. There is nothing in film making — and therefore not the idea of the director — which is precisely formulated initially and is to be filled out by other workers, with only those alterations which stay within the area of what was originally conceived. "What the *auteur* theory demonstrates is that the director is not simply in command of a performance of a pre-existing text; he is not, or need not be, only a *metteur en scène.*" [2]

Films grow in the course of their making. Inevitably they demand a replacement of an original, guiding idea by another which reflects what in fact had already been produced. Were nothing made in the course of the production of a film which required the replacement of a director's original idea, were he to succeed in making all others just give a visual and audible shape to what he initially wanted, the film would be a "think piece," a concept in a sensuous form, not likely to elicit and satisfy emotions. But then he will have produced what is less than an art. "A director . . . must know how to create emotions: before each film, each scene, and each shot, he must stop and ask himself how he can create the particular emotion he desires." [3]

Cinematic values should not be suppressed for the sake of making one grasp what a director had in mind. A director might, of course, think in cinematic terms, anticipate what is to be visually and audibly produced, but if he did not allow for the outcome of the interplay of other workers, with their material or with one another, his film could be only a vehicle, a public conveyance for what he wished to say. Alert to this consideration, a director might be willing to give up one idea after another in order to do justice to what is produced, all the while maintaining absolute control over the way things are done. He would then use an idea that had already been achieved, to dictate what next was to be done, only to abandon that idea for still another, reflecting the next achievement, and so on until the end. He would have made himself a leader of a parade who changed his direction constantly so as to be able to continue to be at the head.

A director who is the only begetter of a film can not make a great film. Such a film requires him to maintain control, initially on behalf of a vague idea and later on behalf of an articulated, clearer one realized in the course of the actual film making by a cinemaker and others. It also demands that he be consistent with himself and, therefore, that his initial and final ideas be relevant to one another. If an only begetter is to maintain control of a film that actually is made, he must inconsistently take up one idea after another; if he is to maintain a single, consistent position, he must ignore much of what is in fact filmed, and finally shown.

b. The defender of the view that directors are the "authors" of films would do more justice to the facts were he not to deny that others beside the director might be creative and contributive. He would not have to assert that all great films require a director who reigns supreme; all he would need do is to affirm that such films are distinct in nature from those made when a director alone enjoys a privileged position. The affirmation would be justified; it is possible, we have already seen, to have great films produced when a scriptist, a performer, a cinemaker, or a montagist, rather than a director has the dominant creative role. The director would then, as Panofsky observed, be like the chief architect of a cathedral: "It might be said that a film called into being by a cooperative effort in which all contributions have the same degree of permanence, is the nearest modern equivalent of a medieval cathedral; the role of the producer corresponding, more or less, to that of the bishop or archbishop, that of the director to that of the architect in chief, that of the scenario writers to that of the scholastic advisers establishing the iconographical program; and that of the actors, cameramen, cutters, soundmen, makeup men and the diverse technicians to that of those whose work provided the physical entity of the finished product, from the sculptors, glass painters, bronze casters, carpenters and skilled masons down to the quarry men and woodsmen. And if you speak to anyone of these collaborators he will tell you, with perfect *bona fides*, that his is really the most important job—which is quite true to the extent that it is indispensable." [4]

A film, where a director was the main but not the only creative contributor, subjects the contributions of others to the condition that they all instance and carry out a persistently held, controlling idea which gives way to another that is evidenced in the film. A script may at times have to be departed from, but it will be never entirely abandoned or neglected; performers may be restrained, without being denied an opportunity to enrich their roles; some incidents may have to be muted, broken down, forced into the background while others are emphasized, in order to give body to what the director has in mind; the montaging may be controlled and guided so that the idea that is finally embodied not only is coherent with that which it replaces but is cinemagraphically vitalized.

The theory that a director is the "author" of a film to which others also contribute can be best defended when it is stated most carefully: a director is the maker of but one type of film, in which his contribution is enriched by the contributions of others. Those who hold to the auteur theory can, without inconsistency, accept this view. "The *auteur* theory grew up rather haphazardly; it was never elaborated in programmatic terms, in a manifesto or collective statement. As a result, it could be interpreted and applied on rather broad lines; different critics developed somewhat different methods within a loose framework of common attitudes." [5]

c. It is possible to take a director to be the only "author" of the film. "Author" will then be equivalent with "provides the unity, continuity, and identity of the film." * Throughout, in the interpretation of the script, the

---

* The man who selects the poems for the Oxford book of English verse provides "unity, continuity, identity." Nonetheless, he is in no sense an author. I do not mean to demote the director of a motion picture to the class of anthologist, but I do mean to suggest we start at the bottom line. If Walt Disney had personally drawn, colored, animated, written every word of the dialogue, dubbed all the voices, written the songs, arranged, conducted, played all the musical instruments, conceived utterly the continuity, and had not conscience about the Brothers Grimm, then, perhaps one might speak of Snow White and the Seven Dwarfs *as an auteur film.* R. T.

---

performances, the cinemaking, and the montaging, there will be a characteristic director style displayed, a signature no one can duplicate. The other film makers will also have distinctive styles, but they will not usually evidence these as clearly or as persistently as he does in the film that they jointly make.

The unmistakability and conspicuousness of the signature of a great director does not suffice to define him to be that film maker who enables film to stand out against all other arts and all other enterprises. That distinction is more properly credited to the montagist. The public and the mass media, the distributors and the producers favor the stars, while some historians, alert to innovations, give the credit to the cinemaker, who at times may be the same man who functions as director. Though there have been those who have pointed up the contributions made by scriptists, no one to my knowledge has claimed that it is he, above all, who distinguishes film from all other arts and other enterprises — except perhaps, implicitly, when one speaks of the author of a "shooting script."

The role that a director plays and the evidence of it that he provides fails to give support to the view that he is the only creative film maker. Were he that, he would substitute mannerisms for style, telltale marks for signature. His style and signature are carried by a work that others also help create. MacCann observes that "Directing involves both collaboration and domination. Even Eisenstein, who was 'all for the collective method of work' confessed that 'there are cases when a director's "iron heel" is not only justified but absolutely necessary.' The process is not a matter of balancing all the elements evenly and democratically. In film, as in life, justice consists of more than simple equality. Within the checks and balances of technical and artistic advice, the presidential leadership of the director must firmly guide the actors, choose the shots, demand a tempo, decide the over-all shape of the outcome. In the clamor of the sound stage, in the loneliness of the cutting room, he must hold his vision." [6]

It would be foolish to claim that the presence of an unmistakable or a conspicuous signature evidences the work of a great director. A poor director can write as clearly as a good one. The most that could be maintained is that a great director provides clear indications of his own great, distinctive contribution. But this should not require one to say that a great director can not allow the other film makers to express themselves most fully and in harmony, or that he can not do this without making his own attitudes and values most evident in the film. His signature could be written by many other hands; his style could be revealed in the way the more conspicuous styles of others support one another. Greatness is sometimes expressed by making oneself small.

Nothing is compromised and no contributor is minimized when it is said that a scriptist makes a film intelligible, a performer gives it focus, a cinemaker enables it to be seen and heard, a montagist distinguishes it from the outcomes of all other efforts, and a director unifies it. "Film," says Lumet, "is a performing, communal art form, and not the work of a single individual. And I think this is still the case even if you've written it yourself, you're shooting it yourself, directing it yourself, and acting the leading part." [7] Together, the various film makers produce a single work, but not without help from technicians and assistants, some of whom do their work well before the acknowledged film makers appear on the scene. Commercial film also needs the support of producers, bankers, distributors, and exhibitors. But now we have begun to move away from the consideration of film as an art to film as an industry — another matter, not now our concern, even though the industry does have a great effect on the creation of works of art.

127

Philosophical Interlude

CHAPTER 8

Elicited Emotions

Film is not just seen and heard. It arouses the emotions and yields them some satisfaction. To see this clearly, it is necessary to turn for a while from film, and attend instead to the emotions themselves, their provocations, their demands, and their pertinence to values, principles, and realities.* It will then be possible to get a firmer grasp of the fact that

---

* *The whole philosophical interlude has authority and is fun to read. Rather like playing a pinball machine and listening to the bells ring and the lights flash.*   *D. S.*

---

each kind of film — popular, dramatic, classical, and innovative — is involved with a distinctive grade of emotion, each with a characteristic strength, role, and final terminus.

A good illustration of an emotion is anger. Anger is mental and bodily at once. A purely "mental anger" is a bitter thought, a state of resentment and animosity, a judgment which is adverse, disowning, antagonistic.* A

---

* *Even a mental condition may already have the glandular and metabolic beginnings of planned action to articulate that anger. I think of blushing, indigestion, sweat, horror, erection, etc. The chase at the last quarter or so of an action movie functions very much on a glandular level.*   *J. W.*

---

purely "physical" anger is a turbulence erupting in a destructive act. To have the one is to have thoughts governed by what they do not contain; to have the other is to have a body uncontrolled, crudely and violently displayed. Not so evidently, but as surely, every other emotion — fear, hope, terror, resentment, pity, love, repugnance, joy — has mental and physical sides. This, Descartes (who is most responsible for the radical separation between mind and body which characterizes so much of modern thought) not only knew but underscored. An unfortunate insistence on what is clear and distinct, though, led him to conceive of a pure mind and a pure body. He thought of them as being equally real, but possessed of radically different natures. As a consequence, the answer with which he in fact began, that mind and body are not separated but are connected emotionally, he abandoned for the sake of acknowledging two abstractions, taken to be realities. Neither he, nor any of his followers, could ever bring these back together again. This is not surprising. Abstractions cannot be added to abstractions so as to produce the unity which enables them to effectively interplay, and, to that degree be more than abstractions. Body and mind have distinctive contents and roles; they function in considerable independence of one another. It is possible to think steadily about mathematical truths while the body hungers; an appetite can grow more and more insistent while the mind continues to think one irrelevant thought after another. But whether they work in harmony or at cross-purposes, they are not altogether independent of one another. Neither mind nor body is a distinct substance. A body is an extended aggregate of tissues and bones, apart from the emotionally toned life that permeates it; a mind is a structure apart from the emotional energy which enables it to conceive, imagine, believe, and infer. The emotions permeate the one to make it living, at the same time that they intrude into the other to make it active.

Different grades of emotion come to expression in both mind and body. Unexpressed, they are to be distinguished from their expressed forms as sources from products, the relatively indeterminate from the relatively determinate, the private from the publicized. Expressed, they connect mind and body; unexpressed, they are reservoirs, to be tapped in order to assess, rectify, and redress responses already made.

Four grades of emotion are worth remarking on. *Tone* is at the base of, and can affect them all. *Mood* shades off into tone on one side, and *attitude* on the other; it is more specific than tone, less specific than attitude. Attitude merges into *feeling* — the most specific but least intensive form that emotion assumes, and the most readily elicited. Together the four form a single undivided emotional continuum to be broken up again and again by the individual, when he insistently expresses himself with reference to different types of objects.

Feeling, attitude, mood, and tone are not faculties, categories, or powers but distinguishable grades of emotion. It seems to make as much sense, therefore, to say that there is a single emotion which is freshly specified in different ways on different occasions, as it is to say that specific grades of emotion are separated off at different times. In the one way, power to specify is given to interest, intent, concern; in the other, these, or objects, are credited with the ability to distinguish already distinct emotions. The one adheres more closely to the nature of man as he is by himself; the other, to him as occupied with something outside himself. Since no man is entirely cut off from the world, nor wholly lost in it, it would be more correct, though, to say that a man at his center is an undifferentiated emotional continuum of varying density which he, with the help of external objects, breaks up into regions, each with its own emotional weight and capacity for expression. In any case, different emotional expressions do not achieve full distinctiveness until they are satisfied.*

---

* *This is just fine! The discussion here is clear, humane, refreshing.*

D. S.

That feelings are emotions will perhaps be granted. They begin below the level of thought and yet are not confined to particular bodily channels, or modes of action; they spring up unexpectedly; they mark a departure from equilibrium, calm, quiet; often they escape control; they may not be desired; and they may be unwanted. An emotion, of course, can sometimes be deliberately prepared for, and deliberately spelled out. Frequently emotions are as they ought to be, relevant to what is painful or threatening, pleasant or promising. But they always overrun the borders of ideas, and give a distinctive tone to the tendencies and acts of the body.

What a man confronts affects him. He does not merely see it or hear it or note it; he feels it. The initial expressions are largely uncontrolled, unguided, partial, biased. Normally they first take the form of a bodily feeling having just a tinge of mentality. Because the mental dimension of the feeling is slighted, bodily action too often occurs in the absence of an adequate grasp of what it is on which one acts, or why. To do justice to what provoked the expression of a feeling, an effort must be made to give the feeling a better mental expression. If this is not done, body and mind will not be attuned; one will respond bodily in one way and allow for a mental response in another. Ideally, the two should be in equipoise. But whether they are or are not, when a man feels, he also stands between the extreme of holding himself away from the world and the extreme of immersing himself in it. It is from there that he emotionally responds, bodily and mentally. Some men withdraw themselves too much mentally, others too much bodily. Some are mentally too greatly merged with the world about, others exhibit the same fault bodily. There is little to choose between one who is too *self-centered,* mentally or bodily, and one who is too *externalized.* Neither is at home both in himself and in the world. But if either emphasis is to occur, it is better that it take place only mentally or only bodily, rather than in both ways at once. The intellectual is mentally involved and physically withdrawn; the athlete reverses the stress. Both are to be preferred to the aesthete or the overly practical, the one doubly withdrawn, the other doubly involved.

He who expresses his feelings harmoniously through both mind and body is *sensible;* he who balances withdrawal with immersion is *decent.* Whatever the degree of his approximation to these states, a man expresses himself in the present, but not without exhibiting some influence of his past experiences. If he unduly neglects the past he must painfully learn anew what experience should have taught; if he unduly neglects the present he will pit his rigidities against what will usually prove to be more resistant. Fortunately, considerable neglect of either present or past is hard to maintain. Both always have some role, accompanied by a dim awareness that one is functioning too much as a creature of habit or is too thoughtlessly lost in present existence. The *well-attuned* man lives in accord with a currently acceptable combination of the two; he is at once *habituated* and *relevant.*

A *reasonable* man is at once sensible, decent, and well attuned. He gives both bodily and mental expression to his feelings, supplementing the one by the other. Neither too deeply immersed in the world nor too withdrawn from it, he lives in consonance both with what he had learned from the past and what is germane to the present. These states are not givens but achievements, the outcomes of rectifications of exaggerated expressions. A reasonable man, like every one else, begins by overstressing one of the factors constituting the states of being sensible, decent, and well attuned. He remains reasonable if he assesses the overemphasized factor as not being entirely appropriate to what had been confronted. He is then sensible, decent, and well attuned, not in his feelings, but in his estimates of how he had responded. Almost at once, though, he makes an effort to recover his balance by bringing the neglected factors into play. When he fails to provide the supplement at the right time and to the right degree he normally passes an adverse judgment on himself as one who does not express the feelings that ought to have been then expressed.

2

Because attitudes seem to be inert and capable of being assumed deliberately, or to be products of activities habitually performed, they seem to be unlike feelings or other well-recognized emotions. But, like these, attitudes can not be attributed exclusively to the mind or the body; they are affected by what they embrace, and change in color and emphasis in accord with these. A series of acts will sharpen their boundaries and fix their directions, but will neither produce nor actually control them. That they are emotions becomes even more evident when the generic is distinguished from the specific. Attitudes are generic feelings pertinent to situations; they are inseparable from, encompass, and govern the particular feelings that are pertinent to particular items there. An expressed attitude embraces a multiplicity of distinguishable, connected feelings. Without it, those feelings would be discontinuous, discrete, having no necessary relation to or bearing on one another. But then it would be hard to see how one could confront a single complex situation and yet exhibit different feelings toward the different related items there. The seashore that we approach in an attitude of acceptance is gay in this place and threatening in that; unbounded in one direction it is circumscribed in another. At ease toward it as a whole, we at the same time feel pleasure and dismay, attraction and suspicion toward different connected parts of it.

Feelings have vague outlines and are incompletely controlled. Few neatly fit external occurrences; sometimes they overrun and sometimes they merely touch on some of the facets of the objects to which they are addressed. Each is affected by others encompassed within the same dominant attitude. This, while allowing each feeling to have a distinctive role and place, relates it to the others.

An attitude is the subjective counterpart of a situation in which a number of items are interrelated. The feelings of a *sensitive* man are ordered in an attitude in consonance with the way a situation is taken to order its items. He expresses different feelings, imposes different stresses, varies the way in which he uses his body and mind, depending on the status that the items in a situation have in relation to one another, and what this imports for him.

Some insensitive men take games too seriously. Others treat crimes too lightly. Sometimes they acknowledge these defects in themselves. This is possible only because they are able, not only to express an attitude, but to stand outside it and assess the way it and its encompassed feelings mesh with that to which they are addressed.

Assessment of a dominant attitude, feelings, and a man are possible because one has (a) identified items apart from expressed feelings; (b) accepted the items and the demands that these make on what is to be in accord with them; and (c) used a deep attitude to evaluate the appropriateness of the dominant attitude and feelings that had been expressed.

a. Were feelings the only means for identifying items in a situation, there would be nothing further to be said. The feelings would alight on them, and that is all. Feelings (and their governing attitudes) can be evaluated because the items are grasped in another way as well.

b. To be able to evaluate dominant attitudes and feelings in terms of their appropriateness to situations and their included items, these must be accepted as imposing conditions which the attitudes and feelings are to meet. There must be an awareness, apart from the dominant attitude and its feelings, that the situation and the items in it require the expression of a certain type of attitude and certain feelings.

c. A deep attitude evaluates a dominant as well as the expressed feelings. It takes them to be more or less appropriate to an accepted situation and its items. Measuring what had been expressed by what had been accepted, it tries to make good whatever discrepancy it finds. And, since a dominant attitude and feelings are expressions of an individual, in assessing them he also assesses himself. If his dominant attitude and expressed feelings are inappropriate, he is unreasonable or insensitive. One still leaves over, of course, the question of the legitimacy of the deep attitude and the accuracy of its assessments. But, for the moment, it is sufficient to note that the assessments take place immediately, without reflection, making evident that the foregoing three conditions are satisfied together, in the course of a single act.

Were there only a dominant attitude, there would be no immediate corrections of provoked responses; were there only a deep, there would be no ready responses to what one confronts; if the deep did not supplement the dominant, one might evaluate but would not correct. Self-criticism is possible because a deep attitude is expressed by the very man who expressed a dominant. Critical judgments can also be passed on others by using one's own deep attitude to measure the appropriateness of their dominant attitudes and encompassed feelings. A dominant attitude — and consequently, encompassed feelings — is experienced as being more or less correct for a situation, and is assessed accordingly. There is an effort to make the response be in accord with what is confronted; when the responses are blocked, frustrated, out of gear, reserves are brought up. Their introduction is at once an assessment of the appropriateness of what had been expressed, and a making good of the deficiency. The assessment and correction are made unreflectingly by bringing the deep attitude to bear. The deep attitude imposes itself on the dominant, and through this on the feelings, the confronted situation, and its items. To the degree that the deep attitude corrects the dominant, the total response is proper, satisfactory, right.

There are times when one insists on using a deep attitude to evaluate a situation in terms of its consonance with a dominant attitude and expressed feelings. We then speak of the situation as baffling, agreeable, frustrating, or attractive. Usually, though, we use a deep attitude to evaluate a dominant and its specifying feelings, rather than a situation and the items in it. We then do more justice to the fact that maladjustment is a fault in men and not of the world. A situation can be baffling and a man may be good and wise, but if his dominant attitude and expressed feelings are not appropriate to what he confronts, we blame him, as a rule, and not the world.

The feelings governed by a dominant attitude are directed at the items in a situation. The feelings may be inappropriate; the objects then demand another answer, more in consonance with their structures and careers. It is then that a deep attitude forces itself forward, and calls up feelings which are more appropriate. Beginning further within the individual than the dominant, the deep attitude ends with a more appreciative acknowledgment of what had been confronted.

The use of a deep attitude is rarely noticed. But again and again we recognize that a dominant attitude and its encompassed feelings are undesirable because inappropriate to what is occurring. We become aware of ourselves as getting too much pleasure out of a minor victory, or as responding to an insignificant defeat with too great a despair or anxiety. The awareness of the impropriety of our responses is often followed by more appropriate ones. And sometimes there are radical occurrences — a spectator, a participant, or a passerby dies during a celebration; a family's routine ways are upset by a serious illness; a sudden turn of events changes one's fortunes or prospects. These new occurrences are frequently responded to with appropriate feelings. The pleasure in a celebration at once gives way to pain and sadness; the illness awakens anxiety and concern; the changes in fortune elate or disappoint. Sometimes the new feelings are held in check and even disguised. But whether they are or not, they specify a deep attitude, and have a rhythm and a direction which is in consonance with the new occurrences.

If a deep attitude is not expressed when a dominant and its feelings are inappropriate, one must have misconstrued what is occurring. Relativists deny this. According to them, one response is as legitimate as another; no attitude or feeling could be said to be inappropriate, and none therefore deserves assessment and requires correction by a deep attitude. Their position would be stronger were there a heterogeneity of responses elicited on every occasion. The fact that birth, death, illness, defeat, and victory awaken similar emotional responses in men who have radically different backgrounds, education, and stations, the relativists either dismiss as mere coincidence or as being the product of similar teachings. Let the contention stand. It still remains true that most men respond emotionally to various occurrences in common ways, and therefore confront them as having similar values. It remains true even if one agrees with the subjectivists when they say that emotional responses give occurrences their values rather than — as I think is the case — that emotions, particularly when supplementary and rectificatory, and elicited at turning points in the lives and fortunes of men, match the values that are objectively present. The occurrences to which one deeply responds have emotionally appreciated values to which others also deeply respond in similar ways. So far as emotional response is concerned, the limit of the world is its common, appreciated values.

In wars, prisons, death camps, in times of incredible stress, famine, and suffering, men are able to affirm and do what otherwise would be even beyond their imagining. They are blind to values they once noted, and are alert to others which they had never before acknowledged. We would have no right to judge them, and they would later have no right to judge themselves, if it were not the case that there is a positive or negative value to birth, death, joy, pain, pleasure, victory, defeat, courage, and injustice, which they are able to know. A failure to acknowledge these values reveals one to be defective, debased, ignorant, less than what a man should be. A man is not really inferior or superior to others merely because he does not make the evaluations they do; he just does not fit in with them. He is inferior or superior to them in fact only if he or they miss values that are present which he and they can know. If he did not have deep attitudes similar to theirs which he could and ought to express, we would have to deny humanity to him or them. He who can not value what the rest can is so far not part of mankind. But if he can respond properly to what is present but does not, he, while one of mankind, is less than he can and ought to be. Men are misprised when they are treated as beasts, for they are then denied the power to assess properly. They are grossly maltreated when what has maximum values for them — the objects of their love and dedication, what they take to be sacred or precious — is abused. We rightly assume that if they are human they assess their feelings and dominant attitudes, and those of others, by the same kind of deep attitude the rest use. The values that are acknowledged may occur only in limited situations. There may have to be a submission to authority or a participation in a particular religion before the situation can be understood. But any man who is able to meet those conditions should be able to discern the values that are there. The values are as objective, but not as broadly conditioned, not as readily confronted, as others which men can discern without belonging to a particular establishment and without making special concessions or admissions. But both kinds of values, those available to men who add none, and those available to men who add some special condition to the way a situation is to be approached, are equally open to their common deep attitude.

Operating in the background of a dominant attitude, a deep attitude prompts an uneasiness when the dominant fails to mesh with what elicits it. The uneasiness reflects the discrepancy between the dominant attitude and its encompassed feelings, and the attitude and feelings which should have been expressed. This is one with saying that it reflects the difference between what in fact had been expressed and what the deep attitude should provide in place of or to supplement it.

3

There are a number of attitudes below a dominant. All, in relation to the dominant, are rectifying. Some of them may reflect the fact that one is functioning as a member of some limited group — professional men, club, union, society — aware of values not discernible from the position of the dominant attitude characteristic of men without special training or experience. Only the deepest, a *basic* attitude, reflects what is appropriate to what men face in limited, group-defined situations, as well as in those situations which others also can confront.

A deep attitude characteristic of the members of a group challenges and measures the dominant attitudes that are expressed in group-defined situations. In turn, it is challenged and measured by a still deeper attitude. At the limit is the basic attitude. This is aroused by the most radical turns in daily affairs. Normally, it enables one to attend to occurrences as having values not entirely confined to particular situations. And it makes it possible for one to judge himself favorably or unfavorably, because of the way he is involved in particular situations, or even for having the attitude characteristic of some group.

The deeper an attitude the more rarely does it come to clear expression. Still, deep attitudes are always operative, always involved with the dominant; the dominant, consequently, is assessed in being expressed, and may be altered or supplemented without delay. But it usually takes a sudden destruction or benefit to throw one out of accustomed ways, thereby making possible the distinctive operation of the basic attitude, or one quite close to this.

Governing the use of the basic attitude is a center involved with what is real. The intensity of satisfactions and dissatisfactions privately felt, and the laughter, tears, joyousness, and despair publicly exhibited, provide evidence of the presence and nature of that center. References to a sense of humor, good sense, and wisdom point up facets of it. A depth grammar presents only a formalization of it. It therefore not only necessarily fails to reach the center of man, but fails to get to his power to assess daily attitudes by a deep attitude.

Comedy and tragedy pivot about the sudden meeting of a dominant, socially conditioned attitude and a deep attitude. In comedy that deep attitude is sustained after a tensed delay; in tragedy it is defied while one continues to hope and need. In both, a crucial occurrence is then emotionally assessed by the basic attitude; normally, the result is joy or sadness, sometimes accompanied by laughter and tears.

4

A man's dominant and deep attitudes are expressed in and through his body and his mind. They can be maintained no matter how he shifts his position along the line from withdrawal to immersion, or to what degree he accommodates the past while keeping abreast of the present. Were he emotionally responsive only to what elicited his feelings, he would live in a world of aesthetic qualities, of pleasure and pain, lightness and darkness, color, shape, and taste. Were he responsive only to what elicited the expression of a dominant attitude and encompassed feelings, he would live in a world of good and bad, success and failure, overlaying the radically malign loss or the benign gain of great goods. But he lives also in a world of truths and realities, as well as in one that is governed by laws and principles and the sources of these. These worlds elicit and are met by emotional expressions, not of attitudes, but of mood and tone. Mood and tone affect the basic attitude and, through this, the dominant attitudes and expressed feelings. They have their own distinctive emotional expressions as well.

If a man is *resilient,* he alters his dominant attitudes in the attempt to make them be in accord with the dictates of a deep attitude. At times, though, a change is produced in a deep attitude because he tries to make it conform to a dominant. The deeper the attitude, though, the less it is able to be affected; the more insistent, too, are its assessments of crucial events and the accompanying feelings. The alteration in either case requires the expression of an emotion below the attitudes. This is the mood.

The degree of a man's resilience has no necessary relation to the degree of his *maturity.* Maturity depends on the attainment of a steady position where selfishness is balanced by unselfishness, whereas resilience concerns only a responsiveness to a disaccord between a dominant and a deep attitude. Two men who had the same attitudes, assessed the same results in the same way, and made the same successful resilient effort to bring dominant and deep attitudes in accord, might diverge in their maturity and therefore in the emphases they gave to their own needs or to the needs of others. Conversely, a mature man, because of his inflexibility, might make no effort to overcome the inappropriateness of his expressed dominant attitude and feelings. He would still express a basic attitude, and assess a dominant attitude; he would still supplement his expressions of a dominant attitude, and even replace them with others. But, so long as he was inflexible, he would not change the nature of the dominant attitude, despite experiences of its disaccord with what his basic attitude demands. He would remain uneasy, adjusting to particular situations, but would not try to express a dominant attitude which was in closer accord with a basic attitude than the dominant attitude that he was accustomed to express.

Both dominant and deep attitudes, whether characteristic of a mature or immature, or of a resilient or inflexible man, are directed at objects which have various degrees of importance in a society. A few men keep themselves primarily directed at what is most important, but they have little time to relax, little interest in anything that is not momentous. Responsible men, they are weighed down with community affairs. Others occupy themselves with trivia and rarely get near to what deserves attention and dedication. The *practically wise* man avoids both extremes.

He could be immature, and be wise only for himself or only for others; he could have little resilience and therefore not try to make his dominant and deep attitudes be in accord. In turn, it is possible for a man to be resilient or mature and still lack the practical wisdom of knowing what roles to give to the more and the less important. A resilient man would do this while trying to adjust his attitudes to one another; a mature man would do it while avoiding the extremes of undue selfishness or unselfishness. He who is all three, at once resilient, mature, and practically wise, is *civilized*. He, too, is an emotional being, but one who starts from a mood, below the level of attitudes, closer to the center of his being.

A mood has its own characteristic expressions, appropriate to truths and realities that are more fundamental and widespread than those emotionally encountered by untutored mankind. The world in which the civilized man lives has values sustained by a domain enriched by human history, discovery, and achievement. His is a world well structured, where truths attained and realities known are preserved and enhanced. That world is broken up into periods. Each period fails to include some truths and realities acknowledged at other times. Aristotle's "high-minded" Greek was civilized in a slave society; the learned men of the Middle Ages had little time or place for science; the Encyclopedists' "philosopher" was civilized in a world where religion was identified with superstition; today's civilized man has little patience with any reference to a final ideal. The illustrations could be multiplied, but these perhaps suffice to make evident that a civilized man sometimes sees himself, and is sooner or later seen by others, to fail to take account of some truths and realities. His world is incomplete and often incoherent. When he tries to overcome these defects, he moves beyond the concerns of his civilization by bringing more of his mood to bear.

A civilized man does not discover the incoherence and incompleteness of his accepted world until he has charged his dominant attitudes with a *belief* in the reality of what he understands. He thereupon finds himself in a position where he comes upon inescapable difficulties which he does not know how to overcome. His intellectual efforts are blocked by paradoxes; he spontaneously responds to men and other realities in ways for which he is not even in principle prepared. Others insist on dimensions of the world of which he had not been aware; there are some who seem to be men like him except for some feature — color, religion, status, sex, economics, age — which he can not take to be essential but yet can not dismiss as incidental; science and technology challenge his naïve trust in his unaided observations, unreflective reason, and habitual predictions. He finds himself with fears, hopes, and anxieties — emotions he did not know he had — not resolvable by anything in his civilized world. What he thought he had understood and assimilated defies him, and he is thrown back into himself, lost and disturbed, until he can find a way to assimilate or justifiably reject what now, brute, obstinate, and insistent, does not fit inside his frame.

A civilized man expresses his mood in an *acceptance* of the known world as the real. That acceptance encompasses, and thereby gives new import to his beliefs, his attitudes, and to his bodily and mental feelings. When discommoded, he is thrown out of his civilized routines. To recover his balance, his original acceptance must be supplemented with another, directed at the uncomprehended, as that which is to be probed and understood. He then stands apart from the civilized world as a man who is aware that he is *finite,* no longer at peace with the world or himself, no matter how well he is in accord with what goes on.

A self-aware, finite man does not necessarily have a good grasp of the position he occupies in the scheme of things. A distinct effort must be made if he is to accept himself as being both dependent and independent of what is outside him. He must so express a mood that it enables him to see himself apart from his civilization, as one reality among others. To have *self-respect* he has to avoid the extreme of taking himself to be wholly dependent or wholly independent of whatever other realities there be. The arrogant and the excessively humble both veer too much away from the position they ought to occupy, wrongly estimating their power, virtue, or reality. Others have a poor grasp of their finitude; they are too ready to accept the world as the measure of their own reality, or themselves as the measure of it. They fail to recognize that men are in a world together with other beings, at the same time that they minimize or exaggerate their own reality. Materialists take the first alternative, existentialists the second.

A man should be alert not only to what is real besides himself, outside the confines of his civilized world, but should take account both of what is individual and of what is common there. Otherwise he will be insufficiently sympathetic or cooperative, no matter how appreciative he is of what is not yet mastered, and no matter how well he knows and keeps his place amongst other realities. A *citizen of the world* neglects neither the singular nor the collective, though he may misconstrue both his finitude and his status in relation to what else there be. The *parochial* man, in contrast, may have a sound grasp of his finitude and the way in which he is both independent of and dependent on what else there be, yet fail to give due weight either to distinct realities or to them as together. Some parochial men neglect individuals to attend primarily to communities; others are alert to individuals but miss the ways in which they are together; there is little to choose between them.

The more justice that is done to all three demands — finitude, self-respect, and worldliness — the more closely *judiciousness* is approximated. At his best, a judicious man environs his acceptance of the known world with an emotional acknowledgment of something uncomprehended but fundamental, where realities form groups without necessarily sacrificing their ability to be distinct in nature and function. Faced with difficulties and irrationalities in the known world, he supplements the initial expression of his mood with others, and thereby is able to acknowledge otherwise unknown insistent realities which are related to those he had initially accepted. The two expressions of mood together constitute a *concerned conviction* that either himself or other realities — individual, related, known, or unknown — must be altered, if he is to be true to what is in fact the case. That conviction is the analogue of the assessment he made when his deep and dominant attitudes were not in accord.

A concerned conviction is faintly present quite early in life, enabling a child to ask its elders hard questions about itself and the world in which it lives. After a language has been well mastered, and has been clarified through technical additions and uses, the child may learn how to avoid slipshod observations and snap judgments, and think with some logical rigor. This must be done if there is to be deliberate inquiry and experimentation. A concerned conviction will then acquire clear outlines. Persistently expressed, that conviction will make a difference to the quality and direction of beliefs, attitudes, and feelings. But its effects will usually be so slight that its existence and that of the rectifying mood will often be ignored. It takes striking challenges, which attitudes are unable to meet, to provoke men to try to become citizens of a world where they continue to maintain their self-respect while still remaining aware of their finitude.

5

Reflective men refuse to remain where the merely judicious are. They may cling to their convictions as firmly as the others do, but they also try to support those convictions with reasons, arguments, leading to justifying principles. Not content with simple conviction, they want the warranted, the rational, the defensible. Emotions originating in a *tone,* emotions below the level of a mood, are used to bolster the adoption of governing explanations. When these are found wanting, the tone has to be expressed in supplementary and rectificatory ways if one is to be emotionally in accord with what is real.

Most men live out their convictions, rarely bothering to justify them. Sometimes these conflict. Reflective men then make an attempt to see if one set deserves to be maintained, or if there is perhaps something which escapes the limitations characteristic of both. An occasional few do not await the conflicts but freely ask themselves whether their convictions could be justified. Stimulated, perhaps, by new religious developments, scientific discoveries, historic reevaluations, and philosophic criticism, they become alert to the incoherence, arbitrariness, inadequacy, or obscurity of principles with which no difficulty had in fact been found. They forge arguments and seek better principles in order to determine what convictions can withstand the scrutiny of a sceptical reason, and can be counted on in hard cases. Sometimes they find that their accepted principles, supposed to make all else intelligible, just lack a satisfactory justification. This may be enough to have them reduce those principles in status to little more than plausible suggestions or suppositions, which are to be accepted in the absence of anything better, or because something like them proved useful in some other enterprise. Sometimes the principles are taken to be idle, thin abstractions, requiring grounding in and enrichment by experience, or to be fragments of some more fundamental, yet to be discovered principle in which they are supplemented by other fragments. In these different ways it is tacitly admitted that the principles that had been used do not sustain a rational approach to an intelligible world.

The more insistent the desire to have a justified rational approach to the world the more is one led to look for sound principles, underlying all others. Some of the principles, which had been accepted and for which no adequate justification had been provided, could then conceivably be justified; others might be abandoned; new ones might have to be acknowledged. It is not possible to determine in advance which of these possibilities will be realized. Not until one has adopted justified principles is one qualified to meet both familiar situations and untoward occurrences with a confidence that one's methods and explanations are warranted and right.

We are all part of a persistent, obstinate world whose nature we have not yet understood. That world tests all principles. When we find that the principles we have accepted are not in accord with that world, we are prompted to retreat toward the center of ourselves and creatively articulate this in the shape of more fundamental, better principles. If we do this, we will be able to assess, rectify, and perhaps replace those we had been using.

Fundamental principles, in effect, provide standards in terms of which accepted principles are graded as more or less justified because more or less adequate to a real world. They provide such standards because, despite their emotional origin at the center of ourselves, they are in accord with what in fact is. They function, therefore, somewhat as deep attitudes do in relation to dominant attitudes and an unprobed world does in relation to an accepted one.

The more one inclines toward altering principles to make them in accord with others that are better grounded and more in consonance with what is the case, the more is one engaged in a *controlled acquiescence* to reality. The more there is an emphasis on obtaining more fundamental principles, the more is one engaged in *reflective inquiry*. Sometimes acquiescence is to the fore; then, without becoming more deeply involved emotionally than one had previously been, one alters explanatory principles so that they are in better accord with what is real. At other times, reflective inquiry may be pursued, and reality articulated in accordance with principles which promise a more successful grasp of reality than the old. A stress on one of these adventures does not altogether free one from the other.

To those who might object that contentions such as these are only arbitrary suppositions, it is to be remarked that the objection is presumably being made on behalf of all men, guided by a desire to speak the truth about what is the case. But to speak for all men is to speak on behalf of what they have in common, and this is below the expressions of feeling, attitude, or mood. To desire to speak the truth is to open oneself to the final demands of a reality to which one acquiesces and inquires into. The objection, therefore, conforms to the very conditions which it is trying to question.

Acquiescence and inquiry are interlocked, though at times one may have such a slight role as to be hardly noticeable. A *boldly submissive* man gives full weight to both; he is not persistently biased in one direction or the other, but instead redresses imbalances in one direction by imbalances in another, somewhat as a sailing ship tacks now here and then there in order to move in a straight line. He is best able to carry out a single *philosophical investigation* into accepted and fundamental principles, and the reality which tests them. With the help of an effective method, the investigation may, over the course of time, follow a fairly steady course.

A boldly submissive man may put more emphasis on the question of how one comes to know principles and the world, or on the question of what it is to be a center or be outside this. Consequently, he may function primarily as an *epistemologist,* analytic and critical, or as an *ontologist,* sympathetic and constructive. Neither of these types of philosophic investigation can be carried out in complete abstraction from the other. The one is directed to the achievement of a satisfactory account of knowledge, but only for real men in a real world; the other seeks to grasp what is real, but in a way which will be able to withstand critical scrutiny. A systematic philosopher, *critically sympathetic,* does justice to both sides. He wants to know as a real man who is among real men in a real universe. But if he is not also boldly submissive he will engage in epistemic and ontological investigations without adequate regard for the way he is in fact involved with the objects of principles and their ground, or without adequate regard for the demands of a proper inquiry into those objects. He will then be as partial as one who does justice to the requirements of a proper acquiescence and inquiry but fails to provide an ontological base for his theory of knowledge, or a theory of knowledge for his ontological account. It is possible to be boldly submissive and critically sympathetic, and yet fail to be sufficiently original or sufficiently considerate of what is the case. A *creative thinker* qualifies originality with considerateness, considerateness with originality. He may fail to be boldly submissive and overstress acquiescence or inquiry; he may fail to be critically sympathetic and overstress knowing or being. A *speculative* man is all three — boldly submissive, critically sympathetic, and creative. He acquiesces and inquires epistemically and ontologically with originality and considerateness.

No one maintains this high pitch continuously. In between, everyone falls back into a position where these expressions are indistinguishable components within a tone. It is the existence of that tone which reveals the most accomplished of philosophers to be at root one with the most naïve and unreflective of men. These express that tone as surely as he does, but less often, less consistently, less persistently, less effectively, less self-consciously. But the expressions of tone by both qualify their acceptances, attitudes, and feelings in mind and body to make them men who do not merely confront what is outside them, or just react to it, but who approach and deal with it, with at least a dim and flickering awareness that they both are and know, are both original and constrained, neither just acquiescent nor inquiring. Were this not the case, the philosophers or the naïve would not only belong to different realms, but there would be no position from which anyone could begin to survey both what is and what is known, what is to be both accepted and examined, what is to be approached with originality as well as with considerateness.

There could conceivably be expressions of something deeper than an emotional tone. But what this could be we can not know until speculation is faced with challenges which it can not meet, and then if it provokes an emotional supplement which answers that challenge. All we can now count on are new speculations designed to overcome difficulties beyond the reach of the old. There is of course a history, and there could be a psychology, sociology, and logic of speculation to which one could turn to account for speculations, their timing, and their interrelationship. But to appeal to these is both to look for explanations after the fact and to make use of accounts which themselves are to be ultimately grounded in some speculatively developed philosophy which shows how the supposed explanations are interrelated, and what their final warrant is. To get behind speculatively attained results, we must invoke what is itself another speculation, or what is to be ultimately justified by one.

6

It is possible to affect feelings so drastically that the attitudes, mood, and tone that qualify the feelings are themselves disturbed. This art can do. It makes an immediate emotional appeal, sometimes affecting men in their deepest recesses, and this whether they be good or bad, ignorant or knowledgeable, foolish or wise.

It is, of course, just as arbitrary to say with Schopenhauer, Schelling, and Heidegger that art knows more truly or surely than speculation does or that art is closer to the heart of things than speculation can attain, as it is to say with Russell, Carnap, and Sellars that this is instead the privilege of science; with Croce and Collingwood that this is the privilege of history; or with Augustine and Aquinas that it is instead the privilege of theology. No none of these contentions is warranted; it could not be before its author speculatively arrived at the very objects which he is claiming had been arrived at in other and better ways. No philosopher can know that art, science, or any of the other disciplines best knows what is ultimately real, except by self-contradictorily speculatively arriving at those realities, and then discovering that they are better known when dealt with in these other disciplines.

Art does offer itself as self-sufficient, at the same time that it so affects the emotions that men become alert to what might not have been encountered in other ways. Consequently, speculative thinkers can justifiably say that there is something that art teaches them, and that it does give them root material on which to work. But this they can rightly say only if they engage in speculative adventures which allow them to recognize what it is to which art has brought them. If it is speculation that acknowledges the achievements of art, speculation can not conclude that art knows what speculation can not, but only that art grasps it in a distinctive way. If art could reach what speculation can not, speculation can not evidently tell us what this is, and therefore that it is there to be known. But speculation can understand how a different approach to the same realities — one more emotional, more experimental, more formal, or better grounded — might exhibit new nuances and different textures. Speculation will not be able to claim that this is to know better or more than speculative thought permits, but only that, since it differs from thought in power and action, it yields a content which is faced and grasped in a nonspeculative manner.

It is because speculation reaches to everything, that it can know that there are other ways of dealing with realities, which it can not duplicate. But it can not, without defeating itself, claim that what it can not duplicate can not be known or that it is grasped in ways that are superior to its own. Art takes one to final realities along one route; speculation knows the route and the terminus but, of course, only as objects of thought. The knowledge that it has tells us that these objects can also be dealt with in art and in other known ways.

Art can bring us to ultimate realities with a directness and emotionality no other approaches permit. It provides speculation with data which it is to articulate and systematize. That there are such data to be so used is known only because one has a sound speculative grasp of art. And use can be made of the data only because one has speculatively reached to it. All the while it remains that which art emotionally reaches in a distinctive way.

The life of a man, the vital energy he expresses in and through mind and body and which he exhibits in his emotions, is the energy of the world, condensed, epitomized, humanly contoured. It is existence, an endless space-time-dynamics brought into focus and intensified. Expressed in and through the body, given articulation and pace, definiteness and direction by works of art, those emotions are finally terminated by the very existence from which they issued and to which they gave a distinctive human guise. Art, by eliciting man's deepest attitudes, mood, and tone makes it easier for him to come to know realities below those objects at which his dominant attitude and encompassed feelings terminate. It does this best when it is not only pleasing, dramatic, classical, but innovative as well. If what is here said of art obtains independent support in an experience with it, it has as solid a base as one can hope to obtain, for we can get no firmer or deeper foundation than one where immediacy and mediacy, feeling and thought, the outcome of creative making and thinking supplement one another.

Chapter 9

Appearances and Realities

What we daily perceive, confront, and speak about are readily taken to be realities. But this they can not be, since they are dependent for their presence and natures on circumstances and on beings which have powers and centers of their own. What we attend to are appearances — *of* realities.

It is customary to speak as though appearances were just idle qualities — colors and shapes, tastes, hefts, sounds. But then one commits a double error: the qualities are detached from their realities, though without them the qualities are not possible; and other appearances — tart apples, large hammers, green trees — are mistakenly taken to be realities, even though they, too, vary according to circumstance and partly depend for their presence and natures on something else.

A commonsense object is an appearance as surely as its perceived qualities are. Both, though, have textures and depths, imperceptibly passing into the realities which make them possible. The color of a tree varies in hue during the course of the day. When we look at it from a distance and with tinted glasses, we see other colors and shapes in place of the green and the rough triangle we noted in broad daylight and nearby. The various colors and shapes are surfaces of the real tree to which they are accredited, but modified and qualified by circumstance, and by the action and presence of other realities.

An observable tree is more than any number of combination of qualities. It is resistant, insistent, persistent, alive, big, opposing other objects. But these features of it also vary, and are dependent on a reality, not conditioned by the presence or action of men or other realities. The observable tree is resistant to the push of a boy but not to a high wind; it is small for the lawn, but large for a man; and its traits are aspects of a real tree, outside the reach of commonsense categories and uses. It is the real tree's interaction with real men and other beings that enable it to appear as an observable green tree.

In the ordinary course of life different kinds of appearances are roughly distinguished in terms of their reliability to guide effective action. No one of them is a detached, floating, inert item, or the true creation of a perceiver. Each is the product of an interplay of realities. That product is overlaid by social conventions and perceptual conditions. Appearances tell us something about the realities to which they are accredited, but not very clearly. Even those appearances which we denigrate as illusions, distortions, misperceptions tell us something about a reality, but the appearances are so particularized and overpersonalized that they can not serve as reliable indices for action. They may, though, be as well grounded as other appearances on which we find it possible to rely. In both cases, we are inclined to ignore whatever intimations of reality the appearances provide, contenting ourselves with making a good practical adjustment.

Some appearances are deliberately produced by altering and relating others. The most interesting are the work of artists. Both the paints of a painter and the painting he produces are appearances; so are the materials used and the outcomes of the work of a sculptor, poet, musician, or dancer. Each in his own way transforms familiar appearances to produce others that are important on their own account. The work of art builds on but makes no reference to these; instead it leads to what is real. Artistic creation results in new appearances which take us emotionally to what underlies them, and other appearances as well. When it is assumed that what we daily confront are realities and not appearances, or when it is assumed that only science or philosophy deals with realities, it is an easy step to go on to suppose that the arts present us with sheer illusions, which is to say, with appearances that are most alien to what is real. But once it is recognized that what we daily confront also are appearances, and once it is seen that all appearances are appearances of realities, one has little reason for continuing to maintain that art, unlike science, philosophy, practice, or commonsense, is confined just to illusions or surfaces.

Appearances give some intimation of the realities that make them possible; they are continuations of those realities affected by the contributions made by others. As a rule the intimations are too vague to interest us, and we are therefore inclined to ignore the realities we faintly discern beyond the appearances. For most purposes, daily appearances are our realities to which we try to adjust. The appearances that art produces contrast with those with which we are daily familiar. They often shock us. More important, though they also attract us and tempt us to stay with them, it is not very long before we become emotionally aware of a reality beyond them. The appearances lead us to existence, relentless, irreducible, voluminous, and objective. They also tell us something about what men are like, since their lives are existence compressed, individuated, shaped into emotions. It is no less true that art faces us with existence than that it presents us with appearances. It would be more precise, though, to say that it presents us with appearances in such a way that we become emotionally involved with existence.

2

A film is occupied with appearances, but not with illusions. It does not present a series of stills which we somehow blur together to give a wrong impression that something is moving. As was already remarked, there is movement in the film; stabbings, battles, chases, conversations occur there. He who would deny this will have to deny a similar status to what is in the stills as well. The same reasons should also lead him to deny the status of genuine appearances not only to movements in a film and to a chair in a still, but to light and to chemicals. There is in fact no final position to which he could retreat in this way, where he would be justified in saying "here, at last, is a true appearance," or "here, at last, is what is real." True appearances are not found by going from films to photographs, or from photographs to light or chemicals. Nor can realities be found by going from one appearance to another. One must go through appearances to get to what is beneath and beyond them.

Filmed appearances can not be counted on practically as commonsense appearances can; in turn, commonsense appearances lack the intensities and references characteristic of the filmed. If a man is shot in a film, he is shot as surely as he would be were he in a battle. But the wounds he suffers in the one are related to other occurrences in the film, and to nothing else, whereas the wounds suffered in a battle are related to other occurrences there and at home. The different wounds, too, are inseparable from different realities; the second affects the career of a real man, while the first affects the career of a man in the film at the same time that it makes existence emotionally available.

Film has the extraordinary power of being able to make one aware of the endless malleability and power of existence. It creates and connects arresting appearances at the same time that it directs one to the reality which those appearances exhibit in limited, specialized portions of space, time, and causality. Film, as a consequence, is at once opaque and translucent, the opacity being the result of its aesthetic use of appearances, with the translucence characterizing the appearances in their relation to existence. Because it is opaque, one can live with it for awhile; because it is translucent, one can be emotionally moved by it to attend to the overwhelming reality of existence. Conceivably, there could be other arts which were able to create and connect desirable appearances, and bring one to existence as not yet broken up into a distinctive space, time, and causality. We do not know of any such arts. When produced, they will create distinctive appearances and lead one to existence in new ways. But a taxonomic scheme allows us to say some general things about them in advance of their actual production, and therefore in advance of the lessons they in fact alone can teach.

3

In my earlier studies of art [1] I dealt mainly with architecture, sculpture, painting; musical composition, story, poetry; musical performance, theatre, and dance. Each was seen to create appearances that bounded, occupied, or exhausted portions of the space, time, or dynamics of existence. All of them, it was recognized, threw some light on particular actualities too, but incidentally.

These nine arts are obviously to be balanced by others which make one aware of the space, time, and dynamics of individual realities and only incidentally of the corresponding dimensions of existence. There should be three arts of *design* whose created appearances are revelatory of the spatiality of actualities; three arts of *description* which are revelatory of their temporality; and three arts of *exposure* which are revelatory of their dynamism. To match the nine basic arts previously distinguished, these three types of art, which primarily reveal individual realities in depth, break up into *reconstructions, portrayals,* and *imagery; biography, autobiography,* and *lyrics; improvisations, method-acting,* and *self-expression.* These divisions are and will remain little more than headings unless embodied in actual work. But for the present it suffices to observe that the fact that some of them have not been exploited points up the truth that the traditional arts primarily produce appearances which are revelatory of existence, and not, as these do or would, of individual actualities. The two sets of arts are distinct. They prompt the further question as to

whether or not there are or can be other arts which produce appearances
that are revelatory of both individual actualities and finalities at the same
time. The prompting of this question enhances the value of the initial
classification of the nine basic arts, for a good classification not only
finds a place for every existent specimen but has room for discoveries
still to be made. One way of answering the question is to see how the
revelations made possible by one set of arts might be together with those
made possible by the other. Conceivably, what was true of any one of the
nine traditional arts could be united with what was true of any one of the
other nine. Somewhat along the lines of concrete poetry one might perhaps
produce a new art in which one could find the virtues of architecture and
lyric combined; an art of self-portraiture could be taken to offer a unity of
what autobiography and painting offer severally; and so on.
The possibility of an art which dealt with what architecture and lyric or
autobiography and painting dealt with separately, makes evident that
there are conceivable arts which do not remain with only one type of
extension. The initial nine, and the suggested matching set, as a matter
of fact, do not demand that the created appearances oppose one
dimension of extension to others. Nor, as a matter of fact, is a revelation of
existence characteristic of the initial set altogether cut off from a revelation
of individual actualities characteristic of the other. A dance makes evident
the very dynamics of existence, but not as sundered either from the space
or time of existence, or from individual extensions. A created appearance
may reveal one dimension of extension in individuals and a different kind
in existence, not altogether separated from one another. That idea is not
unknown to film.

4

While keeping some hold on more superficial emotions, all arts
immediately engage deeper ones. They refine and contour them more
subtly than they could be refined and contoured when brought into play
in everyday life with its conventions, practical demands, and habituated
classifications. What it produces so affects feelings, and what qualifies
and fringes these, that emotional states, not yet expressed but continuous
with those that are, are immediately elicited.
Art radicalizes appearances. What it produces not only challenges
present feelings but elicits and controls others. Each work can assume any
one of four distinct guises — *popular, dramatic, classical,* or *innovative* —

depending on whether it primarily evokes a feeling, an attitude, a mood, or a tone. Yet the classical can be popular; the innovative can be dramatic; the popular can be innovative. However, the popular, dramatic, and innovative characters will, in these cases, usually be incidental, not central to what is in fact being produced. Though each of these entrenches on the others, one is normally so emphasized and the others minimized that it is desirable to distinguish sharply all four.

An artist tries to produce a work that is self-sufficient, self-contained, final. It may prove to be entertaining because it arouses compensatory mental feelings which are mainly approbative. But if it is a work of art, it is not produced simply in order to provide entertainment; that would make it just a piece of craftsmanship, promoting an end outside it. To appreciate it as a work of art, one must keep within its confines and not view it in terms of some external end it might serve. This is true even when it is primarily popular.

An art is primarily popular if it offers an excellent whole to be sensuously experienced. At its best, it brings bodily feelings to heightened and partly controlled expression, by means of rhythms, divisions, and intensities that force the expression of compensatory feelings through the mind as well. When this occurs there is an appreciation of the aesthetic quality of the work, an appreciation that may run from an immediate enjoyment of what is sensuously undergone to a judgment of the work as aesthetically excellent.

Every artist works within a tradition; no one can entirely free himself from his experiences, background, and acquaintance with the work of other artists. His normal feelings are like those of his kinsmen; he makes his most direct impression on them because his creations build on those feelings, even when they break away from them. There are sounds and rhythms, juxtapositions of shapes, colors, spaces, words, and gestures, and combinations of movements and rests to which most men in a culture are indifferent or to which they respond with repugnance, but these, too, can be so introduced into an art work that it may have sufficient power of its own to overcome the widespread indifference or resistance.

It is possible to produce an aesthetic work of art, in which qualities are interlocked to make an excellent surface, and that is all. If the work is met on all sides with disdain or revulsion, it could still be a "popular" work of art, but by anticipation, awaiting the arrival of some later epoch when men's sensitivities were more acute or better prepared. Even if there never comes a time when the work finds an appreciative audience, it is possible to conceive of its creator as having produced a work in which qualities intensify one another maximally. We can then say that he produced a work of art, and even a popular work of art. But, on the hypothesis, we will not know whether or not this is so, for we can not know this without our appreciatively attending to it.

Though a work may not be designed to arouse and satisfy feelings, there is no other test of its aesthetic value than its ability to arouse and satisfy them. Its excellence consists in the production of a whole in which experienceable qualities are maximally supportive and harmonized. This can not be known without feeling the parts in their interconnection. After an experience with a popular work is over, the feelings aroused by it quickly fade, and soon are no longer. But until they have entirely vanished they continue to be manifest. Freed from the work of art, they are directed vaguely and diffusely toward what might satisfy them. No particular object is able to do justice to what the feelings then are and require. Their lack of outline, their thrust, and their indefiniteness do not allow them to find satisfaction with any specific item. That part of a feeling which is not quieted by the intensively rich content that an art provides can find rest only in indefinite content, indefinite in extent. As a consequence, the feeling that had been expressed toward an appreciated aesthetic whole still awaits the remainder of its satisfaction.

A *dramatic* artist arouses, controls, and directs feelings and attitudes which have no evident practical value. He then so challenges them that he elicits deeper attitudes, usually appropriate to values that are the concern of a multitude. To succeed, he must both take advantage of the attitudes that are daily expressed and prevent their raw expression; the former to enable him to address his audience, the latter to enable it to share in his work. This double task is best performed by his accepting the common grammar and usage of words, the familiar sounds and phrasings of familiar music, the usual shapes and colors, separately and together, and then vitalizing the common environment, the spatial configurations, the temporal spans, and the causal activities by expressions of deeper attitudes encompassing newly awakened feelings.

If an audience is unsophisticated, an artist must take advantage of the devices of popular art to make it possible for the audience to enter readily into his work. If the audience is sophisticated, it has already prepared itself before entering into the gallery, theatre, concert hall, or library. Holding its daily practical attitudes in abeyance, that audience is ready to accept the guidance of the artist. A dramatic artist and his audience accept the same common structures, for this is what remains over when practical attitudes are suspended. The artist fills out the structure with new, specific content, whose shape and pace are not only then and there produced, but which provide a controlled elicitation and partial satisfaction of feelings of joy and sadness. Suddenly, he confronts his audience with occurrences which its expressed attitude and feelings can not accommodate, thereby eliciting expressions of a deeper attitude and feelings, more appropriate to those occurrences. He may provide premonitions of the occurrences, and tentative expressions of the attitude all along the way, but they are present definitively only at special places. Those places are turning points, crucial events, in some disaccord with dominant attitudes. Those attitudes and their encompassed feelings are, therefore, incapable of meshing with what is there, and must be rectified and replaced by deeper attitudes and their encompassed feelings. Deep attitudes fade away when one no longer shares in a dramatic work, but not as quickly as feelings fade when one is no longer involved in a popular art. For an indefinite period thereafter one is aware of the world as a locus of tragedy and comedy, necessity and chance, the rational and the unpredictable, where man is at once a native and an alien. If, by a "purgation of the emotions" one means a sobered awareness of the benign ominousness of the course of the world, one can with Aristotle say that dramatic art purges deep emotions that are deliberately evoked by dramatized, crucial events.

The attitudes that dramatic art arouses are continuous with attitudes unelicited and indistinguishable. Dramatic art is the work of men able to provide occasions for the expression of attitudes not required by daily occurrences. In its arousal of these deep attitudes, the dramatic work is able to make one directly acquainted with what is not open to introspection or observation. The acquaintance, unfortunately, is dim, partly hidden by the overwhelming, vivid nature of the expressions of the attitudes.

A dramatic work of art can continue to exist in the absence of feelings, or an expressed attitude, because its structure continues to be present. It is possible, therefore, for an historian, or scholar, or critic to accurately analyze and characterize a great work of dramatic art—a play, a cathedral, a poem, a dance, a painting, a story, a sculpture, a symphony—without participating in it.

Dramatic art exposes values that reflection will enable one to articulate; reflection knows a world which dramatic art reveals. The dramatic art uses fresher, more intensive, better paced, and purer expressions of emotions than is otherwise possible, and reveals to reflection the values of which it should take account. In turn reflection explicates these, and makes evident how they are grounded in more basic occurrences and objects.

Classical art is great art. It has withstood many critical examinations and comparisons, and many shifts in taste and culture, over decades. There is no one specific date when it became classical. It became more and more classical, sometimes with interludes of doubt and rejection, until finally it formed a part of a continuing tradition and heritage. Initially, like a play of Molière's, it may have been and may still continue to be popular; like a work of Michaelangelo, it may have been and continue to be dramatic. Initially and now, therefore, it may have elicited, controlled, and largely satisfied feelings and attitudes, dominant and deep. But the critical examinations and comparisons, and the shifts in tastes of the culture expose a meaning to it which is not answered by any attitudes. Instead, they require expressions of a mood appropriate to realities, among which a man in fact is and with which he is in fact involved.*

---

* *Film has, of course, such a short history that, perhaps, classical is not to be used, appropriately, at all in its context. Yet is it my experience that if films have been withheld from viewing for fifty years — like many of the best films of Mary Pickford — as opposed to the films of Chaplin or Griffith — they can produce a popular reaction — expressions of emotions — which, one would guess, is not far removed from the original impact brought forth. Mary's* Little Lord Fauntleroy *can elicit tears, laughter, and applause today. Technicians, in the industry, are startled by the illusions she created — not simply because they were created fifty years ago, but because they can not explain how they were arrived at. Much as we are in doubt about how Stonehenge or the Pyramids were built, how mummies were indeed, mummified, so one can find few survivors who can explain how Mary kissed Mary in a double role in* Fauntleroy, *or, more difficult yet, how she could cross past herself in* Stella Maris. *Although the man who created the special effect is still alive, who in fifty years will be able to describe how the locusts descended upon* The Good Earth?   *R. T.*

A classical work of art elicits responses which it orders and controls, and thereby makes one confront realities beyond the reach of comedy and tragedy, or the settled outlooks that men have come to adopt toward the known world. Unlike comedy and tragedy, too, which awaken a need to express deep attitudes to deal with what dominant attitudes can not, a classic awakens a sense of the vast unknown. Unlike comedy and tragedy, which depend on crucial occurrences to force what is not dominant into expression, it continually brings the unknown to bear on the known. Making evident that the unknown both fringes and permeates the known, it tells us that reality is at once intelligible and mysterious, settled and unreliable, promising and ominous.

Classical art presents an epitomization of the world as at once known and unknown, in such a way as to elicit fresher, more vital expressions of a mood that is possible to obtain either through reflection or through an actual struggle with the difficulties that beset one's acceptance of the known world. The expressions, which the classical work of art elicits, may long outlast the experience of the work, and may enable one to face the very realities that reflection remarks upon, and which a struggle with difficulties may terminate in. These residua of the expressions of the mood allow one to be in touch with reality's unfathomed immensity, but they do not give one a good grip on it, or enable one to understand it.

A classical work of art does not depend for its existence on the experience of it. That is a peculiarity of popular art. A classical work, consequently, can be correctly characterized and well understood by one who does not emotionally participate in it. But it can not be maintained in existence, as dramatic art can, merely by preserving its essential structure; it has a meaning and an insistence, an effectiveness and a reach not possible to structures.

The classics are present in the outlook of today, coloring it. They are time-binders, historic coalescences, controlling occurrences. Were they destroyed, neglected, or misunderstood they would, of course, not be able to make the same impact that they now do, but they would continue to have a kind of being as long as they made any impact at all. When experienced they are present in a way they otherwise would not be, for they are then localized and lived with. When not experienced — even when no longer available — the mood-grounded emotions they once aroused can still be manifest, keeping us in some accord with a world whose nature is not yet fully understood.

Classical art is a constitutive part of our heritage, and this is a double sense. It affects the outlook and therefore the lives of men, sometimes directly, but more often through imitations, simplifications, and the establishment of canons of taste and value. These agencies do not enable men to have the heightened experience which the original makes possible; therefore they do not allow for as good a grasp of the world as the residua of the original elicited expressions permit. But they do enable one to make some acquaintance with it. Classical art is a constitutive part of our heritage, too, in the sense that it allows one today to become immediately aware, through the expressions which outlast the experience of a work, of the same reality that other generations knew.

There are great classical artists who innovate little. Shakespeare is an example. On the other hand, most innovators are not great artists. Their novelties have to do with technical advances and, when they do not, the results are so surprising and upsetting even to their practitioners that they preclude exploration and subtilization and good use. These innovators normally prepare the way for other artists, some of whom become classical in a way that the innovators do not. Occasionally, though, an Aeschylus, a Stravinsky, or a Joyce appears who produces great innovative art, making new use of old material, bringing in new material, using new instruments, alerting one to new problems, and pointing the way to new solutions, while creating excellent, self-sufficient wholes which promise to achieve the status of classics.

The works in which innovations first appear cease to have more than an historic interest unless perchance those works become classics. Sooner or later, in any event, the innovations are set aside or are taken for granted. Initially, though, the great innovative works broke through the crust of established feelings, attitudes, and moods, to provide interplaying expressions of the tone that lies beneath these and their latent forms. At one and the same time, those works made strikingly explicit the kind of principles that have been customarily accepted, and altered and added to them, with the result that new principles were generated, more appropriate to what is real and known.

Despite his evident originality, an innovator often takes himself not to be a primary agent but, instead, to be under the dominance of a more fundamental impersonal force. He usually does not attend to principles, new or old, or to the powerful source which enables him to correct or replace them. He is disinterested in principles and awed by the power, content to go in a new direction, with little regard for older canons and demands. It is we who come later who, more often than not, find that he has brought into play a new set of principles under the effective dynamic governance of an unprobed reality.

An innovation controls the expressions of a tone. It touches this more immediately than speculation can, and has the expressions in a more intensive form than a dissatisfaction with the operating of accepted principles permits. The innovator sets himself, other artsists, and, hopefully, his audience in a new direction. Though the new direction is rarely followed in inquiry or in life, the work makes such following possible. The change in direction, which comes about because of the innovative work, is not to be undone. The work blocks the return, and will do so as long as the past is a past for a present. The innovation can therefore be examined dispassionately, and its distinctive contributions exposed, almost as if it were an historic document.

An understanding of what is ultimately real needs the guidance of appreciation, and appreciation needs the clarification and justification that only thinking can provide. But each develops in its own way, and brings about results not within the provenance of the other. A thoughtful man comes closer than others to knowing the world that all face but grasp only inchoately, particularly if he allows himself to be directed by an innovative great work. The innovative artist, in contrast, is content to make what is at once new and excellent; he uses but does not examine the power that governs his creation and which elicits expressions of the tone at the center of himself and others. A thinker is less excited, not as daring, not as provocative as an artist, but the artist does not have as wide a range, is not as controlled, and is not as clear as the other.

A great innovative work of art elicits and partly satisfies an expression of the creator's tone. As appreciated and not merely analyzed or understood, the work provokes and partly satisfies a similar expression on the part of its audience. To make the work of art or to appreciate it, therefore, is to come close to making evident the tone of any man. It should make a philosopher more aware of the limitations of long-established principles and of the power beyond them. The expressions art arouses, and which remain after the work has been experienced, should suggest to him the path he is to follow in his own way, inquiring while he acquiesces, facing the world epistemically and ontologically, and cross-graining his originality with humility.

Philosophers rarely attend to great innovative works of art, in part because most philosophers are historically minded and therefore primarily interested in classical works, and in part because they prefer doctrinal grounds to emotionally tinged suggestions as to where their creative efforts should be directed. Most of them study their great predecessors. They do not see them primarily as innovators, for their innovations have already become part of an inherited world. Looking at the history of thought as though it were a grand progress or development, or as a sequence of corrections of solutions to continuing problems, they often fail to follow the lead of the men they study, and therefore fail to move forward in their own time as the others did in theirs.

In modern times most philosophers are more aware of the recent great innovations in science than they are of those in philosophy. But instead of attending to the world with the same boldness that characterizes the scientific innovators, they take the results of the scientists to provide a solid base on which to erect a philosophy. As a consequence, their views do not outlast the epoch when a particular scientific doctrine prevailed. Great scientific discoveries are stimuli to which the proper response is not submission but an awakening to the limitations of established principles, and the need to resubject them to the power which originally gave them birth. Precisely because art is so different in structure, effects, and power from science and philosophy, its innovations can be more readily faced as innovations, and therefore can more readily lead one to follow new paths into the world of which all men are a part.

Film, because of its involvement with all the extensional dimensions of actualities and existence can challenge expressions of established attitudes and feelings from more sides than anything else can. If it is the work of a number of dedicated creative cinemakers, at once independent and cooperative, it could conceivably provide a guide to speculation greater than that provided by other arts. But for this to occur it must not only be popular and dramatic, as it so often is today at its best, but must become classical and innovative as well. It will have to be produced without regard for ends external to itself by men able to create a sensuously experience-able, self-sufficient unity out of visual-audio recordings of incidents. This will require the defeat of a temptation to serve a purpose, no matter how noble. To yield to the temptation is to make a propagandistic, educational, escapist, disclosive, or documentary film. These, too, produce new appearances, and elicit and partly satisfy controlled feelings and other emotional expressions. All, though, fall short of being genuine works of art. From their standpoint, of course, other types of film, even great ones, are so occupied with what is useless but arresting that they necessarily betray the very emotions which they so effectively arouse. From their standpoint, all art has a purpose—that of turning man away from practical concerns and stirring up desirable emotions. The purposive arts take the realization of this end to make possible the realization of their own purposes.

To adjudicate between the claims of film as an art and film with a purpose, it is necessary to become clear as to just what the purposive arts are and do. One will then find, I think, that films with a purpose lack the self-sufficiency and power that characterize whatever is excellent. They can be improved, but only by getting rid of their externally directed purposes, and replacing these with a concern for making something which can be appreciated only to the degree that one attends solely to the work and what its perfection demands.

Each work of art is bounded off from all else as a completed unit. It enables one to look outside it and come to be at and know what is real and abiding. But if it be made or viewed as that which is to serve some external purpose — even that of knowing what is real — it will be less excellent in itself and eventually less revelatory of what is real than it could be.

Films with a Purpose

CHAPTER 10

Propaganda and Educational Films

A film can be excellent in three ways—as a work of art, complete in itself; as a work of craftsmanship, a means serving some external end; and as a component in a larger whole. These are not incompatible. Great works of art are produced by those who are also great craftsmen, and they can contribute to the careers, wealth, and status of their creators.

Craftsmanship, at its best, produces the graceful and pleasant, while making possible the attainment of some other objective. It ends with a chair that can be sat on, with a spoon that can be used. These are not consequences which a sculptured chair or spoon need promote. A sculptured chair or spoon may be made of paper or fur; the one could have fifty legs, the other fifty handles, none of which could be held. An excellent component instead is the fitting, that which is interlocked with others. A chair, usable or not, can be a component in the furniture of a room; a usable spoon is a component in a table set.

Neither craftsmanship nor components have a controlling role in the making of a work of art. They may be dominant in the beginning, they may surface every once in a while, and they may come out clearly in the end, but if they are not on the whole subordinated to what a created excellence requires, decisions will be made which do not promote the production of a work of art. These require emphases and choices at every moment among a number of alternatives, all contributing in different degrees to the making of what is at once sensuously experienceable, self-sufficient, and revelatory of existence.

Films, produced by those concerned with providing entertainment for a multitude and, at the same time, with making money, though they may involve considerable craftsmanship, are primarily components.* Of them-

---

* *This is wrong in two ways. First, the commercial film, the film made for a wide audience and for profit, is not merely a component. That kind of film is the central object of the whole art form. Films are different from poems or*

novels or paintings or even plays, because films cost somewhere between half a million and four million dollars to make. No artist, nor group of artists, can afford to fool around as an amateur. And your last sentence in this paragraph, "They are not being pursued here," is a great strategic error, limiting the usefulness and relevance of your book, and excluding those considerations about film that are vital and interesting. To talk about the art of film without producers and money is to talk about the modes of being without God. *D. S.*

---

selves they do not bring about the desired entertainment; they need the help of advertising, media recognition, distribution, and audience receptivity. Together these constitute a viable unit, the concern of entrepreneurs, impresarios, and heads of studios. Such men are not artists but craftsmen who see to it that the films mesh with the other agencies. If successful, these craftsmen make available a film that can both entertain the mass and make money. A study of the ways in which these films fit together with the other components, and the success they together entrain, are topics for showmanship and economics. They are not being pursued here.

A film which functions as a component may be a work of craftsmanship or a work of art. So far as it functions as a component these aspects of it are made subordinate to a different whole. Excellent works of art or craft have their values muted when they are joined to other components. The result could be quite ugly, even when the film was not. And, of course, poor works of art or craftsmanship can be components in attractive entertainment packages. In all the cases, the film is treated by those concerned with bringing about those wholes as material to be utilized and worked upon.

A film with a purpose is made in order to enable one to achieve an end uniquely or best served by film. It is usually designed to bring about certain results, with the subordinated help of financial backers, distributors, and advertising. But, unlike a film in the role of a component, it is not made to accommodate or mesh with these others. With good fortune a film with a purpose may succeed in entertaining a multitude and may turn out to be profitable, but these are not its controlling objectives; nor is it made to promote these outcomes. A film with a purpose is an agent, directed by forces it does not control, for an end still to be attained; that end is relevant to it as a film. Like all other types of film, the purposive film requires the independent but cooperative work of various film makers. Unlike the other films, however, it has a role that mimics that of a film maker. A propaganda film takes on something like the role of a performer, an educational film that of a script, a disclosive film that of a cinemaker, an escapist film that of a montagist, and a documentary that of a director. Since, in each case, there are limits externally imposed on the film, each type provides an illustration of the way in which the works of different film makers are modified when subject to conditions not pertinent to the making of a work of art.

2

"Propaganda" once had a rather narrow use. It referred to the college which Pope Urban VIII set up in the seventeenth century to educate priests for missions, where they were to propagate the faith. It is commonly used today to refer to the persuasive presentation of doctrines, usually political in nature, overstated and perhaps false, with the consequence that people are led astray.* But propaganda, as was originally intended, can be con-

---

One should consider Triumph of the Will, *a film of the Nuremberg rallies, made on a prodigious scale by Leni Riefenstahl for Hitler. It was designed to impress the world (pre–World War II) with the infinite might and majesty of the Nazi regime. Few film historians, despite the film's obvious intentions, would preclude it from a consideration of great (if there are any great) films. In the same context, one must examine Olivier's* Henry V, Noel Coward's In Which We Serve, *D. W. Griffith's* Intolerance, The Birth of a Nation, *and* Isn't Life Wonderful. *Almost all the films of Frank Capra must be considered propaganda, and Howard Hughes's magnificent* Scarface *introduces itself as such (however speciously).* All Quiet on the Western Front *must be so labeled. The list, indeed, is long. Michaelangelo's* Last Judgment, *one assumes, falls under this category, as does Milton's defense of God.*   R. T.

---

cerned with what is thought to be true. The important and central fact, though, is that it is designed to alter the beliefs and tendencies of people, and to do this, not by cold objective argument and the marshaling of evidence, but by appealing to their emotions. Viewed in this light, propaganda turns out to be a branch of rhetoric, "the discursive means of obtaining the adherence of minds." [1]
A work of propaganda may contain nothing but fictions; it may emphasize certain occurrences and objects, and neglect others equally important; it may be crude or subtle; it may hide or it may expose the faults of that on whose behalf it is made; it may be at the service of a large group or a small, of a strong or a weak. There is no set of conditions which it must

meet in order to be propaganda, except that of having the ability to alter beliefs and tendencies. What is significant is not what it says, not the truth or the falsehood of stated doctrines, not the excellence or defects of what it represents and presents, but only how it serves the desired end.

Films, as we have seen, appeal to the emotions. But they are not all propagandistic, for they are not all, like propaganda, designed to make a difference to the beliefs and tendencies of their viewers. They arouse the emotions, but also keep the expression of those emotions directed toward themselves. After the filming, those emotions continue to be expressed in a less intense and more diffuse form; they then enable one to become alert to realities outside the film, and beyond the reach of ordinary perception. One could keep that fact in mind, and produce a film in order to lead men to learn what is real. The result would be a film with a purpose — perhaps educational. It would not be a propaganda film, since unlike this it would not be directed at controlling the elicited emotions in order to make viewers change their particular states of mind, prompt them to get ready to act, and perhaps have them change some particular object or situation. A propaganda film does not elicit emotions for the sake of having one appreciatively grasp what it presents. Instead, it seeks to function more as a sign does, directing one toward something distinct from itself. It is the better the more it is able to turn attention away from itself, for then it can better promote the doctrines, ideas, values, ideals, or aspirations of those for whose sake the film was made.

A propaganda film may be designed to act on the common unreflecting states of men. It then appeals to their sense of what is desirable and what is to be avoided — glory and danger, victory and defeat, heroism and villainy, justice and injustice, pleasure and pain, the good and bad opinion of others. But it may also be directed at men in a special state at which they have arrived in the course of experience, or to which they may have been deliberately brought by training, education, ceremonies, and other tested means for changing the outlooks of men. If the very same men are to be brought to a particular state on different occasions, they may have to be worked on differently at different times. Neglect of that fact is one reason why effective propaganda at one period or for one audience is often ineffective at other periods or for other audiences, and then is no longer propaganda, but just an oddity or an idle suggestion.

A propaganda film is made to work on viewers who are assumed to be in a certain state, natural or induced. This state may have been brought about without regard for what the film is intended to accomplish, or in order to enable the film to be effective. Often the propaganda is presented in a setting which is conducive to the attainment of the state on which the propaganda is to operate. But a setting may also promote the operation of the propaganda itself; one might be lulled and gulled by incense, lush surroundings, quiet music, uniforms. These can properly be taken to be part of the propaganda. That possibility accentuates the fact that propaganda need not be expressed in a story or message. Stories and messages are vehicles, sometimes only of minor efficacy in achieving the result for which the propaganda is employed.

A propaganda film, like other types, elicits and answers to expressions of feeling, attitude, mood, and tone. It also provokes and partly satisfies rectifying expressions of these. But, unlike an art film, a propaganda film points the elicited rectifying emotions away from itself to occurrences and prospects outside the film. It is a stimulus calculated to produce a response toward what is other than itself. The response is appropriate to a specific object — a government, a product, a situation, an event. When that object is not available in a form which fully satisfies the elicited emotions, the emotions are expected to continue to be operative after the viewing, still directed toward the objects at which the emotions had been pointed by the film.

The emotions that an art film elicits continue to be operative in a diluted form after the viewing; they then make a final reality discernible. That reality might occupy one later, but that fact is not of concern to the film. A propaganda film, instead, is concerned with having the emotions fully expressed apart from itself; it then and there directs them toward particular objects and events, or manipulates them so as to change the audience's mentality. An art film would satisfy the emotions then and there if it could; that the emotions which it elicits point to a reality beyond it is a by-product, not within its purview. A propaganda film does not seek to satisfy the emotions it elicits, but to have those emotions vitalize activities which are to be carried out after the viewing is over. The one satisfies emotions in good part and is indifferent to what happens to the residuum; the other satisfies the emotions hardly at all because it aims at having them satisfied apart from it.

Propaganda makes one attend emotionally to what the film itself does not present. Were one to stop a dramatic production halfway, and ask that its resolution be found outside the theatre, one would have something analogous to what a propaganda film demands. A propaganda film, though, makes the asking for the resolution part of its own presentation. It is designed to dictate to the feelings, beliefs, and tendencies of its viewers,

171

usually on behalf of a still further end — the aggrandizement of those for whom the film was made. The viewers are to be made more insistent or content; they are to be led to buy or sell something, to use or discard it, to identify themselves with it or to destroy it and thereby, perhaps, improve the fortunes of someone else. The emotional response that a propaganda film elicits is satisfied by changing the kind of relations the viewers had to that further end. Though the changes that can be made are apparently endless, all can be brought under three headings: they depend on the action of others, on the action of the viewers, or on some combination of both.

Viewers may be comparatively passive, in an attitude of expectancy or longing which is to be quieted by an object's presence or absence, by its operation or cessation, and the like. They wait for others to bring about changes in them — approval or condemnation usually. The viewers are to have some belief, or are to be satisfied by some object. Or they are to be kept passive up to a point and then made active. A state of expectancy is to be induced which is satisfied perhaps by their seeing an object, at which time the desire to act toward it, and perhaps to use, destroy or possess it, is to take over. Since it is action which is the end here sought, this case can be reduced to one where the primary objective is to get the viewers to do something after they have been exposed to the propaganda.* A propaganda film not only provokes emotions which it does not

---

* A really great propaganda film — Triumph of the Will or Potemkin — is great primarily because it has used the art of film so well. You don't have to be a Communist to admire Eisenstein's work.   A. K.

---

intend to satisfy, but tailors them so that they can be satisfied by a change in the relation which the viewer has to something outside the film. The desired outcome is promoted by conveying a sense of urgency, for this intensifies the state of expectation or the need to act. The viewers are to be made to sense dangers, delays, obstacles, threats, and denials of satisfactions of the elicited emotions. The effect on the viewers will then be something like that produced by a dramatic work with its evocation of deep attitudes that counterbalance others initially and immediately elicited. But the propaganda film would not have to have a dramatic form. It is sufficient if it so works on the viewers that they emotionally respond in the way they would were they faced with a dramatic performance. Indeed, because of the interest that dramatic presentations arouse in their own unfolding, dramatic films are not good propaganda vehicles, unless radically simplified and turned into an interplay of types, characters, exemplars. This fact was well understood and well used in medieval morality plays with their deliberate propagandistic intent to turn men from evil ways to good, or from secular affairs to those ecclesiastically approved.

Propaganda film is a stylized performer trying to make itself at once effective and invisible so that viewers can be brought into direct relationship with something outside. Neglecting roles other than performance which a film might assume, it takes viewers to be just instruments to be played upon. At the same time, it demands a disinterest in the nature of its performance so as to effect a change in relationship between the viewers and other things.*

---

* *There is a fair possibility that most films are propaganda films. The economic base, and the requirement for large audience acceptance tends to limit film making to a narrow range of possible attitudes that a society finds acceptable. The biblical epics of Hollywood, the Russian boy-meets-tractor films, the World War II military films are the most striking examples, but the impact of film on the masses is enormous and obvious, and most societies are aware of this impact and more or less eager to control it and use it. The social aspect of film is worth a more serious discussion than your categories seem to allow. Simply to correlate propaganda films with performers — while witty — does not address the issue nor grapple with it in a satisfactory way.* D. S.

Propaganda film is subject to restrictions which are relevant, not to excellence, but to efficacy. A study of it should make one alert to the truth that when performers in the film are at the service of other film makers they, like the film as a performer, are subject to restrictions not designed to promote the art of performance but only the use of performers for an end alien to their art. A performance *in* a film, and a performance *by* a film, of course, differ considerably. The one is part of a film, the other is part of a viewing; the one is subject to the film, the other makes use of the film as a single whole. One would have to separate off a performance in a film from the other contributions if the comparision with the film as a performance is to be maintained.

When a performance has an overwhelmingly dominant role, a script is just an occasion, a cinemaker an opportunity, a montagist a challenge or a danger, and a director a guide. Viewers play no role, despite the fact that they are most aware of film performers, and idealize them, at the same time that performers often try to obtain parts and to perform in ways they think most viewers would endorse. Since an audience sees a cinematic performance from the position of a cinemaker, indirectly, then, or at one remove, a performance in a film is for an audience, despite the fact that the audience does not, as it does with a play, interact with it.

Though an audience does not have a direct effect on the making of a propaganda film, any more than it has on the making of any other, a viewing, and therefore an audience, is needed if the film is to have its distinctive character. Without an audience, it would be confined to the screen; with it, it can have an effect. Performers enable men to be viewers; viewers enable propagandistic films to be performers, and thereby to attain their purposed ends.

A propaganda film can become a topic for a film work of art by taking account of the propaganda's bearing, and integrating this with the rest of the film. It may then well lose its capacity to propagandize. The propaganda can itself be a work of art, and this in one of two ways: an art film could be used propagandistically to send the audience in some desired direction; or the propaganda could be taken to be a limit within which an art film is to be made, somewhat as the number of acts in a play limits its creation. In the first way, there is propaganda after the fact, having no bearing on the nature of the film or its making. In the second, one keeps within the confines of a propaganda film while engaged in making a different type of film.

A film which is to perform propagandistically is already completed. What is still to be produced by it is a change in its viewers. What it accomplishes simply by being shown, the propaganda film also aims at. Films made in order to produce a certain change on being shown — as commercial films usually are — are necessarily propagandistic — without, of course, affecting their status as popular or dramatic works. Since the other kinds of film also produce effects on being viewed, they seem to be related to the propaganda film as the uncalculated to the calculated and, so far, to be inferior to it. But it is not necessary, in order to produce a film that is not propagandistic, to ignore the effect that the film will have on its viewers. It will have an effect, and that effect can be anticipated and desired. What is essential is that the film not be governed in its making by the intent to have that effect.

A film has its own internal rhythm, inseparable from the kind of film it is. When regard is had for that rhythm, the showing of the film can be justly compared with a performance. The rhythm, and therefore the incidents of the film as integrated into a single whole, works on the viewers. It is as so working on them that the propaganda film has the role of a performance. A performance before a cinemaker, it has already been observed, need not involve any interactions of the performers, even in those cases where they are eventually shown to be talking to and acting on one another. It need not, therefore, have the kind of power that characterizes acting on a stage. There the interplay of the actors provides an opportunity for the discernment of a fundamental connection, below the level of practical life, between different men. It is this to which the audience is alerted by the acting.

Separate incidents, and the film as a whole, enable viewers to sense their solidarity with one another, under the guidance of the incidents shown. A propaganda film is concerned with the beliefs and tendencies regardless of that solidarity. It is often thought, though, that propaganda film, particularly when made on behalf of political powers, brings about a sense of solidarity among its viewers. The thought is based on a confounding of the actual binding of a limited few so as to bring about some public result, with an awareness of solidarity — which may not be exhibited in action — characterizing an indefinite number of men, not only viewers. The one may be the purposed object that a propaganda film is to produce; the other is the inevitable by-product of the viewing of that or any other film. Were a propaganda film made to bring about the latter, it would be deliberately designed to do what other films inevitably do — allow it to be viewed just as a film. A propagandist might think this most desirable, hoping that somehow the propaganda would work in subterranean ways. This apparently was the way in which the Nazi-sponsored Olympics were filmed. That film had little or no propagandistic value precisely because it was so successful in its presentation of the games.[2]

3

Education is not propaganda; educational films are to be distinguished from those that are propagandistic. But it is not entirely correct to say, with Perelman: "Whereas the propagandist must, as a preliminary, gain the good will of his audience, the educator has been commissioned by a community to be the spokesman for the values it recognizes, and, as such, enjoys the prestige attaching to his office." [3] "In education, whatever its object, it is assumed that if the speaker's discourse does not always express truths, that is, theses accepted by everyone, it will at least defend values that are not a matter of controversy in the group which commissioned him. . . . he need not adapt himself to his hearers and begin with propositions that they accept. . . . While a speaker engaged in popularizing ideas must become a propagandist for the speciality he is concerned with and must fit it into a framework of a common knowledge, when a teacher sets out to introduce a particular discipline he will begin by stating the principles particular to the discipline involved." [4]

Much of what is called "education" is, to be sure, thinly disguised propaganda. Some propaganda is for the sake of education. Neither educates. Propaganda and education differ as the active and the interactive, alteration on behalf of some power and alteration for the sake of the taught. Propaganda films have something to inculcate; educational films communicate. Education operates on individuals who vary widely in their ages, preparation, interest, values, and abilities. And it operates on them in uncounted ways. It, too, may fit in "a framework of common knowledge"; it, too, may "as a preliminary, gain the good will of its audience." And the community may commission not the educator but the propagandist because it is interested in encouraging beliefs and promoting action rather than in increasing knowledge or understanding. This does not justify an identification of education and propaganda.

An educational film is also to be distinguished from a didactic film. The didactic instructs, and does so by presenting what is to be learned, but the educational teaches, and does so by engaging the mind. A didactic film is a special type of disclosive film (chapter 11); an educational film may not disclose anything. At its most extreme, a didactic film is a series of instructions to do something; it is not concerned with and usually does not affect the character, interest, growth, outlook, or intelligence. It is a teaching machine, with little educational value. At the other extreme, an educational film leads the viewer to become critical of what he has already assumed, and to dedicate himself to the task of mastering what is just beyond his grasp. It is a guide, containing no information, except so far as this serves to stimulate, evoke, or suggest. Such an ideal educational film can perhaps never be realized. As a matter of fact, it is necessary for an educational film to be didactic to some degree. Viewers need background, material, and preparation in order to become educated. Consequently, an educational film must present some facts, truths, illustrations, and instructions, in order to give the viewer a base from which to start to inquire and grow. But this is far from equating the two kinds of film. Education takes different forms at different ages. [5] A child learns first by playing. It moves on from there to learn from stories. These epitomize for it the hoped-for conquest of good over evil, innocence over trickery, kindness over brutality, youth over age. The child will be lost in dreams, though, if it is not also made to master the techniques of reading, writing, and thinking. It gets ready to be an educated youth so far as it has become disciplined, and is ready to master what skills, techniques, and its own maturation bring within its compass. Its early enjoyment of simplified drama has to be replaced by accounts serving to inspire and ennoble. The youth is thereby helped to find himself and to grasp the major outlines of the world in which he is to live. New skills must be acquired and a better use of reason developed if he is to get to the point where he is ready to become a man with a stable character, a sure sense of what is important, a steady idea of what is just and unjust, and an interest in what is worth the devotion of a lifetime. At all stages there must be pleasure and a sense of accomplishment, or there will be reluctance, resentment, even at the cost of self-denial. At the same time, there must be dissatisfaction, a sense of incompleteness, a thrusting outward, or the educational process will come to an abrupt end.

No one is properly educated who merely has the proper feelings or a sound sense of what is right and wrong. All are to be brought to the stage where they can be clearly aware of what is reliable and unreliable in what has been assumed and inherited; each is to be helped to look, beyond the practical necessities and obtrusive realities which are present every day, to the ultimate sources of principles governing and explanatory of all there is.

These ends, we have seen, are promoted by great classical and innovative art. Film, though, is too young to be classical, or both great and innovative.*

---

* I have already indicated my essential agreement with this statement — except that I have reservations in denying film has not innovated. This, it is my belief, has already been done, proven itself capable of. From the camera obscura of Leonardo Da Vinci to Fred Ott's Sneeze, from the first close-up to Griffith's true (or rather integrated) use of close-ups (Mary Pickford) to Griffith's crosscutting, I think, movies, like the special art of the stained-glass window, began on a roller coaster of innovations. R. T.

If film, because it is not yet classical and not yet both great and innovative, can not take one to the stage where fundamental principles are generated, it does not make sense to suppose that educational film can. This, because it is at the service of an end making demands which may be in conflict with, and are surely often indifferent to the requirements of art, can not directly elicit those pure expressions of the most deeply grounded emotions which it takes the greatest works of art to reach.* When education

---

* A well made educational film can be a work of art, and is an effective educational tool because it has made good use of a work of art.   *A. K.*

---

cuts through to deep emotions, it does so only so far as these have already been expressed within the contexts of feeling and dominant attitudes. Education is a process which usually brings less pleasure than some others do; rarely does it arouse one's sense of right and wrong to a high pitch.* When it appeals to what is behind these it does not get to it cleanly

---

* Although the opening of The Birth of a Nation *caused both rioting and murder in the supposedly staid city of Boston. And my own film,* Wild in the Streets, *was cited by Mayor Daley of Chicago for the reason he had barbed wire put up around the reservoirs of his fair city during the disastrous Democratic convention of 1968, along with regular police patrols. Both of these films were meant to be educational. I can speak for one. The original ending of* The Birth of a Nation, *not seen since two weeks after its opening in New York — but documented — can surely speak for the other.*   *R. T.*

---

and directly; it touches the mood and tone of a man, only as these are expressed in and through attitudes and feelings.

A disturbance of even casual feelings has reverberations in a man's very depths. Usually these are slight and hardly noticed; the depths themselves are not forced to fuller expression. But an educational film engages the mood and tone of men as already expressed in feelings and attitudes. It answers to and partly satisfies them. At the same time, it reveals the inadequacy of the feelings and attitudes, their incapacity to match what is being suggested. By presenting content that the initially expressed mood and tone can not match, an educational film awakens within the individual a need to express his mood and tone in more appropriate ways.

Educational film, like a script, must be translated into other terms. But where a script structures the production of a film, an educational film suggests prospects to be realized. By being made visual and audible, what a script states is made more determinate; by being shown, what an educational film suggests is made more indeterminate, since it is turned into a prospect governing what is to be done subsequently. Unlike the viewer of an art film who is led to express himself in consonance with the film, and unlike the viewer of a propaganda film who is led to change his state, the viewer of an educational film is led to make the very content, that is faced by expressions of his mood and tone, to be a prospect that he is to realize. What the educational film suggests does not, therefore, just answer to assessing and rectifying emotions; it provokes the individual to accept the answer as his own.

The knowledge and realities that classical and innovative art make available to men, a viewer of an educational film has before him as a prospect. He is therefore able to keep the expressions, that were appropriate to the educational film, in existence after the film is no longer viewed. His position toward the end, which an educational film promotes, is the analogue of the position he takes toward knowledge and realities after he has viewed a great classical and innovative work of art. But the prospective end is rarely clearly seen or formulated. Nor need it be. It is sufficient that it begin to do for the awakened expressions of a mood and the tone what the educational film began to do for them. The satisfaction that an educational film partly provides on being viewed is then capable of being completed, after the viewing is over, by activities directed at the full realization of the entertained prospect.

Were one content to confront the prospect that is promoted by an educational film, as a kind of congealed memory of the satisfaction which the emotions found in the course of a viewing of the film, one would be content to have a satisfaction provided for mood and tone only so far as they were involved with and were qualified by feelings and attitudes. But this would still leave an emptiness; deep emotions would have been engaged but would not have been brought into full expression and not, therefore, entirely satisfied.

Drives to criticize and to inquire are desirable outcomes of an educational process. They are sustained by the need to give the deepest emotions full expression and satisfaction. The more that knowledge is acquired and the more definitively that inquiry is directed at the sources of known and used principles, the more readily realized are the prospects which the educational film makes possible. As a consequence, the emotions aroused are given the satisfactions they require.

The purpose of an educational film is to make the viewers actively take for themselves the task of holding on to a presented prospect, and acting in terms of it. Where a propaganda film seeks to have the viewer transformed, perhaps so that he will act for the good of some power, an educational film

seeks to have him transformed in order that he do what he presumably
ought to do.* It puts a dedicated individual in between himself as viewer

* *Doesn't the educational film assume an authoritative role rather than an*
educative one — you can't ask it questions, and get answers or reactions?
                                                                    J. W.

and some desirable result it would have him bring about. Were a propaganda film directed at the attainment of that result, it would ignore the
individual's interest in attaining it, for, unlike an educational film, a propa-
gandista film has no concern for the free, creative internalization of a
prospect to whose realization one is to dedicate oneself. Both types of
film have purposes, but only the educational has as its purpose the getting
of the viewer to have a purpose of his own.

A script embodies an idea, carried out under conditions it does not control. It suffers limitations, but for the sake of a film produced through the
help of other agencies. As a rule, an educational film makes use of a script
and gives it a visual-aural form. Since that script is offered as a contribution to the making of a work of craftsmanship, able to help men become
mature civilized beings, the film itself will be subject to the limitations that
its purpose defines. It is to contain nothing but what promotes the making
of men; that condition governs its production and, so far, precludes the
following out of inclinations to produce a work of art.

An educational film can be a work of art if the purpose which it serves is
made integral to the production; the purpose will then be just a factor
taken account of in the course of a genuine creation. A work of art, too, can
be used for educational ends. The purpose which controlled the making
of an educational film will then be attached to the work of art. That film, no
matter how successfully it performs an educational function, will not,
though, be an educational film since it will not be made with education as
its primary objective.

When school children are taken to see a filmed Shakespearean play, they
are presumably to be educated by being exposed to a work of art. They
will surely be able to learn something about the plot, and will hear, with
perhaps a salutary effect, some splendid lines. Since the educational
purpose is not part of the film, it will have to be added to it, most likely by
the teacher. So far as the film is used by the teacher to change the
thought and imagination of his charges, as well as to increase their store
of facts, it will serve not an educational but a propagandistic end. To turn a
Shakespearean play into an educational work, one must control the filming

of it by the prospect of making viewers become more mature. But the children, in the supposed instance, are merely changed in belief and tendency so as to be able to make reports which justify their being exposed to the film.

Propaganda has been used successfully in politics and commerce. Films have been designed to get men to assume certain attitudes and engage in certain acts, and the men have, when exposed to the film, believed and acted in the way desired. They have supported regimes, attacked enemies, bought products, been aroused and subdued by skilled masters of the technique of persuasion. But, despite the fact that education has been the concern of men who are at least as intelligent as the propagandists, despite the fact that a great number of approaches and techniques have been tried, and despite the fact that there has been a constant checking and rechecking of students, no one seems to know how best to educate. There seems to be little knowledge even on how to get students to become self-motivated, to become interested in what is now beyond their grasp, to think, to reflect, to criticize, or to analyze.

The greatest successes in education have been attained with preschool children, particularly underprivileged ones looked after by indulgent types who loved them. These children do not seem to be able to benefit from exposure to films as much as they do from exposure to adults who enjoy their presence and ways. Since we do not have a sure grasp of what will educate more privileged children and those who are older, it does not make much sense to expect anyone to have a sound knowledge of what a good educational film should contain, how it should develop, and when it should be presented. It is too much like a script, which we not only do not know how to translate into cinematic terms, but which is not adequately supported by performance, cinemaking, montage, and directing.

CHAPTER 11

Disclosive and Documentary Films

Cinéma vérité, or "direct cinema," attempts to make film which blinks at nothing and sees everything. If preparation, performance, or organization are restrictive, arbitrary, or conventional, they are to be eliminated or minimized. There is to be a recording of untouched reality, reality as it exists at a particular moment in front of a cinemaker. Fact is to be presented without an attempt to persuade, to influence, or to make a work of art. It is to be a film without a purpose except that of exposing what in fact occurs to an impersonal cinemaker. No one is to direct the action, or to alter the events taking place (beyond the minimal unavoidable alterations caused by the film maker's presence); there is to be only a "capturing and preserving a picture of time as perceived through unstylized events."[1]

Similar to the claims that are made on behalf of *cinéma vérité* are those made on behalf of newsreels, realistic films, and "candid cameras." All seek to make evident what is actually taking place in the world. But they are different types, and are not to be identified. A newsreel restricts itself to presenting events of public interest; realistic films try to show things in the rough; a candid camera reveals what happens when people are caught off guard, usually in embarrassing situations. *Cinéma vérité,* instead, emphasizes facts, naturalness, and the cold eye.

Despite disclaimers, these different types of film all select from, interpret, and reorganize what is confronted. At the very least, their cinemakers are set up in some place; they begin filming at one time and stop at another; they attend to only some confronted items and set them at some distance from a cinemaker and, therefore, from viewers. Nor are they purposeless; all have the well-conceived purpose of giving focused items their due. Art, propaganda, and education are to be given no consideration. The film is to expose, present, make evident, and that is all. An appropriate name for all would be "disclosive film," since in their different ways, they all try to allow things to show themselves as they are.

Justice is achieved in many ways. Three stand out: courts of law, ethical decision and action, and randomness. For the courts, justice is to be brought about through the impartial administration of laws. What those laws do not encompass — the affections and affinities of people, their social promises to one another, the differential treatment of different children in the same family — the courts do not consider. Ethics, instead, takes account of what individuals intend, how they behave both in legally governed and in nonlegal situations, and what it is that an absolute good demands. It judges the law no less than it does every other set of rules. Finally, *I Ching,* tarot cards, dice, the use of random numbers, and the open market are agencies for increasing the opportunity for every item to present itself on a footing with all the others. Though they are thought of as yielding unpredictable results, the outcome of their full and prolonged play can be calculated.

All three ways of attaining justice are in accord with the traditional way of viewing it — a blindfolded figure holding a pair of scales, evenhanded, assessing things in abstraction from the dignities of those involved, deciding all questions impartially. The disclosive film seeks to give it a cinematic role, uniting the impartial and the unpredictable in an effort to act indifferently, insisting on nothing, selecting nothing, demanding nothing. It is hoped that, in this way, it will be able to disclose what is there, not what had been prearranged, interpreted, already evaluated. But this requires it to accept what is objectively selected. Some things are pushed to the fore and others into the background by the course of the world; some possibilities are now realized and in this way, and other possibilities later and in another way. Since the disclosive film refuses to accept man's selections, it must accept the world's. Yet, willy-nilly, due to the limitations of the place, time, structure, and functioning of the agencies of which it makes use, it will necessarily make selections among these. A disclosive film is not a documentary, for a documentary does not disclose, and may even distort deliberately or introduce fictional elements for the sake of conveying some state of affairs or truth. A documentary stays away from what has no unity, from what makes no sense or does nothing, and, instead, makes a choice of a topic and then, within the compass of this, chooses items which make most evident what that topic is. A disclosive film, in contrast, is interested in making evident what things are, in their full unpredictable concreteness. Gregory Battcock asks: "Certain discoveries of the Abstract Expressionists produced the liberating concept that the object need no longer be, in the traditional sense, entirely the artist's own creation.* But if his control

---

* *Neither object nor performer ever was nor even can be. This was recognized in the most tightly-controlled Louis B. Mayer or Harry Cohn situations. A quaint way of expressing it — at least in regard to performers — was given us by Elinor Glyn. She invented the word (or re-invented the word): It! Either a performer had It or he didn't have It. No cameraman, no makeup man, no director, no publicist could furnish It. This is still true. But the subject opens up a lane down which no respectable film historian has traveled well.*   R. T.

---

is now no longer total, to what extent should it be exerted? . . . What is the role of the accidental?"[2] A disclosive film seeks to get to that extreme where film makers have no control at all; everything is to be "accidental." Of course, it does not get there; if it could it would be without boundaries, as open-ended as a world in which almost nothing imaginable can be precluded.

A disclosive film has a purpose. But unlike the purpose of a propaganda or educational film, it seeks to produce an effect, not on the audience, but on history. Since it resists the tendency to refine, limit, expand, contrast, introduce, or cut out, it can not be a work of art. Instead it tries to assume something like the presumed role of a cinemaker, acceptive of whatever might occur before it.

A cinemaker can adopt the position of any of the objects in a situation, and make evident what other objects are like from the position of the chosen one. The viewer is then made to adopt the position of that object, without thereby becoming a performer. A mother's tearful joy at seeing her long lost son might be conveyed in a nondisclosive film by blurring the picture of the son in the doorway. A viewer is thereby given the opportunity to be at the position of the mother. But the disclosive film will not do this. It will show the mother's tearful joy, and it will show the son in the doorway, but not the son from the position of the mother, or the mother from the position of the son. Ideally, the cinemaker would be swung about at random, and take in whatever it happens to alight upon, though this may result in missing the mother and the son altogether, or in having them in view for a moment or so, with many incidents in between.

A disclosive film is obviously an ideal to which one can approximate but can never fully realize except with an endless amount of film, time, and disinterest. Its purpose — uninterpreted, impartial acceptance of a plurality of items — might be best achieved mechanically with a cinemaker whose lenses, distances, angles, are determined by the apparently random operations of a computer. It would not have to attend to more than a very limited situation, chosen perhaps at random; this itself has richness enough to justify a disclosure of unlimited duration.

At one and the same time, a disclosive film makes cinemaking the only film making that is to be done, and denies it any controlling role. A cinemaker's presence is to be allowed to usurp the places of other film makers, and the cinemaker is to function without control. Its purpose is to be realized by having it act purposelessly.*

---

* It seems to me that cinéma vérité is an absolute misnomer when used in this sense. I think every film critic knows this is the case and uses the phrase, actually, to describe a certain kind of controlled but infinitely circumscribed improvisation — i.e., Marlon Brando's reminiscenses about his life in Last Tango in Paris. The phrase is as far removed from a literal meaning.   R. T.

Every film whatsoever, is disclosive, for each shows what something is. This is one of the reasons, perhaps, why it is often said that all film is naturalistic. But, of course, the setting that is accepted, even if it be in the wilds, is artificial, betraying the selections and values of men. And all selection involves interpretation, evaluation, and, most likely, exaggeration.

Someone acting self-consciously before a cinemaker is doing what supposedly is "artificial." That self-conscious acting can be made the object of disclosure as surely as any other. If a performance is affected by the fact that it and a cinemaker are together the object of a disclosive filming, the latter can itself be treated as part of a single situation together with the performer and the cinemaker. That triad can in turn be the object of another disclosive filming. To avoid an infinite regress, or at least a regress with constantly diminishing returns, one might hide the final disclosive filming so that its operation has no affect on what is disclosed. Strictly speaking, the situation that is caught by a disclosive film cannot stop with a cinemaker or with any object with which the performer is ostensibly interacting; many other objects have some role in determining the way in which a performer functions. Past and future, near and remote objects contribute to the meaning and being of the simplest act. Nothing less than the whole film might have to be devoted to the encompassment of all the objects which play a part in having the act occur then and in that way. If by complete disclosure of what in fact is occurring, one means a disclosure of what something is in a world with other objects whose relationship to it must be shown, no film is ever long enough.

If it be recognized that, at the very least, a great number of objects and relationships must be encompassed in order to let one see an incident as it objectively occurs, and that no film could ever be long enough to take them all in, it becomes obvious that a disclosive film, like any other, dislocates and abstracts, and therefore is never completely objective or impartial. Still, there is a difference between a disclosive film and all other kinds, that keeps them forever distinct. Where other films seek to show a performance in some relation to a cinemaker and, therefore, to an audience which will eventually assume the position adopted by the cinemaker, a disclosive film tries to absent itself at the same time that it makes filmed items present. Concerned with presenting a performance as it might be seen by the indifferent eye of eternity, it offers a standard that nothing else measures, a limit inside of which all else is. Because all filming makes a difference, telling us not what is there but what is there so far as it can be caught on film, the absenting of a disclosive film can be only partially successful.

The one thing that a disclosive film can not do is to disclose itself,* except

---

*Not entirely true if one wants to take this category seriously. In The Chelsea Girls, Bridget Polk, for example, frequently addressed, abused, shouted at the cameraman. The cameraman's responses were recorded and allowed to remain in the film.   R. T.

---

at the cost of ceasing to be a disclosive film. If it were the object of a disclosure, it would be by means of a different disclosive film, which itself was not the object of its own disclosure. One can imagine a disclosive film being filmed through the aid of mirrors and similar agencies, but if those mirrors are not also filmed, there is no adequate disclosure, while, if they, too, are filmed there is no direct filming of their being filmed. Were a disclosive film directed solely at what was mirroring it, not it but only its mirror images would be disclosed. All this underscores the fact that a disclosive film stands outside that which it discloses; what is disclosed is disclosed for it, or before it, never to it.

A disclosive film has realized its purpose before it is viewed. This allows it to be given another purpose afterwards. It can be used as an instrument of propaganda or education (and, to anticipate, for escape) as, of course, other films, even works of art, can be. It can be used as raw material which is to be subject to montaging, so as to produce a film that is to entertain, or which is thereby to be made into a work of art; but, because the film pays no attention to what such montaging needs, it would be only by the sheerest accident that it would contain much that could be used.* Too

---

* *Von Stroheim for the orgy sequences — almost entirely censored — of the* Merry Widow *and* The Wedding March *did, however, use* cinéma vérité *in this manner. He would lock his* chosen *extras* and *principals on a sound stage for two or three days at a time, supply them generously with liquor, drugs, caviar, force them to stay awake. He had four and five cameras following the celebration at the same time. From the miles of film he exposed, he got some fascinating results, intending in each case to cut from what had developed into a real orgy, an artistic orgy. In both instances, Von Stroheim was, as things go, fired from the films before he had the opportunity to do this. A certain Hollywood montagist, getting hold of the cut takes, did it for him, producing a privately shown feature* One Delirious Night. *The editor died when his home burned to the ground.* That *is another story. But future historians will, undoubtedly, find dupes of* One Delirious Night *and we will, perhaps, then better understand what could come out of paying attention to and montaging disclosive film.*   *R. T.*

---

little attention would have been given to questions of lighting, positioning, distancing, angling, negative spaces, silences, and obstacles. Or, where proper attention was given to them, they would be dealt with disclosively, and their instrumental roles obscured.

A disclosive film can, of course, attend to something exercising an instrumental role. When it does, the disclosive film will sacrifice one topic of disclosure for another. An instrumental object is something by itself — as everything else is — but to see it as such it is necessary to disconnect it from its instrumental role. To catch it only in its instrumental role, is to attend to its functioning but not to what it is itself. A golf stroke is to be disclosed in one manner if what we wish to exhibit is the way in which a ball is to be hit; it is to be disclosed in another if what we wish to exhibit is the transition from the beginning to the end of a stroke. If it is broken up into parts for easier understanding, the one will have parts related as condition to conditioned, where the other will have them related as before to after. The one will disclose the hitting of a golf ball, the other the nature of a golfing stroke — which may be allowed to come to an end before the ball moves.

Each thing has an instrumental or mediating role. At the very least, it separates or connects other entities. A disclosive film, consequently, can disclose only one side of whatever it is that it focuses on; it must neglect either what the entity is or how it functions, in order to attend to the other side. If full disclosure is the objective, it would therefore be necessary to make use of no less than two disclosive films of the very same occurrence, the one facing it in its full concreteness as something objective, the other facing it in its role as an intermediary between other occurrences of objects. The question of how the two disclosures are to be related would still be left over.

This tangle of logical, philosophical, and methodological problems is in part a consequence of the fact that the idea of a perfect disclosure conflicts with that of a film. To make a film satisfy the extrinsic purpose of disclosure is to sacrifice the making, the election, and the interlocking of its elements in a sensuously experienced excellence for the sake of objectivity and impartiality.*

What is a disclosive film? Name one! I can't think of any films that fall into the category. In all these cases, you should be citing examples. Aristotle deigned to talk about particular plays; you should not be so shy about mentioning real films, just to allow readers to get the categories straight.   *D. S.*

Objectivity and impartiality are desirable but not completely attainable; neither is the primary concern of one who would produce a work of art. A film, to be sure, can be made in order to realize them to an unusual degree. The realization will be maximally achieved, however, not by foregoing the effort to make a work of art, but by producing one, for this shows what things really are. If truth is what one seeks to obtain by means of film, the film must be so made that it can tell well what a film can. But this requires that one not even seek to have a truth presented. Truths are inevitably portrayed and conveyed in films that are works of art.

2

Propagandistic, educational, and disclosive films all have conspicuous realistic aspects. So does a documentary: "a documentary picture is a fact film in which the story stems out of a real and, therefore, realistic locale, photographed on location at the actual scene of the story and using the actual people concerned with that story."[3] It is not disclosive. "Strictly speaking, the information film is not a true documentary; the great artists who have developed the form are not primarily concerned with conveying information or aiding future research. They are engaged in 'the creative treatment of actuality.' "[4]

Documentary is a distinctive type of film with its own purpose. Since it offers a primary meaning which the viewer's world is to instance, it takes on something like the position of a director whose idea of the whole guides the ways in which other creative film workers function, without loss to their own independence. It is not itself, though, the exclusive work of a director. Usually a script is used; certain incidents and performers have to be focused on; there is definitely a technical and, hopefully, a creative use of a cinemaker; and montaging is unavoidable. Were all of these blacked out, the result would be a sequence of photographs, not a film, and surely not a great film.

When Warhol allowed his cinemaker to run on for hours facing the Empire State Building, he had already decided to be a director. He had something like a script in mind which told him when to begin and when to end, to focus on the building and not on those who might use it, and the like. He placed his cinemaker at a certain position, set it at a particular pace, equipped it with a specific type of lens, attended to the performance of lights and shadows in interaction with the building, and made the montagistic decision to allow the incidents to remain in the order in which they were filmed. He produced a film by assuming the positions of the different film makers, and carrying them out in some harmony.

A documentary is focused on individuals or objects which sustain and help constitute unit incidents. The individuals or objects need not be performers; they could be just factors in a "realistic" performance to which setting, background, lighting, and other parts of a scene made the major contributions.* It is the documentary's purpose, and not its "realistic"

---

* *It is also interesting that performers in documentaries, not being trained actors, can not vary the style of their performances very much. Policemen, therefore, in* Law and Order, *beat up blacks even though there was a camera and a sound rig operating within a few feet—because that was what they generally did, and they believed it to be correct behavior. The making of documentaries relies on an inability of mankind to change*

behavior very much — and I should think that was interesting enough to
mention.   *D. S.*

performances which make no use of professional performers, that mark
it off from other kinds of film.* It seeks to convey the truth of what occurs,

* *Which makes me think of the discussion of performers, earlier on. If*
Cagney is always Cagney, because he can not possibly be other, then
the simple fact that his appearance continues from one film to
another tends to make him a star (in the generally accepted sense — not
in your sense). If he succeeds as a star in the generally accepted sense,
it is likely that he will become a star in your sense.   *D. S.*

and that purpose is often best realized by attending to "realistic"
performances produced by nonprofessionals.
"The most succinct and widely quoted definition is that of Mr. Grierson.
'Documentary,' he says, 'is the creative treatment of actuality.' [*Cinema
Quarterly*, vol. 2, no. 1, p. 8.] There is to be no limit to its practical powers.
Mr. Rotha explains: 'Documentary defines not subject or style, but
approach. It denies neither trained actors[5] nor the advantages of
staging. It justifies the use of every known technical artifice to gain its
effect on the spectator. . . . To the documentary director the appearance
of things and people is only superficial. It is the meaning behind the thing
and the significance underlying the person that occupy his attention. . . .
Documentary approach to cinema differs from that of story-film not in its
disregard for craftsmanship, but in the purpose to which that craftsmanship
is put. . . . [*Ibid.* vol. 2, no. 2, p. 78.]"[6]
Because documentaries are designed to convey truths, they would seem
to be ideal agents for recording historically important events, for reporting
what is of current interest, and as educational aids. But if nothing else
is done but to allow the events to make an imprint on a negative roll of
film, no documentary is made; and if a documentary is made, those events
will have been interpreted, dramatized, reordered, condensed, expanded,
and creatively interrelated. "No documentary can be completely truthful,
for there can be no such thing as truth while the changing developments
in society continue to contradict each other. Not only this, but technical
reasons also preclude the expression of a completely accurate
representation. It is often suggested that documentary has close similarity
to the newsreel. By the trade they are naturally confused because they
both, in their respective ways, deal with natural material. But there the

likeness ends. Their approach to and interpretation of that material are widely different. The essence of the documentary method lies in its dramatization of actual material. The very act of dramatizing causes a film statement to be false to actuality."[7]

Films that provide reports, recordings, and lessons may be propagandistic, educational, or disclosive. These, too, can attend to performances which do not involve the assumption of roles by performers; these, too, can be creatively produced by film makers working coordinately, or with one of them in a dominant role. A documentary, like these others, is controlled by its own noncinematic end. Its object is to have the viewer learn by having him see a truth exhibited, not in some imagined world which has no bearing on ours, but in a part of our world, which for the moment is being governed by that truth.

"For Flaherty, however, all film making was an exploration. He consistently refused to work from prepared shooting scripts, or preconceived stories, preferring to discover his theme, his characters, his settings with his camera."[8] The result was a more accurate report of what occurred than a mere recording could provide. Such a recording makes no provision for the dramatic translations that must be made if one is to learn what is irreducibly desirable and undesirable.

It would seem at first as though a documentary could not be used to portray the malignant, the excellent, the regrettable, the wanted, the tragic — and that does not appear to be the case. A documentary, though, is concerned, not with the particular incidents which it in fact films, but with what allows one to see that the regrettable is indeed what ought not to be, and that what ought to be should be. Normally it tells one more about what the maker of it cherished than it does about what it portrays. Ideally, it conveys what everyone should cherish, and in terms of which what is filmed and what is not are to be measured.

A documentary seeks to make its audience look at the actual world in a new spirit. Its "realism" is for the sake of enabling viewers to grasp the entire import of what is, and to become aware of the obstacles which are in the way of its realization. They are to be presented with an honest account which requires them to pass beyond what is seen and heard to a value that deserves to be preserved. Its message is promoted, not by attempting to approach the "realism" of the disclosive film, but by emphases, omissions, and translations, all at the service of the value celebrated. The audience is not to accept what it sees as that with which it is to identify itself; it is not to take it as something to be acted toward or to be known or believed, or as providing an occasion for an escape from unnecessary limitations, but as instancing, positively or negatively, what ought to be.

A documentary can be known to do justice to what it confronts if one is able to match the filmed with the unfilmed, a separated with an un-separated occurrence. The two are different and remain so; otherwise no matching occurs. But the two must be identical in meaning, or there is no translation of the one into the other. The two conditions are met if the incident in the documentary contains the meaning of what it had been dislocated from.

A filmed incident is as distinct from the incident, as apart from the film, as an isolated fragment is from an organically necessary element. The fragment is denied its neighbors, its functioning in relation to them, its support of or for them, and the way it and they interplay. What occurs in fact has whatever neighbors it happens then to have. To do justice to what occurs in fact, one therefore would have to compensate for the dislocation the film introduces, by producing new neighbors and new connections. Only then could one hope to approximate what the occurrence was in the world.

With every film we face the same task that we do with a play, a concert, a dance, a poem, or a story — or even a sentence. Over the course of an encounter with any of them, it is necessary to retain and alter whatever meaning had been obtained from what had gone before, and to revise what had been supposed in the light of what is later discovered. The import of a film undergoes changes in the course of its unfolding, hope-fully in such a way that the final outcome is in accord with what the film makers wanted to produce.

Today one can see double features, at times a documentary followed by a film having only minimal documentary content. Each is a single, completed whole, cut off from the other. That fact points up the importance of the idea of the film as a whole, and its realization in the form of a unity which not only determines what the parts should be and how they are to be related, but the radical separation of each film from all the rest.

Men enter into the world of film, as they enter into all others — episodically. They tend to define the areas of their practical activities as primary, and to speak of their entrance into the others as escapes, or as occasions for relaxation. But one can, with as much justice, give priority to the worlds of religion, speculation, or art, and see the occupation with practical matters to provide an escape, or as an opportunity to relax from more strenuous

and difficult occupations. No matter how inviting other prospects be, and how well defended by great artists, philosophers, and religious leaders, however, everyone takes the familiar, everyday world to provide a base in terms of which to measure the reliability, the reality, and perhaps even the desirability and value of all the others. Both theoretical scientists and speculative philosophers come back to it again and again, not only as individuals but in their professional capacities, to make sure they are not dreaming or spinning out idle hypotheses. The familiar world, though, is somewhat inchoate, overrun with dogmatisms and superstitions; it is imprecise and discontinuous; it needs to be rectified again and again. A documentary, because it offers an accurate translation of what is in that world, and does this better the better it is made, provides one with an unusual opportunity both to remain with the familiar world and to avoid its incoherence, diffusion, and boring intervals. This does not mean that a documentary is superior to other purposive films. The fact that it does not appeal to everyone, or to anyone all the time, and the fact that there are other worthwhile purposes that can be promoted by film, is evidence enough of its limitations. More important, its very purpose, to capture the import of some real occurrence, precludes the acceptance of it as a work of art. Documentaries about scientific methods and results, religious experiences, and philosophic inquiry and knowledge are both possible and desirable. Not many attempts to provide them have been made, perhaps because the audience for them is not large, perhaps because there is a strong tendency to become didactic, propagandistic, or instructive with the available material, perhaps because what is readily graspable in these enterprises is superficial and what is original and important is hard to know without considerable technical knowledge, training, and sophistication. Yet one could conceivably make a good documentary in all three fields. It will not necessarily attend to the methods, results, practitioners, or pursuits of these enterprises, but it must convey their meaning and thrust. Just how this is to be done is a problem. In principle it does not seem to be any more difficult of solution than the problem of how to produce a documentary of a primitive village, a hunt, or a mountain climb. These, too, have their esoteric sides to be mastered only with difficulty. In all cases a documentary must see to it that an essence is conveyed, usually not through a "realistic" portrayal.
There is no topic which could not be dealt with in a documentary. It can enter into a studio or classroom; it can focus on a basketball game, a formal dance, an animal, or even an inanimate object. It seeks to grasp

what they are, but not as they are to the unreflecting glance — though, it can, of course, deal with them as the objects of such a glance. What it looks at may be approached by others naïvely, but it itself is never naïve. As sophisticated as the best of propagandistic films, as insinuating as the best of educational films, as attentive to what is before it as the best of disclosive films, it tries to make the viewer see what is essential to what is observed, and thereupon to see what is essential to the world in which he lives.

Documentaries begin and end with what is freshly observed; what they present is a translation of what is there encountered. They are as purposive as disclosive films, but, unlike these, seek to communicate the import rather than the obtrusive aspects of what is seen and heard. Unlike the propaganda films, they do not try to make viewers change their minds or relationships, or to engage in certain actions. Unlike the educational film, they do not try to help the viewers mature. Instead, they aim at having men look at the world in a new way, not on behalf of some power, or in order to improve themselves, but on behalf of what is there.*

---

*Your treatment of documentaries is pretty good, but even so could be improved. Discuss some particular documentaries! Flaherty and Wiseman never use scripts, shoot at ratios of seventy or eighty to one, do all the discovery in the cutting, and impose upon the raw stuff of external reality (and uncut film) the mood and tone of their own personalities. Inasmuch as a documentary is mostly a process of selection and elimination, it is the most highly personal of all film making. Other kinds of theatrical film, being inclusive, are collaborative and less personal. By being intentional, and by having scripts and performers, their range is that of attitude and feeling, highly structured. The depths of personal tone are seldom touched.   D. S.

CHAPTER 12

Escapist and Experimental Films

Incidents are filmed in an order dictated in part by a script, and in part by finances and circumstances. Sequences intended to follow on one another are sometimes filmed weeks and miles apart; sequences making use of the same performers and scenes, though they deal with unrelated incidents, may have to be filmed one after the other. That is not all. For dramatic purposes, for the sake of clarification, in order to heighten or to change the import of an incident, an incident may have to be related in specific ways to certain other incidents, which may have been filmed in different circumstances and times, and associated with positions quite remote from it.

The inescapable selections of a cinemaker, which are determined by the mechanics of production, and the effective use of time, money, and men, must be subjected to further selections governed by the effort to make the best use of some of the film that has been made available. The result is a new import for the incidents finally selected, with a consequent distinctive meaning given to the film as a whole. These changes are produced by montaging. It creatively subdivides, interpenetrates, connects, and synthesizes incidents already filmed. The escapist film offers an analogue.

The escapist film is made for the purpose of getting viewers to achieve positions from which to assess encountered regions. Travelogues, historic spectacles, "futuristics," "horror" pictures, sexist films, and comics present other places, times, causal operations, procedures, and transitions in such a way as to allow one to see that regions are occupied in daily life in only a few of the ways they can be occupied. To show this, the escapist film might deal with the very same incidents on which a propagandistic, educational, disclosive, or documentary film fastens, but it will, in contrast with them, avoid persuasion, enrichment, fact, or understanding, to attend instead to making evident how extended regions could be occupied in other ways. The strangeness of the incidents that are filmed is not its primary concern; it is just a means by which the viewer is most readily led away from an identification with filmed performers, incidents, and situations, to a position from which he can see the familiar world as one of many possible. The odder, the more alien, the more disconnected the film's incidents are from anything with which a viewer is acquainted, the easier it is for him to avoid an acceptance of either what is filmed or what he daily lives through.

Something like this result is approximated occasionally by poor films, with their stylized characters and routine plots. They do not provide complete escapes, in part because this is not their purpose, and in part because they do not discourage the viewer's identification with some part of what is filmed. Offered as entertainment or as dramas, they fail to do more than present special ways in which regions can be occupied. More often than not, these are treated as good and strong, or as weak and bad. The different modes of occupation are offered for acceptance and rejection, but not as challenges to the finality of what daily occurs.

An escapist film is designed to permit a full effortless escape, by enabling one to take up an endlessly specifiable position. This is best done by enabling the viewer to see that what is on the film is alternative to what is familiar. By escaping *into* an escapist film one begins a move *from* a blind acceptance of daily modes of occupying extended regions. It is such a beginning, though, only when it is lived in as though it were complete in itself and, therefore, seems not to be a beginning at all. Otherwise it would not be participated in, but just looked at. The emotions that it is to excite and satisfy may be emotions excited and satisfied by other films. But the oddities that the film exhibits are there for contrast, not for living through or with; they allow one to recognize that the familiar ways in which extensions are occupied could be different—not necessarily better, not necessarily worse, but sufficiently different to make one aware, as one had not been before, that they could have been otherwise. One might lose oneself in an escapist film, as one might lose oneself in a daydream; one might excitedly share in the strange doings as one might share in an imagined adventure. But such losings and sharings in the film come to an end, and one finds oneself no longer free from the familiar. If one is to escape by means of a film, one must both become aware of incidents as alternatives to what one in fact lives through and accept those alternatives as privileged standpoints.

An escapist travelogue takes the viewer to exotic, new places, with strange foliage and activities, inhabited by beings whose ways are at odds with his own. It is not primarily concerned with conveying information about another people, or even with making one acquainted with new places. It seeks to show what space is able to contain, and that space is capable of being intensified in ways other than those we daily know. A film could be used to portray some historic occurrence for propagandistic, educational, disclosive or documentary purposes. It could portray it, too, as an escape. The more diverse its time and its events are from those with which the viewer is daily familiar, the easier it is to become aware that both the portrayed and the viewer's own times are specifications of a common temporality. The film will not give history a visual-audible form; a reenactment of history is exactly what is not wanted on the screen. Filmed historic spectacles are not re-presentations of history; they could not be without being overrun with details and irrelevancies, with tedious periods, with confusions and waitings beyond the capacity of anyone to endure, if he is not one of the principals. Nor do they take one into the past, for one can never go backward in time. Or into the future, for one can not get there without living through a series of present times. They do not even lead a man to imagine himself in the past or future; he remains here and now, spellbound perhaps, earthbound surely, and distinct from what he sees. But historic spectacles, by showing what might have been or could be, enable him to see all particular times as alternatives to one another.

What had been, what will be, and what is, all fill out temporal stretches. To readily confront odd ways in which the stretches can be filled out, it is desirable to give them dates other than our own, usually by portraying incidents which are related to but can not possibly occupy the present. The more dissimilar the temporal occurrences are from any of those we live through, the more surely are other dates emphasized, and the more difficult it is for us to imagine ourselves to be in fact present at them. But we can escape into them on the way to an escape into the time which all limited times specify.

"Horror" films are part of a large class of escapist films designed to dislodge viewers from the limited causal chains with which they are familiar. These films use a highly general idea of causality by means of which familiar causal sequences can be directly contrasted with others, having a different pace and effect. The films do not seem to have the kind of undesirable consequences that are sometimes attributed to them, usually by adults who do not look at them. "Horror" films do not turn the audience into fiends or perverts. The effects, more likely than not, are salutary, since they alert viewers to some of the possible specifications to which a highly generic causality can be subject. At its best, the film will lead to an awareness that causality can have an indefinite number of instantiations.

Films with sex as their main topic could be propagandistic, educational, disclosive, or documentary — surely so, for the innocent, inhibited, and young. Those who oppose their viewing take them to be essentially propagandistic, leading men and women to engage in odd and disruptive sexual practices on behalf of some anti-establishment, disruptive freedom of individuals. The films, consequently, are strongly opposed by conservative governments, and by those who adopt their ideology and programs. They are said to be "pornographic," i.e., obscene, repulsive, deserving to evoke disgust on being seen, and in some cases to be capable of awakening undesirable appetites. Taken to be intrinsically repugnant and to produce an intrinsically repugnant expression of lust, they are nevertheless recognized to be films that many people want to see. It is for their own good, those in power decree, that the people are to be denied the opportunity to see them, no matter how much this be desired. Unlike a work of art, whatever emotions an inferior work awakens can get no satisfaction from that work; instead it leads one to act so that those emotions get some satisfaction elsewhere. Those who object to sex films seem, so far, to be justified. But they overlook the fact that the films need not be propagandistic in purpose or outcome, but might be educational, or just disclosive. A sex film might even be a documentary, enabling the viewer to become aware of values that he otherwise might have overlooked. The objectors also neglect to consider the possibility that a sex film might be escapist in both purpose and effect. This it would be, if it were made to lead the viewer to recognize his own actual or imagined practices as alternative specifications of an ideal sexual performance. That ideal performance would not be portrayed on the film; there, alternatives to ordinary performances would be displayed, but in such a way as to lead one to see them as alternatives, and therefore as specifying something more general. One would then escape into what the film portrayed, and from there to what it conveyed. The film itself would be made to function as a montagist between different sexual practices, actual or imagined, contrasting them, grading them, making some into reasonable variants and others into those which are to be set aside.

A sex film, like a horror film, puts most emphasis on causality, but as limited within the area of a distinctive kind of performance. Other types of performance, alternative to those normally carried out, provide opportunities to produce escapist films to be classified with the sexist.

Western, romantic war, and gangster films show the viewer behaviors alternative to his, not for him to adopt, but as means for an escape to a position where he can look at what he does as only one of the things that could be done.

Travelogues hold tightly to the conventional ways of making use of time and causation; historic spectacles lose their plausibility if they present too odd an account of the occupation of space or the working of causality; horror pictures have their greatest impact when they keep space and time conventional while they play variations on the process of causation; sex films, to be successful, have to show the performances as possible to the viewers. To break with all three dimensions of existence and ordinary activities at the same time, one must have recourse to untrammeled, disconnected occurrences. These the comic films portray. They too, are escapist, playing variations on space, time, and causality indifferently. As in the other escapist films, the viewer avoids identifying himself and his world with what takes place there, but not without becoming aware that he and his world need not have been as they are.

Comic film allows one to escape from the particularized guises which space, time, and causality have been found to take. It introduces one to existence, not as it is in itself, but as that which is daily specified in what one now sees is not the only or the best or the worst of ways. A cosmic montagist, the comic film allows one to contrast the specifications of existence with which one is familiar with other conceivable ways in which it might be specified.

Escapist films are made with a purpose. Unlike the purposes characteristic of propagandistic, educational, disclosive, and documentary films, that purpose often is not known, or deliberately chosen. Yet it is sometimes carried out more successfully than those others are, as a consequence of the fact that its purpose is embodied in it. It seeks to affect the audience by bringing about results exterior and usually subsequent to the viewing of the film. Those results are achieved, not by trying to change the state of the audience, or by trying to do justice to the nature of what is filmed, but by then and there exhibiting alternatives which radically contrast with the ways in which space, time, causality, and actions are familiarly specified. What an escapist film presents is to be sharply contrasted with the familiar world. The makers of escapist films do not, therefore, have to call on any technical knowledge about the ways in which people are influenced, or educated, or about what things are like when least distorted. But they do need the ability to film genuine alternatives to what is daily known, for the purpose not of having the viewers share in those adventures, but of freeing them from accepted contingent restraints. The viewers are not only to distinguish what they daily acknowledge from what they are imaginatively sharing in, but to contrast the two as distinct instances of the same generic condition.

The normal inclination of a viewer is to identify himself with what is occurring in the film, or to adapt or subject himself to its course and values. The escapist film fights that inclination by presenting incidents that are at once "realistic" and unassimilable. The realism allows him to take the incidents to be regions of the same extensions which daily occupied regions also specialize; the unassimilability requires him to contrast what is being viewed with what he daily acknowledges. As the former, the film takes the position of a montagist; as the latter, it provides alternatives to be related to what is daily known or done.*

Either I don't understand, or I disagree with your comments about escapist films. I'd call escapist films directorial, rather than montagist, and I find it puzzling that you have thrown about 80% of all film into one category which gets only a few pages of cursory prose. This may be an unavoidable bind, because if you believe that art leads us toward exist- ence, and most films lead away from existence, then the art film is an intellectual construction, not necessarily a good film, but one that accom- modates to your theory. Most film is escapist, and some escapist film is art film. Horror films, westerns, gangster films, comedies, are all probably versions of the pastoral, in Empson's sense, reducing and simplifying, making diminished models by which, circuitously, we can be led toward reality rather than away from it. You must consider from what these films escape, and to what their escape seems to tend.   D. S.

A montagist makes a film with the help of other creative film makers. Were he to dispense with their cooperation or support, he would lose the benefit of the stable articulate structure that the script provides, the interpretations which a good performer introduces, the even-handed acceptance of confronted items that characterize the cinemaker, and the overall guidance of a director. He would be reduced to the status of a collagist, one who pieces together found objects, to produce a single work which has them together in a way that overrides their distinctive natures. The script would be used just as a set of suggestions, the performers would provide focused content, the cinemaker would give him raw material, and the director would state some general idea which the montagist was to realize in his own way. When a film has the role of a montagist, it, too, has to be limited. Daily occurrences and portrayed incidents have to be allowed to stand on a footing; the common generic situation must be made available, and the purpose — escape into a governing general condition — allowed to control.

2

The purpose of experimental film is to lead one to escape into it in order to escape from the limitations of other films. It is intended, therefore, to be an escapist film in the world of film. Consequently, it must attend to the different conditions which govern accepted film making, and provide alternatives to these, thereby prompting an awareness of what film as such is, film as a generic meaning instanced by actual films. Some of the alternative possibilities have been brilliantly exploited;[1] some have not even been tried out. To know those possibilities is to extend one's understanding of what film might be and do.

Script: An experimenter may refuse to take any written guidance. To avoid having some plan in mind or even having it held to unconsciously, he might have recourse to the operation of machines, to random selections, to arbitrarily isolated pieces. He might take some previously used script and use it in a new way, perhaps by exaggerating some parts, minimizing others, or by introducing spacings and joinings neither specified nor forbidden. He might make use of material not intended for a script — newspaper clippings, letters, conversations overheard or remembered; he might interlard one script with another; mix up different languages; reformulate or even produce a script by using a computer, or add to what is written further instructions about gestures and placings. He might make use of a number of scripts which have no evident relationship to one another, and interrelate them in any one of an indefinite number of ways. He might incorporate ideas, turns, narrative lines just conceived in the course of a filming. His script could restate what had been filmed for the sake of making still another film. It might be used for a part of a film, for a number of films at the same time, or to provide suggestions and directions which are to be denied. It could be deliberately expressed ambiguously, or in such a way as to permit the user to make any one of a number of choices; it could be presented as a series of disjunctions, or as capable of being begun at any point and proceeding from there in any order, each requiring different incidents and performances. It might be set to music, expressed in diagrams, codes, or made into a puzzle. Different cinemakers could be given different scripts to follow. These, and other treatments of the script, might be followed by conventional film making. One or more film makers might add their experiments to the experiments explored in the script. But, whether others experiment or not, a script could alert them to possibilities not normally envisaged. The primary contribution that an experimental script can make, though, is enabling writers to grasp the essence of what a script as such is, and therefore to see all actual scripts as so many alternative specifications of it. They will then have escaped to where they ought to be — where great scripts can be made. Great scripts catch the import of the primal script that all of them instantiate.*

The economics for such film making do not yet (if they ever will) exist. Nor is there a place — politically — for such experimentation. It is perhaps the duty of philosophers to daydream, but anyone engaged in film making must convert daydreaming into a financially viable career, unless they begin, like Conrad Rooks, as multimillionaires.   R. T.

Performance: An experimental film could be made without performers. Even with all conditions fixed, there would still be a minimal performance produced through the accumulative effectiveness of the past in the present. The result would be alternative to the usual performance carried out before a cinemaker. So also would a performance be, which was produced by attending only to the background, to the setting, or to passing occurrences.

Performances would be produced even if one focused on the same object for an indefinite time; even if one eliminated all changes in lights and shadows, all motions, and whatever occurred in and about the object or which was produced in the course of a filming. There will always be an accumulated effect. Even a fixated object on a film does not yield a mere still, since it thrusts beyond the screen and is counterbalanced by an audience. Performances can also be produced by placing objects on the film itself; by cartoons, drawings, and puppets; by changing the positions and angles of a cinemaker; by increasing or dimming lights; by beginning, interrupting, and ending actions arbitrarily and abruptly; by repeating or utilizing previous filmed performances; by filming films; by attending to the outputs of computers, chemicals, electricity; by using microscopes, telescopes, distorting mirrors; and by filming the visible effects of sounds. Some of these experiments are hardly to be distinguished from experiments with a cinemaker. Indeed, one might deliberately seek to blur that distinction as well as those between performers and scriptists, montagists, or directors. A script itself might even be turned into a performer. Montaging could be, as it was with Eisenstein, a way of making the inanimate appear to be animate. A director himself could be a performer, or be made part of the performance he was directing. An individual could be treated as though he were a number of different performers, all carrying out the same incident; a number of different performers could be taken to be different aspects of a single individual. A performance might have a portion elided by the simple expedient of having it continue, but stopping the cinemaker for a while. A performance could be made to overlap others by having the same film run through the cinemaker again and again. It could be given different settings, meanings, paces, supports, caught in slow time or fast, or carried out as though it were on a stage with characteristic theatrical emphases, exaggerations, and rhythms. It could be produced by one who showed that he knew he was being filmed; the performer could be self-conscious; he could deliberately look at the cinemaker and listen to the director; he could be seen being instructed and guided.

Anything that can be recorded on the experimental film is a performance for it, distinct from the performances characteristic of other films, and enabling one to become aware of a generic performance, of which all actual performances are specifications. It can lead one to know what a performance ideally is and, therefore, what every actual performance makes evident in a limited guise.

Experiments have not been carried out as far as they might be if Renan is correct when he says: "The ultimate to date in the nonobjective film is Tony Conrad's *The Flicker*. It has only black and white frames. They are alternated in varying patterns, and the resulting strobe effect can set off strong reactions in the mind of the viewer. It can cause the illusion of color, of spreading light, and of lacy patterns." [2] The limits of possible performances extends as far as the cinemaker's use allows. A "nonobjective" film which showed various shades of blue or lines of different sizes, shapes, and colors, or which recorded random drippings on a lens, would be just as "ultimate" as Conrad's. And so would combinations of these experiments and of others, only some of which are here outlined.

Cinemaker: In the course of the discussion of experiments with script and performance, some experiments with a cinemaker were also indicated. It is not always easy to draw a line between what is done in one of these areas and what is done in the others.

One might use old film, overexposed film, mutilated film; one might overexpose and underexpose it; one might deliberately dirty it, treat it with chemicals, tear it, mark it up; one might try developing it in new ways with various kinds and degrees of lighting, kept steady, constantly changing, or varied at random. There could be many cinemakers used for the same performance, set at many different angles and at various distances. They could be made to work together haphazardly or under the direction of arbitrary decisions, codes, or musical cues; they could be used to shoot from above or below, from under water, behind slits, through changing barriers, at different speeds, distances, and angles, determined without regard for what in fact was occurring. They could interact with the performers, be directed at themselves through the aid of mirrors, made to function erratically, be allowed to include all the lead-ins, the sprockets, and any other auxiliary aids which are utilized but not normally shown in a well-controlled film.*

---

* Again, all these techniques are employed — the inclusion of lead-ins and sprockets as late as Ingmar Bergman's Persona. There was a famous "dirty" camera at M.G.M., which was used for the glamour shots of female stars. One day an apprentice made the mistake of cleaning it and Garbo never looked so good again.   R. T.

A cinemaker is a machine whose capacities and promise, whose development and modifications are as limitless as the ingenuity of engineers allows. Though there are experimentalists who have had a cinemaker run without any film in it at all, or who have tried to use it as though it were an ordinary camera, it seems reasonable to say that its minimal use requires the passing of film under some light to record something that contrasts with something else.

No one knows what a cinemaker can do until he tries to use it in new ways. And when he does, he will make evident to others how narrow the limits are within which the cinemaker has been used. There is a generic meaning to "cinemaker" which an experimental film can let us know, if we boldly use cinemakers to provide recordings that are alternative to those with which we are familiar.

Montaging: Some theorists have distinguished different types of montaging. A collision montaging has been contrasted with montaging as linkage, and these two with montaging as collaging, a superimposition of images.[3] The distinctions seem not to be important, except so far as one wishes to mark out the characteristic styles of different montagists.

Montaging is the art of relating different incidents to one another. One can bring incidents close together or keep them far apart; relate parts of one frame with those of another; connect the parts of different films; relate the same incidents through the agency of different intermediaries; or relate the same incident to itself with the help of different intermediaries. One might refuse to engage in any montaging at all, and let the cinemaker record what it happens to come upon, though this effort, as was earlier remarked, can be taken to be a kind of montaging, since it does involve some selection (at least initially) and involves decisions (certainly at the end) as to just what is to be cut off and therefore just what is allowed to be in different parts of the film.

A number of cinemakers could be employed to film the same incident, related incidents, or incidents having nothing to do with one another. Any one of the results could be taken to provide a montaging agent in terms of which the results of the others were related to one another. Though the chosen film was not made to be a montager, since it was subsequently elected to function as one, it would be turned into an escapist film after the fact. In a related way, an experimenter can use any film, made by himself or others, as that which is to affect the import of what he is to do with respect to all other films, including the film he is about to make.

An entire film, serving the purpose of escape from the everyday world, takes on something like the role of a montagist. At its boldest and best, what it conveys is used to grade and relate what in fact occurs outside the film. An experimental film is an escapist work which grades and relates other films.

Director: Emphasis on experiment in film, though it usually has to do with the use of a cinemaker, requires the governance of a man who deals with film making as an occasion for the exhibition of something he has more or less clearly in mind. This is true even when resort is had to machines and random movements, or when one tries to avoid all supervision and control. Such a man is a director, but one who follows, as far as he can, none of the established routines. Renan seems to take his work to be of the essence of the experimental film: "there is a certain kind of film . . . made by a single person . . . primarily for reasons of personal or artistic expression. . . . Avant-garde, experimental, independent, and underground are all terms used to describe this kind of film." [4] But he is only one of many experimenters.

A director could deliberately try to oppose himself; he could try to negate what he had in mind or what he had already expressed. He could make use of other workers — even scriptists, performers, cinemen, and montagists, interrelating these in new ways, making them interact with one another arbitrarily, or allowing them to work only on certain parts of a film. Out of the many parts he might try to obtain a new film. He could try to subordinate himself to one or more of the other film makers so as to explore the ways in which the different varieties of art film, or the different purposes of film might be carried out resolutely. He could join together with other film directors and see what comes of their deliberate, accidental, or random interplay. He could try working cooperatively or in other ways with painters, dancers, composers, computers — with anything in fact, so that the film is freed not only from the limitations characteristic of any one man, but of those peculiar to directors. As is true of almost all the other alternatives, there are well-known films in which one or more of these have been carried out.

The very idea of experiment could be experimented with, by deliberately getting in the way of novelties and breakthroughs. The interferences could be at random, or in deliberate and random combinations of these. Experiments might be permitted only at certain places or times; they could be restricted to particular phases of film making. Employed on the experimental film itself, they allow one to escape from it, either by taking one to the world outside the film, or to films which are not subject to the conditions which govern experiments. In either way they enable one to stand at a position where one can see everything — films and nonfilms — as instances of an excellence that ought to be.

The Viewing: All film makers have some awareness that they are making what is to be viewed. Films with a purpose often take account of the conditions governing viewing; other films are made with some awareness of the kind of audience to which they are to be shown. An experimental film maker can take viewing and audience to be problems.

The screen on which a film is shown could be made smaller or larger than it now is. It could be shaped differently; it could be placed in positions other than straight front. It could be made to vary in size, shape, and placement, punctuated or broken up arbitrarily throughout a showing. The same film could be shown on many screens at one time; it could be shown at the same time on screens of different sizes, placements, or colors; its speed and direction could be altered at will. It could be supplemented by other films on other screens; those others could be more or less relevant to it, and might be shown with or without regard to it. A number of films could be shown simultaneously on the same screen. The screening could be stopped at arbitrary times and for arbitrary periods, or at times and for times which had been prescribed in advance. The same film could be screened in such a way that it would have a different meaning on different occasions; the pace at which it was shown, the placing of it, the light, distance, and collateral occurrences, all could be changed. "That the motion picture is a static work, that it is exactly the same work every time it is shown, and that motion pictures should be made to universal specifications so that they may be shown on given machines under given and never changing conditions. . . . these ideas . . . are on the way out now." [5] The screen itself could be behind water, oil, gratings, or partly behind another screen; it could be given many different or varying colorations; it might be marked up; it could be separated and reunited during the course of a filming. The projector could be experimented on; the same film could be put through different projectors operating under different conditions. A film could be shown partly on and partly off the screen; it could be made to play on the audience itself, or before a mirror; it could be folded back or forward, bent down or up, placed against a fluid surface, allowed to billow out or to be subject to wind and pressures. During a showing, an audience could be pushed forward or backward, up or down, or sideways. It could be undulated or whirled about; have the film blocked from view at various times or in varying degrees; be subject to a series of conditionings with smells and lights and sounds; be altered by drugs; be subject to intrusions and disturbances. An audience could be made to view a film in isolated chambers, be given tinted or distortive glasses, or be forced to look through peepholes or tunnels. It could be filmed watching a film, and could be introduced into the film that is being viewed.

Many more experiments than these could be tried. A good number of them will have trivial outcomes. The final films may be hard on the eyes, the ears, the nerves, the sensitivity, and good sense. To experiment does not mean that what one does is necessarily a success. But unless the experiments are made, we will not know what film can do. No one has the right to say in advance that such and such an experiment will not be worthwhile, for it is one of the functions of experiment to discover whether or not it was good to have engaged in it. What might be we can envisage and sometimes predict, but what actually is or will be, no one can know until he comes upon it. Experimentation is an effective way of promoting the discovery of something unsuspected which it might be desirable to know. To experiment with film is not only to discover what film can do, but to get a better and better grip on what film is in itself, as that which every actual film specifies in limited ways. One will then be in a position to make films with a boldness that otherwise would not be possible, and film makers at last will be brought closer to the stage where they could produce classical works of art, able to withstand the criticisms and changing tastes of generations. The best escape that experimental film can provide is an escape into a world where good films are made.

To learn what film is able to do it is desirable to see what alternatives there are to the way film is now understood and made. Those alternatives the experimental film is designed to provide. To escape into it is to escape from unnecessary limits within which film is usually made. If the escape is successful, it not only will offer something other than what had been done, but will use this to enable one to take all actual films, experimental and conventional, works of art and works of craft, as so many different related instances of film. It will also enable one to look at all films from a position of the most general idea of what a film is, and of which every particular film is a special instance. The actual film, in the one case, will mediate the rest; in the other, it will yield a generic idea which is instanced not only by that particular film but by every other.

Film is a created (audio) visual whole of ordered incidents. We can escape into one of those wholes, and we can escape from any of those wholes. We can escape from anything into which we have escaped. It is good to do this, for it enables us to get a better and better grasp of the essence of film, and therefore of what is concerned with all time, space, and causation, able to be occupied, specialized, and limited in endless ways.

References   Notes   Indexes

References

Arnheim, Rudolf, *Film as Art.* Berkeley and Los Angeles: University of California Press, 1960.

Avakian, Avram. "On the Editor," In *Movie People,* edited by Fred Baker and Ross Firestone. New York: Douglas Book Co., 1972.

Baker, Fred, and Firestone, Ross, eds. *Movie People.* New York: Douglas Book Co., 1972.

Balshofer, Fred J., and Miller, Arthur G. *One Reel a Week.* Berkeley and Los Angeles: University of California Press, 1967.

Battcock, Gregory. *The New American Cinema.* New York: E. P. Dutton & Co., 1967.

Bazin, André. *What Is Cinema? Essays Selected and Translated by Hugh Gray.* Berkeley and Los Angeles: University of California Press, 1967.

Bluestone, George. *Novels into Film.* Berkeley and Los Angeles: University of California Press, 1961.

Bobker, Lee R. *Elements of Film.* New York: Harcourt, Brace & World, 1969.

Brakhage, Stanley. "The Art of Vision." *Film Culture,* no. 30 (Fall 1963).

Brownlow, Kevin. *The Parade's Gone By.* New York: Alfred A. Knopf, 1968.

Coppola, Francis Ford. "On the Director." In *Movie People,* edited by Fred Baker and Ross Firestone. New York: Douglas Book Co., 1972.

Curtis, David. *Experimental Cinema.* New York: Dell Publishing Co., 1971.

Durgnat, Raymond. *Films and Feelings.* Cambridge, Mass.: M.I.T. Press, 1967.

Eisenstein, Sergei. *Film Essays with a Lecture.* Edited and translated by Jay Leyda. London: Dennis Dobson, 1968.

_____. *Film Form: Essays in Film Theory, and The Film Sense.* Edited and translated by Jay Leyda. Cleveland and New York: World Publishing Co., Meridian Books, 1963.

Farber, Manny. *Negative Space.* New York: Praeger Publishers, 1971.

Fielding, Raymond, ed. *A Technological History of Motion Pictures and Television.* Berkeley and Los Angeles: University of California Press, 1967.

Fowler, H. W. *A Dictionary of Modern English Usage.* 2nd ed. Revised by Sir Ernest Gowers. Oxford: Clarendon Press, 1965.

Geduld, Harry M., ed. *Film Makers on Film Making.* Bloomington: Indiana University Press, 1969.

Herman, Lewis. *A Practical Manual of Screen Playwriting.* Cleveland and New York: World Publishing Co., 1963.

Higham, Charles, and Greenberg, Joel, eds. *The Celluloid Muse: Hollywood Directors Speak.* New York: New American Library, 1969.

Houston, Penelope. *The Contemporary Cinema: 1945–1963.* Baltimore. Penguin Books, Pelican Books, 1963.

Hughes, Robert, ed. *Film: Book I: The Audience and the Filmmaker.* New York: Grove Press, 1959.

Jacobs, Lewis, ed. *Introduction to the Art of the Movies.* New York: Noonday Press, 1960.

Jones, Quincy. "On the Composer," In *Movie People,* edited by Fred Baker and Ross Firestone. New York: Douglas Book Co., 1972.

Kennedy, Margaret. "The Mechanized Muse." In *Film: An Anthology,* edited by Daniel Talbot. Berkeley and Los Angeles: University of California Press, 1970.

Knight, Arthur. *The Liveliest Art: A Panoramic History of the Movies.* New York: Macmillan Co., 1957.

Kracauer, Siegfried, *Theory of Film: The Redemption of Physical Reality.* New York: Oxford University Press, 1960.

Lawson, John Howard. *Film: The Creative Process.* New York: Hill & Wang, 1964.

Levinson, André. "The Nature of the Cinema." In *Introduction to the Art of the Movies,* edited by Lewis Jacobs. New York: Noonday Press, 1960.

Lindgren, Ernest. *The Art of the Film.* New York: Macmillan Co., Collier Books, 1970.

Lumet, Sidney, "On the Director." In *Movie People,* edited by Fred Baker and Ross Firestone. New York: Douglas Book Co., 1972.

McBride, Joseph, ed. *Persistence of Vision.* Madison: Wisconsin Film Society Press, 1968.

MacCann, Richard Dyer, ed. *Film: A Montage of Theories.* New York: E. P. Dutton & Co., 1966.

MacDonald, Dwight. "Notes on Hollywood Directors." In *Introduction to the Art of the Movies,* edited by Lewis Jacobs. New York: Noonday Press, 1960.

Manvell, Roger, ed. *Experiment in the Film.* New York: Macmillan Co., 1951.

Mekas, Jonas. "Notes on the New American Cinema." In *Film: A Montage of Theories,* edited by Richard Dyer MacCann. New York: E. P. Dutton & Co., 1966.

Montague, Ivor. *Film World.* Baltimore: Penguin Books, Pelican Books, 1964.

Nichols, Dudley. "The Writer and the Film." In *Film: A Montage of Theories,* edited by Richard Dyer MacCann. New York: E. P. Dutton & Co., 1966.

Panofsky, Erwin. "Style and Medium in Moving Pictures." In *Film: An Anthology,* edited by Daniel Talbot. Berkeley and Los Angeles: University of California Press, 1970.

Perelman, Ch., and Olbrechts-Tyteca, L. *The New Rhetoric: A Treatise on Argumentation.* Translated by John Wilkinson and Purcell Weaver. Notre Dame, Ind.: University of Notre Dame Press, 1969.

Pudovkin, V. I. *Film Technique and Film Acting.* Edited and translated by Ivor Montague. New York: Grove Press, 1960.

Renan, Sheldon. *An Introduction to the American Underground Film.* New York: E. P. Dutton & Co., 1967.

Reynertson, A. J. *The Work of the Film Director.* New York: Communication Arts Books, 1970.

Roberts, Kenneth H., and Sharples, Win. *A Primer for Film-Making.* New York: Pegasus (Publishing), 1971.

Robinson, W. R., ed. *Man and the Movies: Essays on the Art of Our Time.* Baltimore: Penguin Books, Pelican Books, 1967.

Rotha, Paul. "Basic Principles of Documentary." In *Film: An Anthology,* edited by Daniel Talbot. Berkeley and Los Angeles: University of California Press, 1970.

Salter, James. "On the Screenwriter." In *Movie People,* edited by Fred Baker and Ross Firestone. New York: Douglas Book Co., 1972.

Sarris, Andrew. *The American Cinema: Directors and Directions, Nineteen Twenty-Nine–Nineteen Sixty-Eight.* New York: E. P. Dutton & Co., 1968.

―――. *Confessions of a Cultist: On the Cinema. 1955–1969.* New York: Simon and Schuster, 1970.

Sitney, P. Adams, ed. *Film Culture Reader.* New York: Praeger Publishers, 1970.

Southern, Terry. "On the Screenwriter." In *Movie People,* edited by Fred Baker and Ross Firestone. New York: Douglas Book Co., 1972.

Spottiswoode, Raymond. *Film and Its Techniques.* Berkeley and Los Angeles: University of California Press, 1959.

―――. *A Grammar of the Film: An Analysis of Film Technique.* Berkeley and Los Angeles: University of California Press, 1950.

Stephenson, Ralph. *Animation in the Cinema.* New York: A. S. Barnes & Co., 1967.

Stephenson, Ralph, and Debrix, J. R. *The Cinema as Art.* Baltimore: Penguin Books, Pelican Books, 1969.

Talbot, Daniel, ed. *Film: An Anthology.* Berkeley and Los Angeles: University of California Press, 1970.

Truffaut, François. "We Must Continue Making Progress." In *Film: A Montage of Theories,* edited by Richard Dyer MacCann. New York: E. P. Dutton & Co., 1966.

Vorkapich, Slavko. "Toward True Cinema." In *Film: A Montage of Theories,* edited by Richard Dyer MacCann. New York: E. P. Dutton & Co., 1966.

Weiss, Paul. *The God We Seek.* Carbondale: Southern Illinois University Press, 1964.

―――. *The Making of Men.* Carbondale: Southern Illinois University Press, 1967.

―――. *Modes of Being.* Carbondale: Southern Illinois University Press, 1958.

―――. *Nine Basic Arts.* Carbondale: Southern Illinois University Press, 1961.

―――. *Religion and Art.* Milwaukee: Marquette University Press, 1963.

―――. "A Response." *Review of Metaphysics,* June 1972 supplement, pp. 144–65.

―――. *The World of Art.* Carbondale: Southern Illinois University Press, 1961.

Wollen, Peter. *Signs and Meaning in the Cinema:* Bloomington: Indiana University Press, 1969.

Youngblood, Gene. *Expanded Cinema.* New York: E. P. Dutton & Co., 1970.

Notes

CHAPTER 1

1. Vorkapich, p. 172.
2. Bazin, p. 15.
3. Ibid., p. 166.
4. These characteristics of sound are examined in my *Nine Basic Arts*, pp. 171 ff. But no detailed discussion of them is needed in order to make the point that the visible can be supplemented by the audible, but not conversely, if we remain within the world of art. Outside that world, where sounds are fragmentary and serve to carry messages, of course, sounds need supplementation by other agencies.
5. Montague, p. 155.
6. Other disciplines, I have tried to show elsewhere, provide similar introductions to what is ultimate, by first engaging, not the emotions, but understanding, faith, or reconstructive inference. Each yields only a partial truth and part of reality, but each also, in addition to partly satisfying a distinctive set of demands, leads one toward that which will complete the satisfaction.
7. Mekas, p. 337.
8. See Weiss, *Modes of Being,* chaps. 1–4.
9. See Weiss, "A Response," p. 146*n*.
10. See Weiss, *God We Seek,* p. 18.
11. See Weiss, *Nine Basic Arts,* p. 34.

CHAPTER 2

1. Coppola, p. 57.
2. "The definition generally accepted by the animators themselves: *an animated film is one that is created frame-by-frame.*" Stephenson, p. 13.
3. Bluestone, p. 62.
4. Nichols, p. 82.
5. Kennedy, p. 100.
6. Coppola, p. 58.
7. Ibid., p. 77.
8. Bluestone, p. viii.
9. Lawson, pp. 206–8.
10. Jones, p. 153.
11. Herman, p. 4.

12. Ibid.
13. Ibid.
14. Lindgren, p. 69.

CHAPTER 3

1. Nichols, p. 77.
2. MacDonald, p. 194.
3. Ibid.
4. Lindgren, p. 202.

CHAPTER 4

1. "To create them is a grave misdemeanor; and the greater the need of the word that is made the greater its maker's guilt if he miscreates it." Fowler, p. 49. I think this is not a "miscreation."
2. It is astonishing to see how few there are. Ernst Haas is almost alone in his understanding of what a camera can and should do. This is surprising, particularly when one considers the fact that the practice of photography is widespread and that photography is older than film. The emphasis on the pictorial, the daily, and the familiar has evidently hobbled its development.
3. Levinson, p. 149.
4. Ibid.
5. Lindgren, p. 167.
6. Panofsky, p. 28.

CHAPTER 5

1. Montague, p. 110.
2. Lindgren, p. 59.
3. Ibid., p. 94.
4. Spottiswoode, *Grammar of the Film*, p. 202.
5. Ibid., p. 203.
6. Weiss, *World of Art*, pp. 134–41.

CHAPTER 6

1. Sarris, *American Cinema*, pp. 25–26.
2. Ibid., p. 30.
3. Ibid., p. 37.
4. Wollen, p. 104.
5. Salter, p. 95.

6. Southern, p. 75.
7. Ibid., p. 78.
8. Avakian, p. 137.

CHAPTER 7

1. Avakian, pp. 133, 137.
2. Wollen, p. 112.
3. Truffaut, p. 374.
4. Panofsky, pp. 28–29.
5. Wollen, p. 77.
6. MacCann, pp. 15–16.
7. Lumet, p. 48.

CHAPTER 9

1. Weiss, *World of Art;* idem, *Nine Basic Arts;* and idem, *Religion and Art.*

CHAPTER 10

1. Perelman and Olbrechts-Tyteca, p. 8.
2. It could be said to be a successful documentary. But then it would have been made to serve another purpose (see chapter 11). The more successful a documentary is the more it too serves an end other than that of just producing a fine film with which viewers are to live emotionally for a while.
3. Perelman and Olbrechts-Tyteca, p. 52.
4. Ibid., pp. 53–54.
5. See Weiss, *Making of Men,* chaps. 1–3.

CHAPTER 11

1. Youngblood, p. 107.
2. Battcock, p. 13.
3. Herman, p. 79.
4. Lawson, p. 260.
5. The apparent contradiction between the present claim that the documentary tries to avoid the use of performers and Rotha's assertion that it may make use of trained actors vanishes with the recognition that the "trained actors" are made to function as subordinate parts, so as to convey a truth cinematically.
6. Spottiswoode, *Grammar of the Film,* p. 284.
7. Rotha, p. 245.
8. Knight, pp. 142–43.

CHAPTER 12

1. See, particularly, Renan; also Youngblood.
2. Renan, pp. 31–32.
3. Youngblood, pp. 84–85.
4. Renan, p. 2.
5. Ibid., p. 227.

Index of Names

Index of Subjects

Absence: film and, 57; disclosive film, 186
Abstract expressionism, 183
Abstractions: body and mind, 132
Acceptance: understanding and, 143
Accidents: disclosive films, 184
Acquiescence: inquiry and, 146–47
Acting: time and, 53; propaganda films, 175; mentioned, 40
Actors: confrontation, 39; film actors, 41, 42; rehearsal, 44 directors, 45, 100; roles, 48; spatiality, 52; dynamic activities, 56, 58; occurrences and, 70; performers and, 103
Actualities: incidents and, 12–15; art and, 154
Aesthetics: satisfaction, 62–63; experimental films, 114; mentioned, 15
Alternatives: escapist films, 198–200; experimental films, 201–2, 204
Ambiguities: scripts, 25
Anger, 131
Animals, 46
Animism, 52
Antecedent: consequent and, 69
Anthologists, 126
Appearances: and realities, 151–64; documentary films, 190
Architecture, 123, 125
Art[s]: film and art, 3; existence and, 21; works of art, 22, 167; satisfaction and, 62; cinemaker and, 65; film art, 74; and object, 77; 'auteur theory,' 87; emotions and, 97, 155–56; art films, 102–27; as montage, 122; feelings and, 148; speculation and, 149; appearances and, 152, 154, 155; actualities and, 154; extension, 155; innovation in, 162–63
Artists: freedom and, 76; culture and tradition, 156

Association: causality and, 68
Attention: audience and, 66
Attitudes, 132, 134–43, 146, 158
Audience: sound and, 7; screen and, 8–9; film and, 10; causal process, 15; money and education, 17; internationality of, 18; emotional response, 19, 34; actors and, 42; scripts and, 43; director and, 50; attention, 66; causality and, 71; montagist and, 74; present and, 81; camera and, 93; performance and, 95; stars and, 110–11; popular art and, 157–58; propaganda films, 170–71, 173; educational films and, 178–79; documentary films, 191; escapist films, 199–200; experimental films, 206
'Auteur theory,' 87, 123, 125
Author: director as, 87, 122–27
Awareness: existence and, 21

Beat the Devil (1954), 94
Beginning: of film, 24–25; directors and, 98
Behavior: escapist films, 197–99
Birth of a Nation (1915), 5, 7, 8, 18, 82, 178
Black and white films, 6–7
The Blue Angel (1930), 106
Body and mind, 131–33, 135, 140
Boldly submissive man, 146–47

Cameramen, 67
Cameras: script and, 33; audience and, 51, 93; animism, 52; photography and, 59; rhythm and, 61; mentioned, 5–6
Camille (1936), 106
Cancellation: confrontation and, 54
Candid camera, 182
The Carpetbaggers (1964), 110